Praise for *The Inner Voice*

"With plain spoken honesty and a wealth of technical detail made reader-friendly, Fleming has fashioned a manual that should be required reading for all young singers."
—*Boston Herald*

"Fleming's book is not only an indispensable asset to those who want to know her better, it's also a huge asset to aspiring young singers."
—*The Seattle Times*

"The tone of her writing is as elegant as the tone of her voice."
—*The Baltimore Sun*

"Renée Fleming writes almost as well as she sings. . . . [A] revealing account of how an opera career is launched and sustained. Fleming is particularly good at describing the physical demands and mental challenges of making beautiful sounds while at the same time trying to act. . . . Illuminating."
—*The Charlotte Observer*

"Beautifully written, elegantly told."
—*Pittsburgh Post-Gazette*

"As decorous as the author herself . . . Renée Fleming continues to make much of her great gifts."
—Terry Teachout, *Commentary Magazine*

"Fascinating"
—*Women's Wear Daily*

"[A] candid account . . . A realistic portrait of what it takes to succeed and a volume intriguing for its advice and honesty."
—*Publishers Weekly*

"Her perceptive account of what it takes to become and continue to be a great performer will resonate with all those who dream big. . . . A beguiling self-portrait of a great artist at work."
—*Kirkus Reviews*

PENGUIN BOOKS

THE INNER VOICE

Renée Fleming's vocal artistry is acclaimed worldwide as "the gold standard of soprano sound." An international artist for more than a decade, she is recognized for her compelling artistry, beautiful sound, and interpretive talents. A sought-after performer onstage and in recordings, she has won two Grammys and has been nominated eight times for the award.

RENÉE FLEMING

The Inner Voice

THE MAKING OF
A SINGER

PENGUIN BOOKS

To Amelia and Sage,
who give me reason
to sing

PENGUIN BOOKS
Published by the Penguin Group
Penguin Group (USA) Inc., 375 Hudson Street, New York, New York 10014, U.S.A.
Penguin Group (Canada), 90 Eglinton Avenue East, Suite 700, Toronto,
Ontario, Canada M4P 2Y3 (a division of Pearson Penguin Canada Inc.)
Penguin Books Ltd, 80 Strand, London WC2R 0RL, England
Penguin Ireland, 25 St Stephen's Green, Dublin 2, Ireland (a division of Penguin Books Ltd)
Penguin Group (Australia), 250 Camberwell Road, Camberwell,
Victoria 3124, Australia (a division of Pearson Australia Group Pty Ltd)
Penguin Books India Pvt Ltd, 11 Community Centre, Panchsheel Park, New Delhi – 110 017, India
Penguin Group (NZ), cnr Airborne and Rosedale Roads, Albany,
Auckland 1310, New Zealand (a division of Pearson New Zealand Ltd)
Penguin Books (South Africa) (Pty) Ltd, 24 Sturdee Avenue,
Rosebank, Johannesburg 2196, South Africa

Penguin Books Ltd, Registered Offices: 80 Strand, London WC2R 0RL, England

First published in the United States of America by Viking Penguin,
a member of Penguin Group (USA) Inc. 2004
Published in Penguin Books 2005

17   19   20   18   16

THE LIBRARY OF CONGRESS HAS CATALOGED THE HARDCOVER EDITION AS FOLLOWS:
Fleming, Renée.
The inner voice: the making of a singer/Renée Fleming.
p.   cm.
ISBN 0-670-03351-0 (hc)
ISBN 0 14 30.3594 0 (pbk.)
1. Fleming, Renée.   2. Sopranos—Biography.   I. Title.
ML420.F565A3 2004   2004051757

Printed in the United States of America
Set in Fournier
Designed by Francesca Belanger
Frontispiece: Renée Fleming as Massenet's Manon, Paris Opera, 2001.
Photograph, copyright Jacques Moatti.

Acknowledgments

WITH THANKS TO:

Ann Patchett, whose silent work on paper is the equal of the most colorful songbird. I would never have had the courage to undertake this project without her friendship and help.

Richard Kot, my editor: patient, kind, and, fortunately, enormously knowledgeable about opera. His hieroglyphic attention touched every paragraph in this book.

Darrell Panethiere, my ever positive muse, inspiration, dear friend, and consultant on all things musical. I was your dependent for the length of this project.

Mary Lou Falcone, who has advised me every step of the way and in all things. You gave me the courage to be honest.

Alec Treuhaft, who made this possible and who convinced me that I had something to say right now.

Evans Mirageas, for solving my existential dilemma during a long afternoon in Köln with the complete history of recorded sound and the voice in twentieth-century culture.

Christopher Roberts, president of Universal Classics and Jazz, in whose crystal ball and fearless leadership I implicitly trust.

My family and especially my sister, Rachelle, for a lifetime of love.

Alison Heather and Mary Camilleri, for their daily support, patience, and humor.

At Viking: Patrick Dillon and Bruce Giffords, for their meticulous attention to every line in this book; Herb Thornby and Francesca Belanger, for their elegant jacket and interior designs; and Alessandra Lusardi, for managing very complicated traffic.

The following friends and colleagues, who helped me in the final stages with their thoughtful comments: Matthew Epstein, John A. Fallon, Ann Gottlieb, Mary Jo Heath, Matthew Horner, Pat Kingsley, John Pascoe, Costa Pilavachi, Jacob Rothschild, Sue Schardt, Dr. David Slavit, Ann and Bill Ziff.

Contents

Introduction

I AM NO STRANGER to having my luggage searched. Like any other international traveler, I have spent a good portion of my life waiting in customs lines while people I did not know rifled through my musical scores and peered inside my shoes. But the dogs were something new. I wasn't in the airport, after all, but in my dressing room, waiting to rehearse Tchaikovsky in St. Petersburg, and the bomb-sniffing dogs had come in to make sure that I wasn't a terrorist disguised as an opera singer. German shepherds shoved their muzzles into my purse and nosed between the gowns hanging in the closet. They sniffed at the makeup, the wigs, and the piano and then looked back at me with heavy skepticism, making me feel vaguely guilty.

I had come to St. Petersburg to take part in a gala performance, a beautiful evening filled with music and dance. I was the only non-Russian who would perform for fifty heads of state for the three-hundredth anniversary celebration of the city, and I was to sing Tatyana's letter scene from *Eugene Onegin* on the stage of the historic Maryinsky Theatre. During the nineteenth century, this elegant theater had been home to the Russian Imperial Opera, founded by Catherine the Great in 1783. It had seen the world premieres of such landmark Russian operas as *Boris Godunov, Prince Igor,* and *The Queen of Spades,* and Verdi's *La Forza del Destino* had been written for the house. The world-renowned ballet of the Maryinsky Theatre had premiered *Sleeping Beauty, The Nutcracker,* and *La Bayadère* all on this stage, and in the orchestra pit had stood Berlioz, Wagner, Mahler,

Schoenberg, and, most important of all to me today, Tchaikovsky, conducting their masterpieces. I took a deep breath. This wasn't the first time history had weighed heavily on my shoulders.

I had never been to St. Petersburg before, and many people had warned me about the dangers there. I was told to watch out for the mafia, potential kidnappings, hotel robberies, and at the very least a mugging, but my information was clearly outdated. Everyone was helpful, and the whole place wore an air of elegance. I found the city beautiful, with its splendid baroque palaces and neoclassical facades set out like a series of pastel cakes along the wide boulevards. The cathedrals, the canals, every street and sidewalk were groomed for the anniversary. The sea itself seemed to have a polished glow, and the government had even sprayed the clouds to keep it from raining during the visit of President George W. Bush, Tony Blair, Jacques Chirac, Gerhard Schröder, Junichiro Koizumi, and other world leaders. It was the city's finest hour, but, unfortunately, it wasn't mine: my translator and guide was a fourteen-year-old girl who lived only for AC/DC, Alice Cooper, and basketball, and my hotel room had no window. When I say "no window," I don't mean that I had a bad view—I mean that I had, quite literally, no window. When I was told that there were no other rooms available, I pulled out my Valery Gergiev trump card and said I would have to call him about getting another hotel. There are many ways in which a soprano relies upon the guidance of a conductor, and not all of them are confined to the stage. As a result of dropping the most powerful name in Russian music today, I got a window *and* a view.

Some aspects of the performance turned out unimaginably well: I was given a beautiful nightgown and robe from a production of *La Traviata* to wear, and they fit me perfectly. Other things didn't go quite so smoothly. There were no plans to block the performance, and I was simply instructed, "Do it the way you did it last time." But I hadn't sung the role for years and couldn't remember where I had been standing on some other stage with a different set. The famous

Maryinsky Theatre was an impossible maze of back passageways that all seemed to lead nowhere. I could have used the assistance of one of those bomb-sniffing dogs to find my way from my dressing room to the stage—a feeling that perfectly mirrored the hopelessness I felt inside the Russian language.

Though my German and French are fluent, and my Italian, taxi-, restaurant-, and opera-interview-proficient, my Russian beyond *nyet* and *da* is nil. I had learned the role of Tatyana by rote years earlier when I first sang it in Dallas, and of all the heroines I've sung, she is the one I feel most closely aligned to: "Let me perish, but first let me summon, in dazzling hope, a bliss as yet unknown." Even if I didn't speak the language, it was still my responsibility to find a way to sound as authentic as a national, especially since I was singing the most beloved soprano aria in the Russian repertoire to a house full of Russians. This requires, first, not only memorizing the words, but taking apart every sentence in order to understand how each word is translated. It also involves a painstaking study of their exact pronunciation and inflection. I pay close attention to how words end, whether the vowels are open or closed, which consonants are doubled. Many of the most challenging sounds for a singer are in the Russian language, and it takes a great deal of time and patience to learn how to make them seem authentic.

Once that's in place, the subsequent task of learning the role comes along much more quickly. When performing an opera, I have to memorize not only my own text, but the text of everyone around me onstage, so that I'm ultimately involved in a dialogue, as opposed to simply staring blankly at my colleagues while they make unintelligible sounds. I've devised many tricks over the years to help with memorization, and although it seems obvious, the most important one is learning to connect the words with their meanings. Ten minutes of concentrated memorization with a full understanding of what I'm saying is worth hours of mindless repetition. Using alphabetization, alliteration, onomatopoeia, and rhyming, especially in languages like

Russian and Czech, and having a visual memory of the music on the page are also essential. I do anything I can come up with to grind the text into the gray matter between my ears. Interestingly enough, the more difficult the etching, the longer it lasts. Six years after learning a role as complex as Tatyana may find me mumbling the confrontation scene with Onegin while waiting in line at the post office, despite the sideways glances of other customers.

Of course, I was hardly the first American soprano to find herself in this position. Our national tradition of pressing ahead and assuming everything will work out in the end dates all the way back to Lillian Nordica, formerly Lillian Norton of Farmington, Maine. She must have been the first true American superstar on the international scene. When she came to the Imperial Opera in St. Petersburg in 1880, she was twenty-two years old and had virtually no career behind her, but the Maryinsky engaged her to sing a dozen leading roles in the 1880–1881 season alone. A dozen roles at twenty-two. Comparatively speaking, I had nothing to worry about.

For this performance, I was coached in Russian by Irina, a smartly dressed and professional musical presence in the theater. Valery Gergiev has single-handedly built up the reputation of the Kirov Opera until it has achieved a towering international position, often keeping his artists employed through more lucrative Western tours. Russia is a society that recognizes artistic potential in children from a very early age, and it has consequently produced not only talented performers but a people with a deep and intelligent appreciation for the arts.

Which only made me all the more nervous about Tatyana. Her letter scene is fourteen minutes long and extremely wordy, and I suddenly wished I could trade my program with the Maryinsky's leading soprano, who was to perform Glinka's Vocalise instead. Singing "Ah," after all, is foolproof! I decided the only way to get through this was to steel my mind and not allow doubts to flood in. Of course, this was nothing compared with the first time I sang the role in 1992 when my daughter, Amelia, was two months old, and uninterrupted sleep was a distant dream. Memorizing between her birth and the premiere had been agonizing, and I felt vindicated when I read years later that pregnancy and a sound memory are mutually exclusive. Now I willed myself to think only of Tatyana and her letter, to forget that this event would be televised around the world and that Vladimir Putin himself would be seated directly in front of me, judging my pronunciation. All I had to do was put on my nightgown and robe, step out onto a stage without any blocking, and begin to sing in a language I didn't understand.

It's impossible, at moments like these, not to stop and wonder how I got there. How does a girl from Churchville, New York, come to be asked to represent her country at a major international musical event, standing on the stage of a theater filled with dignitaries? The answer is unnervingly simple: it all comes down to two little pieces of cartilage in my throat. Those vocal cords—delicate, mysterious, slightly unpredictable—have taken me to unimaginable places. I have slept at the White House after staying up until two in the morning talking music with the Clintons and the Blairs. I have sung for Václav Havel at the end of his presidency and sat beside him at dinner for four hours afterward while he spoke of his life.

Apart from the moments of celebration and commemoration, I have performed at more solemn occasions. I have sung "Amazing Grace" at a ceremony at Ground Zero, only a few months after the attacks of September 11, with nine thousand people crushed into a space that was impossibly small for them, filling up the streets, pressing against one another shoulder-to-shoulder in every direction until they became one single life of sorrow. In the week leading up to that event, I had sung that song again and again, trying to imprint it into the muscle memory of my throat so that when the time came to perform it, I would be able to get through to the end without crying. I remember a young girl who was sitting at the front of the crowd with her family on the day of the ceremony. She was about sixteen years old, and I had no idea whom she had lost, but among the obviously grief-stricken people who carried photographs and signs and wept, her expression seemed utterly empty. Her eyes were dry. It was as if she had lost her own soul when those buildings went down, and when I started to sing I had to look at the sky or I knew I'd never be able to maintain my composure.

Given the fact that most classical musicians are not household names or faces recognizable from television, it's interesting to speculate about why people so often turn to a classically trained musician, and most often a singer, in times of national conflict or grief. Why choose a soprano to represent our collective emotional experience, rather than a familiar singer from the world of popular music who has sold millions of records? Why turn to a far lesser-known voice whose music is appreciated by a smaller audience? I think the answer lies in two places. First, the tradition of music grounds us and connects us to one another through a sort of universal appreciation that transcends taste, particularly in such songs as "Amazing Grace" and "God Bless America." Second, a trained voice has a kind of innate authority that transmits a sense of strength. We can be heard without a microphone. We sing with the entire body. The sounds that we make emanate not just from the head, but from the whole heart and soul and, most important, the gut. The word "classic" has come to be applied to so many things in our culture—cars, rock music, a particular episode of a television show—when in its truest sense it carries the weight of something that has been distilled over time and represents the highest quality in a given field. The music we sing has been loved in many past generations and will continue to flourish and find life and love in the future.

Thanks to the instrument of my voice, I have been fortunate enough to be invited to step onto the stage at great national and international occasions. I have seen the world from the vantage point of the greatest opera houses and recital halls. I have been incredibly fortunate in my career, and people often remark to me, "What a wonderful gift you have—how glorious it must be to open your mouth and have that voice pour out!" While it's a fact that a voice begins with natural talent, any talent must be nurtured, cajoled, wrestled with, pampered, challenged, and, at every turn, examined.

As I set about my education as a singer, I devoured the autobiographies of my predecessors, hoping to find the kind of advice that would improve my singing, but mostly what I found were entertaining accounts of celebrated lives. As much as I enjoyed the stories of intrigue at Champagne receptions, what I desperately needed was practical advice: When did these singers learn what they knew, and who taught them? How did they survive their early auditions, stage fright, and rejection? How did they learn all those roles once they finally succeeded? How did they maintain their voices over the course of a demanding career? I searched for such a long time for the book I wanted to read that finally I decided my only recourse was to try to write it myself. What I came up with in the end was not the story of my life, but the autobiography of my voice. My voice, after all, is my calling and my career, just as any performer's talent—whether singing, acting, or dancing—compels her to find her place on the stage. I hope that *The Inner Voice* will be a valuable companion to anyone striking out in this daunting but exhilarating profession.

The story of my singing has a plot not unlike those of the horse novels I loved in my youth: A child finds a wild horse whose true potential only she can see. She loves it and cares for it, trains it tirelessly. The girl and the horse have a commitment to each other that no one else can get in the way of. She sticks by the horse through injury and doesn't believe anyone who says the horse is all washed up. When the horse is thriving, she turns down all offers to sell it off. In the end, the horse proves to be a winner, and in return for her work and devotion, it takes her to victories she had never dreamed possible.

This is the story of how I found my voice, of how I worked to shape it, and of how it, in turn, shaped me.

CHAPTER ONE

· F A M I L Y ·

I HAVE LIVED A LIFE with a soundtrack. So many of my memories have music attached to them. Sometimes the music is at the center of the story, and other times it's only an afterthought, a song that one of my daughters half-sings under her breath while we're walking to the bus stop in the morning. Music can propel the story in a perfectly quiet room when I'm alone and learning a score. It has taken me around the world and brought me home. I can trace back so many of the dearest people in my life, my teachers and colleagues who became my friends, to a certain set of pitches. My memories so often involve someone singing, or me singing, or someone striking the first notes on a piano, that it becomes difficult even to imagine the precise place where those memories began. So while I can't remember first hearing music, I can at least remember the night when I first fell in love with it.

I was thirteen, and my family was living in a suburb outside of Rochester, New York, in a tract subdivision that had shiny new houses based on one of two models—the ranch and the split-level. It was summer, and the streets stayed light until late. The kids played in their yards, running games of tag through neighbors' lawns, shouting to one another, until it finally grew dark and their mothers came out onto the front steps and called their names and one by one they went inside. It was warm, and because everyone kept the front door open, we could hear the calls of "Good night" and "See you tomorrow" and the slamming of screens, and then the world quieted down again, the sound of voices giving way to the sound of crickets and the cars driving past. On this particular night, I was in our living room and my parents were singing. They were both music teachers, and all day long they listened to singing—the endless scales, the songs learned and repeated again and again, practiced until every note was perfect. My father, Edwin Fleming, a high-school vocal music teacher, listened to legions of voices every day, while my mother, Patricia, taught at a small private college. They sang and listened to singing until you would have thought that by the end of the day every note would have been squeezed out of them; and still when they came home they would find it in themselves to sing even more, as if the music at their jobs hadn't tired them out in the least. On this night they were singing for each other and for me and my younger sister, Rachelle, and brother, Ted. My mother played the piano and my father stood beside her, and together they sang Gershwin's "Bess, You Is My Woman Now." The *Porgy and Bess* duet was one of their greatest hits, a song that was romantic and yearning and completely suited to their voices, his baritone supporting her beautiful soprano. I stretched out on the living-room rug with my dog, Bessie, and felt a kind of perfect contentment.

My father was handsome, with a soft lower lip and shining black hair that fell across his forehead in an Elvis Presley curl. My mother looked like the kind of leading lady Hitchcock always favored, a cross between Tippi Hedren and Kim Novak. They were a glamorous couple, and when they sang together, everything was right in our lives; we were all happy. I always associated the music they made with happiness, because how could the world not be perfectly in balance when such harmony existed in your own living room? I could have lain there forever, listening.

It was something that happened regularly, the two of them singing after dinner, but on this summer evening their voices carried out across the lawns, and the children who had been playing put down their balls to listen, and the mothers who had come out to call them went back inside to get their husbands, and one by one the neighbors made their way to our house. They were moths and my parents were a single, irresistible flame. Some of them stepped inside our screen door, but most stood in our front yard, their faces close to the big picture window. Everyone I had ever seen in our neighborhood was there. It was a street made up of immigrants, mostly Italian families newly arrived in upstate New York. My parents now began to sing to them, popular arias and the first-act duet from *La Bohème*. My mother was working on her master's degree at the Eastman School of Music, and she sang the Puccini arias she was rehearsing for her graduate recital, "Mi chiamano Mimì," "In quelle trine morbide," and "Vissi d'arte." After every piece the neighbors applauded wildly, unable to believe their good fortune that such singing existed right there on our little street. The applause kept my parents going, and they performed until it grew late, holding hands, smiling, bowing, making their way through every duet they knew. Finally, it was over, and the thrilled and exhausted neighbors wandered back to their own houses, and my parents sent us to bed. I was Eliza Doolittle, too excited to sleep. I was the luckiest girl in the world to have parents that other people marveled at, to live in the center of such singing.

"But it didn't happen like that," my mother said recently when I was recounting this memory.

It didn't?

Of course there were plenty of nights when the two of them sang together, and people would come by; but on the particular night that seemed so unforgettable to me, my father wasn't even home. My grandmother was visiting from out of town, and my mother was accompanying herself at the piano.

Memory often works that way, splicing together its own greatest hits, so that the perfect night is matched with the perfect song, and the perfect moments of physical beauty and family harmony are set side by side. I would like to say that I completely trust myself to remember the details of my own life; but it was also my mother's life, my father's, Ted's, and Rachelle's, and each of us would tell a different story. But the most important element would be true for us all: there was always singing. Music was language in our house. It was air. Someone was playing the piano; someone else was setting the needle down on a record so that we could listen to the Schubert and Wolf lieder my father loved. It was practicing, teaching, rehearsing, but it was also spontaneous, unstudied, unconscious, as pervasive as the heat blowing up through the vents on the floor to push back the cold New York winters.

When did my life in music really begin? With my first curtain call at the Metropolitan? My first Elton John record? Or was it my parents' meeting at Indiana University in Pennsylvania? They once held hands while reading a bulletin board in the school's hallway and had their hands slapped apart by an elderly professor who was walking by. "Stop that!" she warned them, but they didn't listen. They married while they were studying to be music teachers, and the three of us graduated from college together, my mother holding me up with her diploma to smile at the camera, the two of them in academic gowns and mortarboards. My mother had meant to be an opera star, or even a movie star—everyone said she was headed in that direction— but the surprise of a baby put an end to that.

I spent my infancy in a playpen beside the piano where my mother gave voice lessons at home while my father went off to teach music at a nearby high school. I remember her students warbling through their lessons. One girl wore a body brace and sang "When Love Is Kind," committed forever to my memory in the sparrow-light voice of this girl who stood unnaturally erect in front of my mother in the afternoons.

I have to wonder now what aspect of that exposure would be more beneficial to a baby opera singer: the music itself or the constant repetition, the never-ending drill of practice. My life might have turned out entirely differently had I been born the daughter of ticket takers at an opera house and so had grown up seeing opening nights, glamorous, glittery productions of the sort that would fill a child's head with big ideas. I count myself lucky to have aligned my own beginning with the beginning elements of music: notes, scales, the constant hunt for the right pitch. I feel certain that if I absorbed any lessons at all in the first months and years of my life, they must have been about the work that went into making a beautiful sound.

My mother says I was late to talk and early to sing, that she could call out a string of tones and by the age of one or so I could parrot them back to her, which is pretty good for a baby who didn't have the skills to ask for apple juice. Before I was three, I was standing on the hump in the backseat of the car (having been born in those pre-carseat dark ages), making myself just tall enough to lean into the front seat between my parents while my father drove. Together we sang three-part rounds of "Frère Jacques" and "White Coral Bells." Learning my part, I planted myself firmly between two wonderful teachers.

So how is it that I had no idea, even at this early age, that I wanted to be a singer? I should have seen it at the very latest by three, when I gave my first solo performance as Suzy Snowflake. I was practically born into the job, and yet somehow it never occurred to me to take it. What I wanted were buckets of approval and love, and to be good. I was a notorious teacher's pet, a straight-A student. Pleasing the English teacher meant producing a carefully written paper, just as pleasing the music teacher meant singing well. Seeing as how the music teachers were my parents, I sang and sang.

For a child, the desire to please can push almost every other consideration aside. I was naturally shy—doesn't every actor, dancer, or musician claim a childhood crippled by shyness?—but if I was told to get onto a stage, then that was where I'd go. If left to my own devices, though, I would always find a book. I could read instead of sleeping, read while I walked, read at the table, read in the car. It drove my father crazy after a while, especially when we took long family vacations, a whole world of scenery shooting past my window while I kept my head in the pages of *Black Beauty*. "Look up!" he would say, watching me in the rearview mirror as he drove. "Stop reading for five minutes and look at something! I don't know why you'd want to spend so much time reading novels, anyway. They don't teach you anything." He was an avid do-it-yourselfer, instruction book always in hand.

So I did look up, for five minutes, and the world was everything he promised it would be: beautiful, green, mountainous. But the novels were teaching me something else: the world I really wanted to look at was in those pages, and in my head. I could imagine myself on the back of Black Beauty, galloping in the rain through an English countryside. And that, of course, is a critical element in an actor's craft—the ability to project yourself into another person, in another time, in other circumstances. No one thought that reading was a waste of my time, just that I was veering toward being a singularly unrounded individual.

My stage triumph as Suzy Snowflake stood alone until Rachelle and I came back as a sister act with *The Ugly Duckling*. In the seventh grade I was cast as the Mother Abbess in *The Sound of Music*. It was a bit of a stretch to play an aging nun in seventh grade, especially after I was nicknamed "Mother Abscess," but I was the only one who could sing "Climb Ev'ry Mountain."

At least that nickname was a change from my usual one in junior high, "Miss Perfect." I wore a stretchy pink headband, three inches wide, to school every day, and that was about as close as I came to making a fashion statement. I longed to be a renegade, to smoke cigarettes in the bathroom and sneak off from school after lunch, but I never had the courage. Instead I kept up my A's. I entered a competition to write a new school song and won with the inspiring verses:

> *Gates Chili Junior High is the greatest of them all*
> *And to her name we all give praise while standing great and tall.*
> *We love thee, alma mater, for showing us the way—*
> *Glory we give to you, we love you more each day.*

Perhaps such a wrenchingly earnest child deserves to be taunted and mocked, but I died a little every day when the school bully sang my song over and over again in a high falsetto on the bus going home. I was all orthopedic shoes and slumped posture, secretly wanting to be something very different, something dazzling.

I got my chance in the next school play, a full-scale production of *My Fair Lady*. At twelve I played Eliza Doolittle and sang every note of the role. Ralph Jurgens, a tall, broad-shouldered man who looked more like a cop than an English teacher, rounded up all the even vaguely musical eighth-graders and gave them British accents to play with. Now for the first time I was really learning a part. Or I thought I was learning one—until my mother came to watch a rehearsal a week before opening night. She waited until it was over and we were safely in the car before she announced that we were going home immediately because there was work to do. A lot of work.

There can be no underestimating my mother's role as a teacher in my life. It was she who first introduced me to the idea of a total performance, that singing did not mean merely standing stock-still beneath a light, closing your eyes, and opening your mouth. She explained to me that the line "Just you wait, Henry Higgins" could not be delivered as if it were being read from a phone book. She taught me how to move, when to look at the audience and when to look away. She would dance my steps and I would dance along behind her. Good student that I was, I had always learned my lines, but under her guidance I came to understand that memorization was not the same as acting.

"Smile!" she told me. "Try to look like you're enjoying yourself."

My mother was an incredibly gifted and disciplined performer. Back then, the Rochester Opera Theater was a thriving operation, based at the Eastman Theatre, a gorgeous old auditorium that seats over three thousand people. I was mesmerized by the giant chandelier that hung over the audience like a bright planet. My father, brother, sister, and I would sit in the front row on the nights my mother sang there, stunned by her voice and her beauty, by how she held the audience so intently.

When my mother was a little girl who sang at church functions, her grandfather would sit in the back row and promise her a dollar if he could hear her—a pretty clever way to teach projection. Was this really the woman who made us breakfast? Her stage makeup could be seen from the last rows: a black line under the eye, another over the eye, a streak of white at the outer edges, and a red dot in the corner, her false eyelashes sweeping her cheeks like Fuller brushes. Her costumes followed her across the stage in great, billowing folds. Heavy makeup and velvet gowns on your own mother—what could be more glamorous than that? Rachelle and I had the most exotic collection of dress-up clothes that any two little girls in upstate New York dared dream of.

Mother sang Marcellina in Mozart's *Le Nozze di Figaro* and Fiordiligi in his *Così fan tutte*. In the title role of Puccini's *Suor Angelica,* she was up there onstage in her nun's habit, crying over her child who had died, and I kept thinking, *She's crying for me!* And then I was crying for her. Of course I was mortified by my outburst, for weeping was sure to be met with unrelenting teasing in my family. Still, secretly, I loved surrendering to the pure emotional display, just as I loved having a mother who was a star. I was certain that all the children in the audience were wishing that she was theirs.

But no matter how much I loved seeing my mother perform, I never had any sense of reverence toward her singing. "You were flat in the first part of the third act," I was telling her by the time I was ten. And while she herself had the tact to take me outside, away from my friends, before critiquing my work, I shared my comments with anyone who happened to be standing around. She was wise enough not to take me too seriously, and even seemed delighted with my precocious musicianship. I know this was the case because of my reaction when my own daughters started critiquing me when they were about eight years old. Even if they were only pointing out that the lipstick I was wearing was not exactly a flattering shade, they made it clear that they were watching me and that they knew a mistake when they saw it or heard it. Like me, they had no intention of letting their mother get away with anything.

It was through my reading that I came to believe that happiness was something that required a horse, and because my mother had also always loved horses, my parents, on their very modest schoolteachers' salaries, decided that I should have one. Her name was Windy, and she lived in the garage for a couple of weeks, until one day she pushed her way into the kitchen, having apparently decided she deserved a more intimate place in the family circle. Finally, someone from the city council came and explained that neither the kitchen nor the garage nor any other part of our tract housing complex was zoned for horses and that Windy would have to go.

My mother and I also fell in love with a spider monkey named Jethro, who made his home in the pet section of Sibley's department store, and so, on my twelfth birthday, he came home—fortunately, on a three-day trial basis. We soon realized that he was a bit beyond our suburban capabilities. Even if neither Windy nor Jethro could continue to live with us in our split-level on Valencia Drive, I learned a valuable lesson: There was no dream too large or too exotic to be realized.

If my mother typically offered specific guidance regarding the shape of a note or a turn of the wrist, and set an example with her unflagging energy, ambition, and work ethic, what my father taught me about singing came packaged in larger life lessons, and many of those lessons had to do with horses. We moved to a house in Churchville, New York, in order to have a proper place for animals, and ultimately wound up with three of our own horses, four boarders, and three dogs on our five acres of land. It was exactly what I had dreamed of, but my father made it clear that with dreams come responsibilities. "Horses can't feed themselves," he'd tell me, and I would be out in the bitter cold mornings before school, breaking the ice in the ten-gallon water buckets, filling them up in the basement, and lugging them back up the steps to the barn. I regularly dragged hundred-pound sacks of grain from the car to the tack room after mucking the stalls. It was hard, heavy, freezing labor, but it was the price of having horses, and horses were what I wanted. I understood that you have to work for what you want, for what you love. Having observed the girls who sang at the piano for my mother, I knew that beauty could occur naturally, but more than likely it was the result of discipline, and so I curried and brushed and picked out hooves. There was no praise for my efforts; hard work was simply what was expected.

Even when we went camping, my mother, who was given to high heels and stockings, packed a vacuum cleaner and a double mattress in the back of the seventeen-foot motorboat that trailed behind our car. When we set up camp for the night after boating to an island, with all of us holding the mattress on board, my mother would ferret out the camp's single electrical outlet, plug in her extension cord, and then proceed to vacuum off the ground the tent would sit on. That was pretty much the point at which my father bade farewell to sleeping outdoors.

I remember how my mother would teach all day and then have everyone in her family over for a giant meal. We would bake and stew and chop and sauté for hours, serve and pick up the plates and wash them and put them away, then scrub down every inch of the kitchen, and when I stumbled off to bed half-blind with exhaustion my aunt would shake her head sadly at my mother. "Renée's a little lazy, isn't she?" she would say.

The women in my family often misused the word "lazy," because they simply did not understand the concept. I can trace that attitude back as far as my great-grandmother, who came to America alone from Prague as a teenager to escape the unwanted advances of a German soldier. To be a girl alone in a new country without speaking the language would be a daunting story of courage in most families, but in my own it was just another example of an occasion to roll up your sleeves and do whatever needed to be done. That great-grandmother from Prague produced a daughter with a beautiful voice who played the piano. Her friends called her "the Girl of the Golden West," after Puccini's opera. My grandmother had wanted to be a music teacher herself, and so she steered my mother into that profession. My mother, for her part, wanted to be a singer or a movie star. We were all so intertwined that sometimes it was difficult to tell who was living out whose dreams.

If a work ethic and a talent for music are transmitted through the genetic code, then I inherited them from both my parents. My father's family was the most inexhaustibly capable group of people I have ever encountered. Need a house? We'll build one! Don't know a thing about foundations, plumbing, electricity? We'll figure it out! It seemed that every one of them could rebuild an engine, shingle a roof, fix a refrigerator. My paternal grandfather was a coal miner in the hills of Pennsylvania, and my uncle Lysle spent five years in the service in New Guinea, surviving on the snakes and insects he caught for food. His stories of rescuing nurses from headhunters and keeping his reconnaissance soldiers safe, thanks to the training he had received from my grandfather in the hills of Pennsylvania, fascinated me. But even in this madly industrious group my father stood out. As a boy, he learned to play the trumpet, and it was the trumpet, along with his love of music and diligent practice, that got him to college, the first member of his family to attend. Even on his teacher's income, he managed to own a small airplane, a Piper Cub, with three other men when I was a little girl, and I thought that taking afternoon flights was what every child did after Sunday lunch.

In the face of so much accomplishment it was hard at times not to feel like a dull penny. I started going to horse shows and competing in barrel races, but like so many other things I longed to do, competition didn't come naturally. The only person I know how to be competitive with is myself. I can push myself to any limit, but I am worthless when it comes to competing against other people. Those early horse shows nearly broke me. For me, fear manifests itself in a nearly catatonic state. The more panicked I feel, the more my eyes go dead. I become so utterly still that I could put down roots and grow leaves. While most animals experience a sense of fight-or-flight when they perceive danger approaching, I always fell into the "faint" category. As a freshman in high school, I was supposed to compete in the state fair horse show. I'd already ridden in a few 4-H shows by then, but they were much smaller events. I looked around at the crowds, the smiling girls with confident ponytails, and I leaned against the stall, mute and motionless with fear and nausea. My father, who saw me hesitating to get up on my horse, thought I wasn't paying attention. He mistook my frozen panic for indifference, an unwillingness to make any effort.

"I didn't spend the whole day and all this money so that you could just stand there," he said to me sharply. "I want to see you at least try."

It's funny to think that my first inklings of stage fright came not on a stage but in a dusty corral, surrounded by horses and people in cowboy boots. But my father was right to lean on me and wisely did not let me give in to my fears. I went behind some bales of hay, threw up from my heavy sense of dread, tucked my shirt neatly into my jeans, and got on my horse and rode. I did my best, which was what my father expected of me, though at that moment my best wasn't very good. It was that quality in my father, his no-nonsense determination, that instilled in me a drive to overcome my limitations. I was lucky to have someone who didn't baby my fears, but was always there urging me on.

I wasn't the only one my father refused to coddle. His church choirs were also held to his exacting standards. He chose music that was very difficult for them, pieces like Leonard Bernstein's *Chichester Psalms* or Bach's long, complicated cantata "Christ lag in Todesbanden." When they complained, he would simply tell them, "We're going to do this. We're going to learn it. It's going to be hard, but you'll make it." If they tried to refuse and told him he had to pick a different piece, he responded calmly that if that was the case, they would have to pick another choral director. What he expected of other people was the same thing he expected of himself: to go out there and try. He didn't look at anyone—not his students, not his children—and think, *Well, you're just not up to this*. It was his higher expectations that pulled all of us up.

• • •

Regardless of whether performing frightened me or I enjoyed it, or whether I was any good at it, one thing was certain: I kept doing it. In high school I was cast in yet another production of *My Fair Lady*, this time by the music teacher, Rob Goodling. In retrospect, I have to say it is nothing short of amazing that I had such talented teachers to work with early on, especially since we were not exactly in the heart of a booming metropolis. Rob was a man with big ideas who later toured groups of talented students through Europe. He cannily populated his musicals with handsome basketball players and track stars, which in turn made our after-school rehearsals the place to be. Suddenly, the popular kids were the ones onstage, and having a good voice made me even more popular. (I'm sure I have Rob to thank for later being chosen prom queen.)

I only wish that all children had the luxury of the arts education I enjoyed. In inner-city schools, for example, where financial challenges are serious and relentless, music programs are considerably less widely available. Conversely, in Texas, music education has achieved a high level of importance, comparable to athletics. In New York State, many public schools operate robust music programs, and some assign them a priority that rivals more traditional academic subjects. This lack of uniformity makes it difficult to generalize about the state of music education, though there is clearly a relationship between the availability of financial resources and the existence of school music programs.

When I was growing up, we crowded onto the school bus with our violin cases, flutes, and trombones and practiced "Twinkle, Twinkle, Little Star" and Chopin's nocturnes as studiously as we drilled our multiplication tables and memorized our spelling words. Everyone knew that we weren't all going to grow up to be musicians, but educators appreciated that the discipline of music, not to mention the joy that understanding it can bring, is both a deepening and a broadening experience in any life. Fostering creativity in children is as important as any other part of the school curriculum because it feeds the soul. A daily dose of creativity helps children imagine a better world and then create it.

About that time I was accepted into a special weekly composition program offered to just a handful of students throughout Rochester. I had written songs and poetry since junior high school, and "Stargazer," the first song I wrote, had become a veritable hit among my friends and family, a favorite at talent shows and holiday functions. I followed with many pieces composed on piano and guitar until my second year in college, when I learned to actually communicate through speech. There's no doubt that composition provided me with an expressive outlet I genuinely needed to compensate for the shyness that kept me painfully bottled up. It was when I started writing music rather than just performing it that I first began to develop a sense of who I was as a person. Composition wasn't about pleasing; it was about expressing. Not surprisingly in those days, my hero was Joni Mitchell, and I listened to her soulful lyrics until I nearly wore the grooves off the records. I thought that I had personally discovered *The Hissing of Summer Lawns* and *Hejira*. Her unique poetic and music voice so perfectly expressed the world I wanted to inhabit.

William Harper, a doctoral candidate at Eastman, taught the composition class and completely opened up my ideas about music. I'll never forget that first session, when we listened to Penderecki's *Threnody for the Victims of Hiroshima*. I couldn't believe that these ideas existed and I had never known anything about them at all. I sat there, thrilled and silent. I remember everything about that moment: the little classroom where we met, the late-fall light coming in through the windows, William Harper sitting there on his desk listening, his chin down, his eyes closed. Everything in the world froze for a minute, and I felt as if I were hearing music for the first time. All of the interest I've had in new music in my life can probably be traced back to that moment, that piece.

The lessons were encouraging, and yet there was still an unspoken understanding at that time that women didn't grow up to be real composers. The best we could hope for was to someday write songs, not symphonies, and so I continued writing songs. That same year, however, Mr. Harper introduced me to a woman who would have a profound impact on my relationship to music for years to come, the mezzo-soprano Jan DeGaetani. I was wildly impressed with the number of scores she was working on. These were not the neat folders of music that were in the piano bench at home, but sprawling, misshapen scores of new music covered with penciled notations. It was almost as if you could hear the piece unfolding just by looking at it on the page. There was nothing static about this work; it was completely, actively in progress. When I sang for her, she listened to me with great seriousness. "Don't train all the naturalness out of your voice," she told me. The very fact that she took the time to advise me at all made me feel important.

When it came time to go to college, I auditioned for several vocal programs. I was terrible at auditioning in those days, and would walk into the room looking guilty for taking up the time of the people on the judging committee. I was nervous and self-conscious, qualities I should have gotten out of my system while I was singing in school plays. My mother had really hoped I'd get into Oberlin College, and I did, but I didn't receive enough financial aid to attend. She was so heartbroken for me that she cried all the way back from Ohio in the car. When I was a child, my family had had to struggle. My father hunted deer and fished to supplement the groceries that his annual schoolteacher's salary allowed. I grew up eating venison, and I thought we were nothing but rich, which was a real testament to my parents' positive attitude. But by the time I was through with high school, we had become a part of the classic middle-class paradox: we didn't have enough money to secure a spot for me in a top-flight conservatory, yet we were no longer poor enough to qualify for some much-needed financial aid—which is how I ended up at the Crane School of Music of the State University of New York, Potsdam. That turned out to be the first great break of my career.

CHAPTER TWO

·EDUCATION·

*T*HERE ARE SO MANY THINGS that go into making a singer—
not just natural talent and hard work but tenacity, resilience, and
luck. When I started my freshman year at the Crane School of Music,
I began work with Patricia Misslin. Had I somehow found the money
to attend any of the better-known music conservatories I had
dreamed of, I probably would have received no more than one private lesson a week. As an undergraduate, I certainly never would
have been onstage except as part of a chorus. At Potsdam, I not only
had the full attention of a talented, dedicated voice teacher, but by the
end of my first month at school I'd been cast as the soprano soloist in
the Bach B-minor Mass. A freshman! No one was more surprised
than I at this upset.

Even though I had garnered a lot of attention as a singer in high
school and was now studying music in college, I was here at Crane
because this was the path of least resistance. I had no burning desire
in my gut to sing, no moment of recognition that led me to this particular destiny. I don't recall my parents' ever having cultivated much
of an independent soul in me. The question was never what I wanted
to be, do, eat, or wear but rather what I *had* to be, do, eat, and wear. I
was only too happy to comply and until graduate school never ques-
tioned the whys and wherefores of my career path. At that point in
time, my voice was a minefield of problems: I couldn't sing softly, I
was physically tense, and I had no high notes. Everyone knows that a
soprano with no high notes isn't going to go very far in the world.

Still, Pat recognized that I had innate musicality, real musicianship, and a genuine eagerness to learn and work.

Pat had short, fine, curly brown hair and usually stood with her feet in perfect turnout, à la Mary Poppins. As she taught, she watched me over her glasses with her chin practically down on her chest, cheeks and eyebrows lifted, humming along as she accompanied me on the piano. She was a crack musician who could play anything. Dressed in crewneck sweaters and plaid wool skirts, she radiated a no-nonsense New England reliability that made me trust her. Somehow she managed to be warm and accepting of me as a person while maintaining a highly critical ear when it came to work, which meant that when she tore me down I always knew it was because she planned to build me up again in better shape. I'd count it as a good day if we got through a page of music in an hour. I'd barely open my mouth before she was stopping me, saying, "Wait. Let's do that again." It was incredibly detailed work, and I ate up every minute of it. I never fought her, never said, "No, I think it's better my way." Not only would it not have been true, but at that stage I didn't want to have to think for myself. I wanted her to tell me how to shape every note, what to do with every nuance.

Pat put a tremendous amount of emphasis on resonance, focus, and placing the voice. These weren't new concepts, but she worked in such minute detail that I was forced to hone each pitch individually. That in itself was a huge task: to understand the concept of actually aiming sound mentally, and to learn how to place the voice "in the mask." The mask, I quickly came to understand, meant the nose and cheekbones— the nasal and sinus cavities where sound resonates. The use of mask resonance, as opposed to the natural tendency to speak with mouth and chest resonance, is crucial to every young singer's development, as it's the only way to project the voice to the back of a hall without strain. It's the "buzz," "hum," or *squillo* that develops the nascent shape of a tone into a full-blown operatic sound.

Pat would further explain that resonance, in simple terms, is a function of the direction of your air. As you're singing, you actually use your mind to direct the air to combinations of certain parts of your body: either to your head, because there are multiple sinus cavities behind the eyes; or to the mouth, which creates a different sound; or to the mask; or to the chest, which results in the lowest kind of sound. Resonance is easily understood by looking at any instrument. Imagine that the sound made by the vocal cords is the same as the sound that comes out of a trumpet mouthpiece: on its own, it's nothing more than a buzz—it's the resonance that creates the tone. What makes a voice what it is, is a combination of the sound from the vocal folds and the blending, or balance, or processing through the resonance tract.

If I send air into the highest resonating chambers, I get a very light, childlike sound: the head voice. This is all that a lot of beginning singers have, a voice with no body to it. The head voice is something we associate with flaky girls, the high lilt of Glinda the Good Witch discussing the positive attributes of ruby slippers. Aiming at the mask makes more of a nasal sound. When someone has a nasal-sounding voice, it's very distinctive: imagine Roseanne Barr speaking. A chest sound would be very low. Sarah Vaughan had a beautiful chest voice, all deep and smoky. In her later years, it was difficult to tell when listening to her in a blind test if it was a woman or a man singing. Ideally, an opera singer will maintain an enormous amount of focus in the mask while using all the rest of the resonance areas as well. The trick is going up and down and blending them all. I always imagine that the voice is a tapestry, and that as one thread goes up, different threads are woven in. Coming back down, those threads are woven back out and other threads are pulled through. What that creates is evenness in the tapestry, up and down, in length and breadth. The picture changes, the colors change, but the quality and texture of the tapestry remain consistent.

"What's your mental picture?" Pat would ask me. "Where are you sending your voice?" At that time I didn't yet know, but I was working fast to figure it out. I was learning to think in imagery that would affect involuntary muscles and cause the body to produce a healthy, even sound. "Inner smile!" Pat would say. "Lift those cheeks!" "Breathe through your nose to find the lift!" "More focus!" "Breathe!" She likewise demanded rhythmic accuracy, complex shaping of phrases, and at least a working knowledge of foreign languages—in short, more musical multitasking than any eighteen-year-old was capable of. I felt infinitely stimulated by the challenge.

I stood at the piano doing my best to keep up with her, trying not only to sing but to follow her instructions with my body and my voice. What parts of my anatomy was I supposed to use to focus my sound so as to have the least amount of tension and gain the most projection? Muscle isolation and coordination are first requirements, taking years to develop fully. I left her studio feeling as if my head were filled with the very resonant buzzing of bees, every one of them trying to tell me something I desperately needed to know. Every time I went to see her it was as if she threw open another window by teaching me how to be mindful in my singing. She was giving me the very foundations of how to think about my voice, an alphabet from which I could begin to build a technique. She instilled in me a sense of vocal health, very bright, with an emphasis on closed vowels. While another student might have felt overwhelmed by her exacting criticisms, Pat and I were the perfect match.

Studying singing is really not so different from studying any other instrument, except that perhaps the exercises sound more peculiar. One of Pat's warm-ups was a long series of undulating scales ending in a descending arpeggio on a single breath—"wa-MA-LOOO-see, wa-MA-LOOO-see." Who knows where that came from, but it worked for the voice in the same way that playing scales helps loosen up the hands, shoulders, and arms of a pianist. A young student might come in with only a kernel of sound that's interesting—maybe an octave or even just a fifth that shows some promise—and it's the teacher's job to take that kernel and develop it, to stretch the range into something both wide and deep and then fill it in with texture and light. In the beginning, the lessons typically involve instructions like "Keep your shoulders down," "Take a low breath," and "Pitches aren't formed with your chin." Young singers have to train the breathiness out of their tones, to rid themselves of the popping veins, the trembling jaws, the faulty pitches, the straining for high notes, and the inability to sing coloratura or move the voice without moving the whole body. I couldn't roll my *r*'s at all. To solve the problem we discussed cutting the narrow flap of skin that attached my tongue to the base of my mouth, a prospect that didn't especially appeal to me, and after several years of practice I was finally able to roll with the best of them.

Even though I was only eighteen when I started working with Pat, I was not in a particularly pristine state. No voice is discovered on a desert island without having been corrupted by the desire to imitate a passing seagull, and mine was no exception. I'd been performing so much and mimicking the mature sounds of my parents and other adults for such a long time that I had developed some bad habits along the way. Pat had to take away my penchant for singing too darkly and maturely, and while she took some things out of my voice, she introduced others to take their place and corrected vocal difficulties through musical means.

In order to reach even this point in a young singer's training, a teacher and a student have to develop a terminology, to find a language in which they can easily communicate. The essential component is rapport. The student has to feel cared for, because singing is such an exercise in vulnerability. The voice, after all, is the only instrument that can't be sold. You can't say, "I really don't like this one, so I'm going to trade it in for a Stradivarius." It's the only instrument that can't be returned, exchanged, put in the closet for a wild night on the town, or—fortunately for me—left in the trunk of a taxicab. For that reason it's also important that teachers be able to navigate through a student's psychology. Criticism can feel extremely personal when you are the instrument that's being discussed.

In most cases, it would take any two people at least six months to build up a relationship that would provide a foundation from which they could really get to work, but Pat and I had to start off faster than that since I had the B-minor Mass to learn. The first thing she said to me after I got the part was, "You're going to sing this well if it kills both of us." In the end both parts of her statement were true: I sang well and it nearly killed us. By the day of the performance, after daily sessions with Pat, I was thoroughly drilled, utterly prepared—and had a bad case of laryngitis. Pat came over to my little dorm room with hot chicken soup, and my new friends and roommates bolstered my morale, telling me I could do it and not to worry, while I spent two hours steaming in the shower. Everyone rallied, and the flurry of activity made me feel momentarily that I wasn't quite the invisible wallflower I thought I was. I adored the attention and went on and sang without the slightest hoarseness.

But what the day really marked was the start of my performance ritual. Some singers have a rabbit's foot, and others depend on a lucky undershirt. Luciano Pavarotti needs to find a bent nail onstage before he sings, and heaven help the singer who wears purple in his presence. Renata Tebaldi was always escorted to the wings by her assistant, Tina, who held a picture of Renata's mother, Giuseppina, which Renata kissed before stepping onstage, as well as a tiny teddy bear whose nose Renata pinched. Lily Pons was *always* sick to her stomach before a performance. Birgit Nilsson liked a cup of black coffee when she came into the dressing room and a bottle of Tuborg beer at the end of a performance. Several singers depended on the bottle to get them through. Sexual superstitions also abound. One conductor's wife was supposedly asked, "What's it like to be married to a famous conductor?" to which she replied, "He won't the day before, he's too busy the day of, he's too tired the day after—and he does three concerts a week!" Not surprisingly, food rituals are the most common, and they are too numerous to list. I happen to like having a lot of people I'm very close to in a state of complete panic, because, frankly, it relieves me of having to carry the performance anxiety alone. It's as if there's a certain amount of worrying that has to be done before any performance, and I can either take it on alone or have other people share the burden with me. For years my sister, Rachelle, was my designated worrier. I would whip her into such a frenzy before a performance, saying, "I can't do this! I'm terrified!" that she would soon be terrified herself. A few years ago, though, she finally retired from the role, complaining that she'd had it with the worry. She knew by then that I was going to be fine, and she wanted to be able to sit in the audience and watch a performance like everyone else without having her stomach in a knot about whether or not I'd be able to hit my high notes without gagging. In fact, by now I've established such a reliable track record that I haven't been able to find anyone who will take on the job, and the function of misery in performance preparation has come fully back into my court. Maybe I should place an ad: "Seeking opera lover with finely honed hand-wringing skills, paranoid hysterics a plus." Fortunately, I now tend to save this particular ritual for only the most high-profile engagements, and the rest I am actually able to enjoy.

Of all the lessons I was taught during my years at Potsdam, one of the things that gave me the most pleasure was learning how to practice. As a child, I had always memorized my part, attending every rehearsal religiously. Practice, though, was something I associated with musical instruments—in my case the piano, the violin, and then the viola. Heaven knows I pulled the string instruments out from under my bed on lesson day and dusted them off, erasing the evidence of not having practiced—as if the teacher wouldn't know. Now that I was studying music fully, I began to understand that I had to put in my time on my voice the same way I would have done were I in school studying the piano. I headed off for the practice room day after day, the tires of my beloved bicycle, George, crunching through the snow. I always loved walking into that small, spare space. As I made my way through the hall, I could hear people in other rooms singing or playing the violin or practicing whatever instrument they were learning, but that room would be mine alone. I would begin by vocalizing for twenty to thirty minutes, using the list of exercises I had conscientiously copied, and then I would practice whatever song or aria I had been assigned, trying to train my ear to catch my own mistakes. The words "practice" and "practical" are almost one and the same, and the more I worked, the more I saw their similarities. It was here that I began to develop my real passion for singing, for the process of exploring every corner of the enigmatic instrument of the voice. I still think it's a miracle that anyone learns how to sing well, since the mystery of coordinating involuntary muscles can seem impossible to unravel. It is a beautiful thing to sing in front of an audience, but singing to myself alone in a room, breaking down phrases note by note, word by word, is even more satisfying somehow, and that is how I began to learn.

Pat's other great influence on me had to do with repertoire. The vast mountains of music she owned represented unexplored terrain for a musical adventurer, much as my mother's music cabinet had earlier held similar treasures. Pat challenged me with Petrassi songs, a Britten canticle I adored, chamber music, Haydn and Handel arias in German. Once she saw that I was a good musician who could learn quickly, she moved me on to obscure song literature. One day, she handed me an old-fashioned and weathered piece of sheet music. The title was the "Song to the Moon" by Dvořák, which I learned in English. Little did we know how much this one aria would eventually forge my future. I was like an open well in the ground, waiting there to swallow up anything that came my way. Pat wasn't just training me vocally; she was also shaping me musically.

Any point she wanted to make about singing could be backed up by the recordings she had, and she was always encouraging me to listen to them. I would sit in her house in the evenings and make piles of cassette tapes: Janet Baker in Handel, Elly Ameling, Pilar Lorengar, Victoria de los Angeles. I still recall watching my first live television broadcast from the Met—*Don Giovanni*—curled up on her couch.

Ameling was my favorite singer then, because the great Dutch artist actually came to Potsdam a few times and performed. I listened to her recordings so intently that her influence could be heard in my singing. But it was also Ameling who, a few years later, taught me the power of a backstage visit, when, still a heart-on-my-sleeve student, I tried to tell her in a single, brief sentence that her singing meant everything in the world to me—even as, completely uninterested, she looked past me to the next person in line. I was crushed. Of course, it's not fair to expect an artist to respond to the needs of all her fans; but as a result, I have tried to emulate Jan DeGaetani, who would make each person in line feel as if *she* were the one who had given of herself that night and therefore deserved to be appreciated in kind. Jan would say, "Oh, I adored the recipe you sent!" or "My, how I love that necklace! Where did you find it?" and we would all stutter with delight, unable to imagine how she could be thinking of anything but the beautiful performance she had just given.

Music was so exciting to me in that period of my life, you would have thought it had been invented the week before. There were two pieces that absolutely obsessed me. One was Anne Trulove's aria from Stravinsky's *Rake's Progress*, "No word from Tom." I would sit in my dorm room every night and listen to it before I went to bed, and then it got to the point where I had to listen to it three or four times in a row. But it was almost like drinking three or four cups of espresso: the energy of that aria and the way it built made it impossible for me to sleep. Its jagged vocal line and its use of English with wrong syllabic accents were so quirky as to seem nearly electric in Judith Raskin's performance. I learned it and I sang it in a lot of auditions, but it was never that successful for me. People weren't familiar with the piece at the time; it seemed too long, and I didn't sing it quite well enough. It was hard for me to know the difference then between the things I madly loved and the things my voice was meant to sing. I operated under the mistaken impression that only an aria that was difficult for me would be impressive in an audition, rather than the correct idea that if the piece was easy, perhaps that meant it was a good fit. Still, this constant stretching ultimately gave me the solid technique I would need to withstand the real rigors of a career. The other piece that lodged itself in my imagination was Jan DeGaetani's recording of George Crumb's *Ancient Voices of Children*. I was so attracted to the mystery of the piece and the vocal writing that the "Todas las tardes en Granada" section—with its marimba tremolo and its exotic-sounding toy piano, DeGaetani's voice resonating directly into the piano, whispering, then the next moment shrieking—became my favorite piece for a while. Years later, when I had the good fortune to study with Jan and had the chance to get to know her better, it made me admire both the song cycle and the artist all the more.

Classical wasn't my only interest in those days. Potsdam was the place where I fell in love with jazz, a love that, for a while at least, I thought would be my life. When I had the chance to audition as a big-band singer my sophomore year, I jumped at it. My mother had taught with Esther Satterfield, who was Chuck Mangione's soloist when his Rochester-based band was enormously popular. Esther sang "The Land of Make-Believe," and that song, with all its sweet exhilaration, had always stayed with me. It was the piece I used for my audition, and I would picture myself as Billie Holiday, my hand cradling an old-fashioned silver microphone, a gardenia pinned behind one ear. I had worn out the soundtrack album of *Lady Sings the Blues* while learning every song from the piano/vocal score. I got the big-band job, which soon led to a weekly engagement with a jazz trio. We performed every Sunday night for two and a half years, developing an incredible following and packing the house week after week.

Singing with that group was a great release after spending school time disciplining my breathing and my resonance. Instead, this music was teaching me about performing. Jazz is, of course, incredibly inter-active, and every time a given song is played, its actual performance is going to be different. Singing jazz was a great way of letting go of my fears, because the music was just going to happen, and I had to make constant decisions about which direction I was going to go. It also taught me to be much more instinctive. As the vocalist, I quickly discovered it was my responsibility not only to sing but to make the friendly patter between numbers. I could handle the vertiginous high notes and the endlessly extemporaneous melodies, but simple sentences like "How's everybody doing tonight?" proved to be almost too much for me. Pat O'Leary, the bass player, would lean forward and smack me on the shoulder. "Say *some*thing!" he would hiss. "Tell a joke!"

A joke? No one had mentioned that in my job description. The worst of it was that at every performance it had to be a different joke, a new direction in my one-sided conversation. ("Pretty cold out there tonight, eh, Potsdam?") It was perfectly acceptable for me to sing the same songs week after week, but my unwritten monologues expired after a single use. The audience was like a shy blind date that expected me to make all the conversation, and so out of sheer necessity I did, but never with any flair. There are a lot of different ways to capture your audience's heart, but learning how to talk to them wasn't a bad place to start.

Jazz was also a perfect opportunity to experiment vocally. Pat came to see me a few times and during the breaks would say, "Do you know you just sang a high D above high C above high C?" Pat had perfect pitch, so she knew exactly what I was doing even when I didn't. I could hit those high notes as a jazz singer, mostly because I had no concept of just how high they were at the time. I was simply improvising. The trouble was that I couldn't yet manage the high notes I actually needed for the soprano repertoire. Anything above the staff, from G to high C, was still difficult, at best. These pitches were inconsistent, still strident and shrill.

Sometimes we would go out on tour. The guys in the group were a little older than I was, a little wiser. Larry Ham taught me how to make perfect omelets, and Eddie Ornowski drove me around the countryside in his big old white Cadillac with a red leather interior while listening to Schubert string quartets. I drank it all in.

My turning point came when legendary saxophonist Illinois Jacquet came to teach a master class and suggested later that I tour with him. (He had teared up when I sang "You've Changed," songs of unrequited love then being my forte.) That offer forced me to decide whether I wanted to be an opera singer or a jazz singer. In my heart, I knew I was too young and too frightened to move to New York, which a career in jazz would have required. I had not been raised to be an independent thinker. I couldn't decide what to cook for dinner without asking someone else for guidance. Jazz is the music of free will, and I still preferred to toe the line. So I stayed with what I knew, which was how to be a student.

After the Bach B-minor Mass, I sang Laurie in Aaron Copland's only opera, *The Tender Land,* the lead in a chamber opera by Gustav Holst called *The Wandering Scholar,* and Elsie Maynard in a great production of Gilbert and Sullivan's *Yeomen of the Guard.* Those roles, along with my jazz performances, placed me before real audiences and not just teachers and classmates. The drama and dance classes I took at Potsdam were incredibly helpful to me too. If I had gone to Eastman or Juilliard as an undergraduate in those days, I wouldn't have been able to study drama, because at that time there was no crossover between different divisions in the conservatories. This changed later when the necessity for fully rounded acting singers began to be appreciated, but by then my school days were behind me.

My major at Potsdam was music education. My parents, forever practical, insisted that I graduate from college with a skill that would ensure me a job. They had confidence in my abilities as a singer, but they had also been in the music business long enough to see that the streets were littered with talented sopranos who couldn't achieve a professional career. I had to be able to support myself on the very real possibility that my big dreams might never materialize. All I can say is that I'm lucky I made it as a performer, since the trials of Mozart seemed minor next to the semester I spent student-teaching in a public middle school. Eighth-graders, with their cracking voices and pinging hormones, remain one of the greatest challenges I have faced to this day. I had always respected what my parents did for a living, and had even thought I understood it, but it wasn't until I did some time in the classroom myself that I came to see what a daunting task teaching in public schools really was. When my brother, Ted, later followed in the family tradition and became a teacher, he earned my greatest admiration.

When the time came for me to graduate from Potsdam, I had a great deal of hesitation about leaving Pat, but she gently though firmly pushed me out of the nest. "Go out there and learn new things from different people," she urged me. I loved Pat and appreciated all she had done for me, and, as I reminded her, a lot of singers do spend their whole professional lives with one teacher. But she was insistent that it was time for me to go. With her encouragement and a lot of nudging, I moved on to Eastman to study for a master's degree in music.

In my first audition at Eastman I landed the role of Zerlina in *Don Giovanni* in another upset, surprising everyone, most of all myself. It was my first bona fide full-scale opera production, and I was thrilled to be on the stage of the Eastman Theatre after spending so much time there when I was growing up. This was an enormously ambitious production, and the baritone and I both worked out madly at the YMCA across the street, because he had to lift me in a dance scene. During the course of my career I have sung all three female roles in *Don Giovanni,* and Zerlina is certainly the place to start, her "Vedrai carino" being that opera's precious jewel of an aria. Donna Anna is the most difficult role to sing, with her two glorious scenes and one of the greatest accompanied recitatives ever composed. Da Ponte and Mozart portray her ambivalence toward Don Ottavio and then subtly allow us to surmise that Don Giovanni's attack unleashed a repressed passion in her, followed closely by the murder of her father and then a torrent of shame and sorrow. Donna Elvira, with whom I made my inauspicious La Scala debut, is wildly temperamental and more obvious: a perfect example of fatal attraction. Mozart was the solid cornerstone of my operatic repertoire for the next ten years, and I ultimately sang nine different Mozart roles, in many different productions. The Countess in *Le Nozze di Figaro* served as my debut role, first as a student at the Aspen Music Festival, then in Houston, at the Met, in Paris, at the Teatro Colón in Buenos Aires, in San Francisco, at both Spoleto Festivals, and in Hamilton, Canada, and I went on to sing her at Glyndebourne, in Geneva, and in Chicago. If anyone needed a Countess, I was the Go-to Girl, and I was lucky to have come to prominence at the commemoration of the bicentennial of Mozart's death in 1991. Frankly, I would have chosen Berio, Puccini, Berlioz, or Stravinsky—anything but Mozart—as my introduction to the international stages of the world. While I would have preferred to avoid having to live up to his requirement of crystal-clear, naked perfection, in retrospect I'm grateful for that repertoire, as it helped protect my voice. I had no choice but to sing well and carefully for that first decade of my career, maintaining a youthful weight and quality to my voice, when the demands of other composers—full-voiced drama over a heavy orchestration—would have used me up by now, and I'd likely be hearing from opera companies, "Thank you very much, but you have a wobble and your top isn't what it used to be." Sheer luck again sent me into Mozart's demanding but safe hands.

Director Richard Pearlman was running Eastman's opera department then, and I'll never forget the day he played a recording of Maria Callas in a class devoted to her art. He had known her, and he loved to tell a story about offering Callas a cup of cocoa during a rehearsal in Dallas. She refused it, saying, "No, thanks, honey, chocolate gives me pimples." The story made a huge impression on me, not so much her response as his reverence for her. All those years later you could still see the power she had over him as a young director. Every soprano in the class sat there thinking, *What would that be like?* As we listened to her singing he would tell us that her voice was beautiful, as if it were an objective fact rather than a controversial opinion. The first time I heard a Callas recording—and, for that matter, one by Elisabeth Schwarzkopf—I didn't understand why they were considered iconic when to my ear they weren't even particularly accomplished singers. Callas's voice seemed unattractive, with its overly covered, steely edge and its wide vibrato on top, and Schwarzkopf's vocal production struck me as uneven and eccentric, however beautiful the voice. But as often is the case with things that are unusual and unfamiliar, we develop a taste for them. We come to love certain voices because of their very flaws, their strangeness, and, most important, the way they can be identified by little more than a single note. After I had listened long enough and thoughtfully enough to these two sopranos, I came to a point where my heart belonged to both of them, along with those of their millions of other fans. I was probably especially sensitive to the idea of flaws at this time because I was trying so hard to iron out my own. Arleen Augér once remarked to John Maloy, who was one of my teachers at Eastman, that I'd be great if I could only get my technique together. I had the talent and the discipline, but I was still learning to sing, which meant I had plenty of kinks to work out if I wanted to make a career of singing. And while I had some successes at Eastman, I had my share of dismal failures as well—the very worst being my first audition for the Met National Council Auditions, a program designed to assist promising young singers in the development of their careers.

My accompanist was Richard Bado, a friend and a fellow student at Eastman. I was a quick study even then, and that talent did nothing but exacerbate my tendency toward procrastination. I memorized Pamina's aria from *Die Zauberflöte*, "Ach, ich fühl's," the week before the audition. My parents were in the audience with several of my friends, and the adjudicating panel, which had flown in to represent the Met, was right in the middle. I was polished and brushed and made up and well dressed, and as I looked out at all the people who loved me and the people who wanted me to do well and the people who were ready to give me a chance, I fell apart completely. We're talking white knuckles. All I could do was fantasize about fainting or falling through a hole in the stage. So many nervous singers long to fall through nonexistent stage holes that I have to wonder why recital halls across the world don't just go ahead and saw them into the floorboards. "Ach, ich fühl's" is a very exposed aria, sung for the most part very quietly. That's always been the thing that frightens me the most: anything that's exposed. Not the fireworks, fioriture, leaps, trills, or chest tones—those I can file my nails by. The terrifying place is that soft pitch in the middle voice. That drenches me in cold sweat. This was one of the first pieces I'd sung with this kind of exposure, so you have to wonder what I was thinking of when I chose it for such an important audition. My throat tightened completely. My breath stopped working, and I had a flutter in my sound that you could drive a truck through. I can still see my family's faces fall, and everyone in the house just sitting there with a look of growing embarrassment. Richard Bado told me later that he wanted to stand up in the middle of the audition and say, "We're going to stop now. She can do so much better than this, and I think we should just try again another year."

When it was finally over, after what felt like twenty years of standing there with my throat in a vise grip, I had my first real existential crisis. I saw a school-appointed therapist for the first time to discuss my growing realization that I didn't even understand what I was doing in graduate school. All I'd ever known was how to please others and how to do the right thing so that I could see a positive reflection of myself in their eyes. I was so steeped in the role of good girl that when I once skipped an opera rehearsal to attend a Bonnie Raitt concert, I couldn't enjoy it for the intense nausea I was experiencing. I'd been the perfect chameleon, becoming whomever the person I was talking to wanted me to be, and I don't mean only my parents or my teachers. I would behave this way with complete strangers. Somehow my botched audition brought all of that crashing down on my head. As a result of it, I started to pull together a genuine sense of who I was and what I wanted. It was then that music became mine for the first time, as I started to take responsibility for what I really wanted to achieve. This was not an amazing transformation, and it is one that many young performers experience, but it was the beginning of my real growth. John Maloy was very supportive through all of this, telling me it was all going to work out, and I believed him.

As much as I struggled with my fears, it never once occurred to me to just stop trying. My parents had drilled into me the code of Never Give Up. In my family, you didn't admit defeat, or change your mind and go on to something else. The core of my mother's philosophy, whether it involved being in a play or taking piano lessons or having a horse, was that you can take on anything you want, but you can't quit.

When I look back on it now, I can see that this crisis was inevitable. If it hadn't been the Met audition, it would have been something else. The passivity of my desire to please was holding me back from going on to the next level in my development. I needed to kick up all this dust and start questioning things so that I could learn the answers and move on. What I finally discovered was that in fact I really did love music, and especially singing, and I loved to learn about singing. It was time for me to stop worrying so much about what other people thought. It's such a simple concept but it was completely foreign to me.

My parents had divorced in 1981, and in the winter of 1983 my mother and her new husband, George Alexander, had a baby, my brother Geordie. I was there at the hospital waiting while she went into labor, and at the last minute I was invited in for the big event. There was my mother, at the age of forty-five, having her fourth baby! It was the moment I knew that I would have children myself one day. This angelic, curly-haired, towheaded baby is now Bryn Terfel–sized and is studying voice. He shadowed me in London last summer to see if the operatic lifestyle was one he could live with. The talent is there, but only time and his own strong desire to sing will tell.

That year I spent the first of several summers singing and studying at the Aspen Music Festival. It was a very sweet time in my life, with blue skies, serious musicians, and endless possibilities. I bicycled seven miles up to the Maroon Bells and back down every day. The glorious scenery was there for me no matter where I looked. After a winter in Rochester, a summer in Aspen is an almost unimaginable reward, and every year I could hardly wait to pack up my suitcase and my bicycle and get back there. I had applied to a lot of summer programs, but the only two that accepted me were Aspen and the Spoleto Festival. I have a noble history of being rejected by a lot of places, only to discover that the one that finally lets me in is in fact the perfect fit.

For two of my summers at Aspen I studied with Jan DeGaetani. She was a tremendous role model as a musician, above all. Her love of music and her gratitude for her art manifested itself through tears at nearly every master class. We students felt as if we had been granted membership in a clandestine and exclusive club, meeting in her crowded living room, singing for one another and discussing in hushed voices the intricacies of a text, the use of dynamics and resonance. I also met Ed Berkeley, who directed me in one of the best theatrical experiences I've had to this day, Conrad Susa's opera *Transformations*, a setting of Anne Sexton's poetry in which I played Sexton. We spent days on end just reading and analyzing her poems. The following summer I was cast as the Countess in *Le Nozze di Figaro*, in which Jorge Mester, who was the festival's director, heard me. It was he who suggested that I go to Juilliard for a postgraduate program, the next step in my education. One of the many reasons that my work is so endlessly exciting is that you never know who is going to be in the audience or the orchestra pit, holding your fate in his hands.

CHAPTER THREE

·APPRENTICESHIP·

*T*HE HEAD OF Juilliard's opera department was Erica Gastelli, an incredibly elegant Italian woman who was always perfectly put together in a way that seemed at once flawless and effortless. Whenever I think of her, I see a beautiful necklace she wore, which was made out of huge chunks of golden amber. The first thing I did when I made a little bit of money as a singer was to buy myself an amber necklace. This is often the way we put together our lives, adding the striking qualities of others into our own character. Whether it was Erica Gastelli's style or Elisabeth Schwarzkopf's ease with languages or Beverly Sills's ability to draw her public close to her, I made a careful study of the qualities I admired and did my best to emulate them. The other students in the program and I used to impersonate Erica's thick Italian accent, mimicking the way she criticized our hair or our clothes, beginning with a finger-wagging "Oh, Renée . . . ," followed by "Why would you wear that *aaawful* dress?"

It was Erica who had called me at my parents' house right after I'd come home from Aspen to announce, "You have been accepted to the Juilliard program. We would like you to sing Musetta in *La Bohème*." She had a very low speaking voice, very formal—the kind of voice that makes you stand up straighter even if you're only speaking on the phone, the kind of voice that under normal circumstances would have demanded a very dignified response. At this moment, though, I had no dignity. I felt as if I had been shot out of a cannon. I dropped the phone and screamed, running through the house, crying, "Juilliard! Juilliard!" My mother was home, as were Ted and Rachelle, and they joined in the shouting. It was pure bedlam, as it would be the three or so times later in my life when the truly great phone calls arrived. When I finally remembered what I had done, I crept back into the kitchen and picked the phone up off the floor, certain that if Erica was still on the line she would inform me that Juilliard had changed its mind. She was not amused; but then, as I was to find out later, she was never amused.

Juilliard had a postgraduate training program then called the American Opera Center. Being accepted there was an enormous boon to me for many reasons, not the least of which was that it was free. For two and a half years I could audit any language class and study voice, perform in opera productions, and coach both music and diction. The only expenses I had to cover were my room and board. I could never have afforded to live in New York City and pay for so much instruction. I would have been lucky to manage the occasional voice lesson, maybe a bit of coaching, but I never would have been able to learn as much as I did. I still had a very long way to go.

After witnessing my heartbreak over the failed Met audition and the tumultuous period of growth that followed, my father didn't want me moving to New York. "You'll end up jumping off a bridge," he warned me. He worried that living in the city would overwhelm me, but I loved it. I found a temp job in Rockefeller Center with a group of opera singers at a law firm, assigned to an enormous asbestos case—a case from which my own grandfather ultimately would benefit. The firm had well-educated, reliable, and honest workers in us, and we had almost complete flexibility regarding our hours. I had earlier acquired excellent secretarial and touch-typing skills while temping, which was probably related to the eye-hand coordination I had developed through years of studying piano. This job enabled me to take advantage of everything Juilliard had to offer. I also added to my income by singing in New York City churches, which used students to supplement their amateur choral ranks.

Jorge Mester was slated to conduct the production of *La Bohème* in which I would appear, and Graziella Sciutti, who had only recently retired from the stage, would be directing it. Musetta would have been her role, whereas I was anything but typecast. My extreme inhibitions prevented me from displaying any of the sass and sway needed for a seductive Musetta. Sciutti finally threw up her hands and said, "I cannot make this girl do anything!" That was when my favorite coach, Ubaldo Gardini, stepped in. Ubaldo would work with me for hours. "Why do you want to bang on that note?" he would whine, as I pressured out the high A in "Dove sono." He also gave me some advice that I follow to this day: "Sing in the mirror. If it looks funny, it's wrong." He was as frustrated with my Musetta as Sciutti was, and he finally ordered, "Just walk across the stage and swing your hips." But I couldn't manage even that. Musetta, of course, is a legendary coquette, and I was a famously shy girl from upstate. Even if I could learn how to talk the talk, I was hopeless when it came to walking the walk. Still, I was confident that once I got my costume on everything would be fine. Back then, I could be Musetta only if I *looked* like Musetta. I had to be physically transformed before I could become a character onstage. Fortunately, I got over that. Learning to quickly assume a role is a necessary part of the profession. In my current rehearsal days, murder, rape, sobs, and vengeance often follow a coffee break. One has to swallow and simply take the plunge, embracing the dramatic, emotional language of opera.

Of course, swinging my hips and batting my eyelashes as Musetta was a minor dilemma compared with what I faced in my next Juilliard production, Gian Carlo Menotti's *Tamu-Tamu*. Then the question was whether or not I'd go onstage topless. *Tamu-Tamu* opens with a middle-class family reading the newspaper, talking about how tragic things are in a third-world country they've never heard of before. There's a knock at the door, and suddenly all the people they've been reading about are standing on their front doorstep, grass skirts and all. I played the suburban mother, and at one point one of the girls, who was sufficiently covered by her beads and long hair, and I were supposed to exchange costumes, which meant I would be going topless. It was a scandal. My voice teacher walked into the office of Juilliard's new president, Joseph Polisi, and said, "Under no circumstances will a student of mine be pressured into performing topless. There must be another solution!" In the end I wore a body stocking, with garishly painted nipples. Who knew that real nipples wouldn't read in the house, and that painted ones would look more realistic?

My memories of Juilliard fall into two distinct categories: On one hand there was the school, the productions I was in, the friends I made, and my beloved diction coaches, Tom Grubb, Corradina Caporello, and Kathryn LaBouff. On the other, there was Beverley Johnson. Certainly I have Juilliard to thank for providing the means for us to work together. But then Beverley became a force in my life so much greater than any school could ever be that when I think of her it's not as part of Juilliard, but simply as part of my life.

All Juilliard students were expected to find a voice teacher, and at that time they were allowed to study only with someone on the school's faculty. Beverley taught there and at the Aspen Music Festival, so I approached her about a consultation. Within five minutes she had me on the floor doing sit-ups while she admonished me about several vocal issues. And that was that. We'd found each other. I was looking for the kind of detailed instruction I had gotten from Pat Misslin, and there it was, on Beverley's living-room rug.

Beverley had an extremely distinctive look, with a very long chin that she was forever, in all the years that I knew her, trying to hide. Not long after I met her, she decided she would never be photographed again. She was a very slim woman with such perfect posture that if you saw her from the back, you would think she was twenty-five years old, not the approximately eighty she probably was. She might not have had much luck hiding her chin, but she hid her age perfectly.

Beverley wasn't a very popular teacher when I began studying with her. Teachers go in and out of fashion over the years, and someone who had taught as long as Beverley had become accustomed to going from being the instructor everyone fights to study with to being last on the list and back again, two or three times in the course of a career. I happened to catch her when she was out of fashion, which was all the better for me because she had more time.

Although Beverley had studied singing, she was trained as a pianist. Her husband, Hardesty Johnson, was a singer, and it was he who had originally been brought to Juilliard to teach. She eventually joined the faculty in 1964. The interesting thing about her being an instrumentalist was that she intellectualized the voice, studying it much more than a singer probably would have, which ultimately led to her becoming so strong a technician.

I had technical issues that still needed to be resolved, and she was so technically oriented and focused on physiology that we responded to each other immediately. Between the sit-ups, her breathing exercises, and the way we were able to communicate with each other, it was almost like hearing the locks on a safe all tumble into their correct sequence. I ultimately worked with Beverley for sixteen years, and it's safe to say that she did more for my singing than anyone else.

Of course, Beverley wasn't the only voice teacher who was asking her students to do seemingly strange things. In one master class, I had to sing before an audience while lying on the floor. Another teacher had me leaning against a wall, then leaning over the piano, then singing while bent in half, touching the floor. Teachers will do almost anything to encourage the body to release tension in some areas while maintaining strength and energy in others. It's a coordination process that is technically complicated and difficult to achieve both physically and psychologically, demanding all available resources to get the necessary elements to line up properly. Beverley used to say that tension in your upper lip could ruin your voice for the day, a connection that you wouldn't even remotely think of making. She would instruct me to take my finger and press down on my upper lip while I was singing, and suddenly the sound would free up. It seemed impossible, and yet I could hear the difference. There are so many different muscles that can affect vocal production that it's almost impossible to check all of them off in your mind, and even more impossible to control them, since they are largely involuntary.

Beverley kept a battered copy of *Gray's Anatomy* close to her piano among the stacks of scores. She was forever pulling it out to explain something about the mechanism of the voice. "See that?" she would say, tapping on the page. She would show me a drawing of the pharynx and the larynx, the epiglottis and hard and soft palates, the breath cavities and the diaphragm.

One of the first issues we addressed was fine-tuning my understanding of the principles of breathing and support. To think about breath, I first had to divide it into three parts. I had to learn the best way to take in a breath and to use the space in the lungs and body efficiently; the best way to control breath release; and the best way to support sound with breath. Unlocking the body's ability to take in the most possible air is a process both of expansion and of releasing tension. Ask a nonsinger to take in a huge breath, and he will usually lift his shoulders and chest, pulling in his abdominal muscles, actions that are followed by a red face and straining neck muscles—not a posture conducive to beautiful singing. Contrarily, a singer learns to release her abdominal wall and back muscles outward, without pushing, as much as is humanly possible, allowing the diaphragm, *involuntarily*, to release down and the lungs to expand to their fullest. Crucial to this process is a release of the intercostal muscles, the ones that connect the ribs; releasing them allows the rib cage to expand outward and slightly upward as well. The chest rises last, but the shoulders and neck remain relaxed. This entire sequence should be carried out with as little tension as possible. Release, expand, visualize your torso as a barrel, imagine a low breath to begin with, release the back of your neck, make space in your mouth and nose, don't suck in air, no tension in your mouth and nose either—these and similar instructions began to enable me to develop breath capacity.

Second, breath control enables the efficient use of precisely the amount of air needed for any given phrase, whether a long, sustained line or a short, powerful burst. Contrary to what one might think, it takes more air to produce low notes than high ones. More air escapes through the vocal folds during the slower vibrations of a lower phrase than in the much faster oscillations of a top C. Think of how different pitches of whistling feel, or even of making sounds by blowing into different-sized bottles. The air flow is more concentrated for a higher pitch. It takes a singer time and physical maturity to develop the deep, sustaining breaths of a swimmer; negotiating a long passage of Richard Strauss is, in fact, a little like being underwater.

The third requirement, breath support, is both the most complicated and the most controversial part of a singer's breathing technique. This was one of the most important pieces of the singing puzzle I received from Beverley. Few are in agreement about the best way to support a voice, but it's the support that allows a singer to manage a "cultivated scream" for three hours without causing herself pain and harm. When a singer uses her body and breath properly to support the voice, it takes the strain completely off the throat. My ear, nose, and throat doctor, David Slavit, marvels at the fact that we can sing for hours—a feat that ought to leave blood on the floor—yet come in the next day with baby-fresh vocal cords, showing no signs of redness, swelling, or strain. The same is rarely true of sports fans, who after shouting throughout a stadium match are generally hoarse or unable to speak. Stage actors have to learn support just as we do, or they could never withstand a regimen of eight shows a week, although the increasing presence of amplification even for plays is reducing the necessity for this kind of technique. Singers nevertheless rest between performances, for our Herculean "weight lifting for voices" needs a day off, just as power lifters would never train the same way runners do. Interestingly enough, the heavier the voice, the more such rest is necessary. A lyric voice such as mine, which less often engages in "extreme singing," actually benefits from regular daily training, with flexibility being the key goal.

How I support my breath is relatively simple to explain, but in practice a difficult process to really coordinate. Once I have taken in that optimal breath, and my abdominal wall is open, out, and expanded, along with as much of the rest of my torso as possible, I resist allowing these muscles to collapse again. "Resist" is the key word: if I continue to push out, I'll lose the connection of the breath and create tension in my throat; if I allow it all to collapse quickly, I'll have a breathy tone and not enough air to sing even a short phrase. Another crucial part of this formula is to keep the intercostal muscles out as well, and to prevent the chest from collapsing. I learned this particular technique from observing other singers, and there is a valid reason that caricatures of opera singers so often portray them as pigeon-chested. When I'm singing comfortably, I can actually imagine that my torso and my breath are doing all the work, while my throat is completely relaxed. Years of practice and experimentation led me to this optimal combination, which enables me to sing high-tessitura pieces, which are not by nature comfortable for me.

While I was trying to understand how my own body worked, there was also music to learn and the entire concept of developing an artistic interpretation to wrestle with. For me, as for most singers, the process required a huge amount of time, energy, and practice. Of course, every now and then there's someone who just happens to come by all of it naturally—the twenty-five-year-old who just opens his or her mouth, and by some miracle it's all there. But even the greatest natural talent in the world needs to learn how to support and care for her instrument. In that respect the voice is like an inheritance: no matter how great it is, you still have to figure out a way to make it last. Everything breaks down at some point, and if the singer doesn't know how to fix it, she will quickly fall by the wayside.

I've finally accepted the fact that singing takes ten minutes to explain and ten years to accomplish. This was all work I had begun as a high-school student. Each teacher brought me further along with different explanations of the same concepts; often my understanding of those concepts was a result of my own experience or discovery, and sometimes it was just plain luck. Learning how to sing is rarely a process that follows a straight line, and it's rarely clearer than fog until one grasps it in its totality.

Most singers are like me, building up every little note, every notch, as if the voice were a mosaic put together one tiny colored tile at a time. It's the puzzle again. Because I wasn't a natural, I had to develop a very intricate understanding of how my instrument worked, with a clear-eyed assessment of its strengths and weaknesses. I had to create a technique that was reliable regardless of how I was feeling. Someone once said that there are probably seven naturally good singing days in a year—and those are days you won't be booked. What we must learn is how to sing through all the other days.

At the start of my second year at Juilliard, I had to make a choice: I could stay where I was, continuing my work with Beverley and singing the lead in Gounod's *Mireille* the following year, or I could accept a Fulbright grant for study in Frankfurt, Germany. I have always been a big believer in auditioning. I knew enough to realize that most of the things I applied for would never come through, so I always thought it was best to just go ahead and throw my hat in the ring for everything feasible and then decide what to do if I won. This was just part of how I worked: if there was a grant, a competition, a scholarship, I gave it a try. For me, it was all part of the Shoulds. I should do this. I should try for that. "Should" was my steady diet my whole life. The Fulbright application was part of the Should diet.

John Maloy, my teacher from Eastman, was on the Fulbright panel that year, and he strongly encouraged me to accept the fellowship. Beverley was equally adamant that I should stay and continue my studies with her, arguing in an almost maternal way that my voice and I weren't ready for the wide world. Fulbrights are extremely difficult for singers to get. Although I would rather have gone to France or Italy, Germany took the largest number of vocalists. In Germany I would also have the chance to study with Arleen Augér, whom I had liked so much when I met her in Aspen and who had fortuitously agreed to accept me as a student.

In order to help me make a decision, I started polling people, which is another lifelong habit of mine. Getting others involved in my decisions is a little like having them worry about me just before a performance. Jan DeGaetani told me I'd be a fool not to go, that it was a great opportunity. "I so regret never having learned a foreign language," she said. I talked over the matter with my parents, my friends, and my boyfriend. I tallied up everyone's opinions, and then I made my own decision. In the end, even if every single person had told me to stay, I still would have gone. Ironically I am actually quite strong in my own judgments, for as much as I crave to hear everyone's advice about what I should do, I always know to listen to my inner voice where my career is concerned. This intuition, along with resilience, has been a fundamental anchor of my professional life.

I kissed everyone good-bye and got on the plane confident that I'd made the right choice, but the minute we took off I was mortified. What had I done? Was I out of my mind? I was shy, I hated being alone, I didn't speak German. It's a good thing that they don't turn planes around, because at that moment I was convinced that what I really needed to do was to move home and get a job as a secretary.

When I arrived in Frankfurt, the first thing I did was to go and find Arleen. She had already warned me in Aspen, "It's fine that you're coming, but I really won't have much time to work with you. My career is taking off right now." She had just sung at Prince Andrew and Sarah Ferguson's wedding, and she was suddenly becoming a big star in the United States. She nevertheless promised, "I'll be here maybe six times this year, and then we'll work." Because I was happy for any attention I could get, I told her that arrangement would be fine with me.

In our lessons, she compared the voice to floors in a hotel, with each tone occupying its own floor. It was my job to find the optimum space and place and position for each tone. She knew what she was talking about. Technically speaking, Arleen sang better than anyone else I've ever heard. She made 150 recordings in her life, and they were all as close to perfect as it gets; her Konstanze in *Die Entführung aus dem Serail* is a particular marvel.

Arleen's floors-in-the-hotel analogy helped me to consciously even out my range. One of the first tasks for a singer looking to develop an operatic range is smoothing over passages, or breaks. A break is a transition in the voice, the best example of which is the kind of high lonesome yodeling that made Hank Williams Sr. a legend. Yodelers go from high to low with a huge, audible break in between, and while it's charming in goat herders and country-music icons, it can sink an opera singer in the course of a single aria. Our breaks may not be as audible, but that doesn't mean they aren't still very much there. What a teacher has to do is to increase the singer's range while establishing an even sound from the top to the bottom of it. We use the word *passaggio,* which is Italian for "passage," to describe usually two transition points in the voice. A singer must make sure the passage is a smooth and seamless one. Within a range of anywhere from one and a half to three octaves, a classical singer, unlike a pop singer, needs to have a sound that's homogeneous throughout, without any breaks the audience can hear. The sound also has to be beautiful, another burden that most pop singers don't carry. In opera, vocal production must sound easy and effortless, and that's where the challenge lies.

I think of my voice as an hourglass. The bottom has breadth and width and a color that is deeper and darker. As I go up through the passaggio, which for me consists of the tones between E-flat and F-sharp at the top of the staff, I must imagine a sound that is narrow, like the waist of the hourglass. The passaggio is slim and focused, and there can be no pressure or weight there, just as you wouldn't want to put any weight on such a delicate passageway of glass. As the voice moves into the top of the hourglass, the sound can open up and blossom. It takes on warmer colors and more breadth again. Every voice is different, and many singers might think of their voices as a column that is even all the way up and down, but for me the defining feature is the curve, the passaggio.

It's in the dangerous straits of the passaggio that many singers come to grief. They try to carry the full weight of the middle voice up through it, muscling their way to the top, or they carry the head voice down, causing weakness and fatigue in the bottom. Singers can also get away with a lot based on youth, strength, and enthusiasm, only to find ten years later that what was once just a niggling problem has brought their careers to an end. Lower-passaggio tones between the chest voice and middle voice are also problematic for women, especially for mezzo-sopranos. When we speak of a singer as having two or three voices, it's because she has allowed these transitions to become abrupt gear shifts, which can be fine for dramatic emphasis or for Hank Williams Sr., but a steady diet of them isn't recommended for a classically trained voice.

I had a great deal of admiration for Arleen, not only as a singer but as a person. She had very high principles and she was always clear about where she stood on every issue. Early in our lessons she said to me, "I will teach you to the best of my ability, but I will not help you professionally, because really, you young singers are breathing down my neck. Professionally, you are on your own."

Coming from anyone else, such a declaration could have been off-putting to say the least, but Arleen presented it as simply a statement of fact, making it clear how she could help and how she couldn't. I appreciated that kind of candor, as it meant that our lessons stayed purely in the realm of learning an art form, and I could, at least for the time I was with her, leave the business of business at the door. Of course, Arleen did help me professionally, not only by improving my voice but by virtue of the fact that I could cite her as one of my major teachers.

I had completely the opposite experience that same year in Germany with a Canadian soprano, a woman I had never studied with, or even met, named Edith Wiens. She had a huge concert career in Germany, and I was fortunate enough to encounter her at a rehearsal of Britten's *War Requiem* in which she was singing the soprano solo. I had taken a seat in the front row, with only a handful of people in the audience, and I loved the piece so much that I must have sat there beaming through the entire rehearsal. When it was over, she came up to me and asked, "Who are you?" After I introduced myself she told me, "I love your face. I love what you gave to me in this rehearsal. How can I help you?" She sat down with me, a complete stranger, and wrote out the names of all the important managers in Germany. She gave me a couple of hours' worth of business classes, telling me all about how to get started as a singer. It was strange and lucky that I found those two halves of what I needed in different people, and that they came together to form such a complementary whole.

I had come to Germany armed only with some French from school, which of course wasn't very useful. I had one month of intense study at a Goethe Institute on the Rhine before my studies began. After braving the train from the airport alone, with my two suitcases, which were meant to hold a year's worth of my belongings, I arrived at my rented room, which belonged to a kindly retired couple. I walked around the village and was immediately picked out as an American by a brash local who spoke a little English and invited me for coffee. I nearly choked on my first taste of *Sprudel* water, and after he left, when I reached for a *Brötchen*, the waitress nearly slapped my hand. I felt like Dorothy, hungry on the yellow brick road, trying to pick an apple only to be angrily rebuked by the apple tree. Needless to say, I had no clue that she was telling me that unlike at home, bread had to be paid for. I scurried back to my room and didn't leave it until classes began the following morning.

I ultimately enjoyed my intensive language study, both for the lessons themselves and for the stimulation of an international student body. I was pleasantly surprised one day before graduation when our teacher pulled me aside and said that if my singing career didn't work out, I could pursue a career as a linguist. So, armed with what I believed was some degree of facility in the German language, I was placed with a family for a month in Frankfurt before my music studies were to begin. At the end of our first afternoon together, I remember thinking, *Okay, this is a nightmare*. I could not understand a word that anyone said—not a single word. And the Schulz family made no concessions to me either, by speaking slowly or simply. They just lived their lives—teaching me how to knit and to pick edible mushrooms and to light real candles on Christmas trees; discussing art and technology—and talked as if I could keep up. And eventually I did. By the end of this year of total immersion, I had learned to speak fairly fluent German, which has only become stronger with time. Whenever I return to Germany, people say to me, "I can't believe how much your German has grown!" But I think that once the foundation is laid, the neurons just keep firing. Languages always improve for me over the years, regardless of whether or not I use them very consistently, in much the same way as music. The roles I have learned deepen and acquire more layers without my studying them or singing them or even *thinking* about them in between performances. The fact that music is as much a language as German or French is one aspect of learning that fascinates me.

After I left my new friends, the Schulzes, I moved into a dorm, a high-rise *Studentenheim,* where I had a tiny room and shared a common bathroom and kitchen with the other students. At the Hochschule für Musik, I befriended a British woman named Helen Yorke, a pianist. We were both so relieved on the first day of school, literally the first day, to find someone we could talk with. Helen and I laughed together constantly. We went to concerts and coffeehouses, endlessly discussing music and home and the future, reveling in the sound of each other's English. Helen played many recitals for me after that.

I applied to the opera department at the Hochschule but was rejected. As was true at so many points in my life, being turned down proved to be a stroke of luck. Excellent opera instruction was easy to come by at home; what I got instead was something much more valuable and rare: a year in which to study exclusively German lieder with Hartmut Höll. I thought he was a musical genius, illuminating for us his unconventional interpretations of the Wolf, Webern, and Schubert songs we were studying, and I'm honored now to have opportunities to share the concert stage with him. Helen and I coached with him as much as he would allow. Though it wasn't a style that would have worked for everybody, I loved his way of dissecting every note. Faced with his method, many students would balk: "I don't want to do it the way you're doing it. I have a different idea about that phrase. Just give me a framework so I can develop my own interpretation," but I used his interpretations as a template for forging my own, years later.

It seemed that everywhere I turned in Germany, another golden opportunity was waiting. I also studied lieder with Rainer Hoffmann that year, combing the vast lied repertoire for undiscovered jewels. He later pointed me to Schubert's "Viola," which became the cornerstone of my Schubert recording and my Salzburg recital debut with Christoph Eschenbach. Imagine a whole year in which to indulge the thirst for the discovery of literature that Pat Misslin had instilled in me. With my *Studentenausweis* (student ID card), I also went to the opera three times a week for three or four dollars, soaking up new repertoire, absorbing every scrap of culture I could. The Frankfurt Opera was under the music directorship of the conductor Michael Gielen, who encouraged truly cutting-edge theatrical work at that time. Ruth Berghaus's productions there were famous, as was an *Aida* in which Aida is a modern-day *Putzfrau*, a cleaning lady, in a contemporary museum of ancient artifacts. Audiences would be *screaming* at the end of performances, whether booing or cheering, and fights would break out—and all over an opera! It was thrilling. My favorite opera was

Strauss's *Capriccio*. I would sit through the entire piece, barely understanding a single phrase, just to get to the final scene. My taste in what constitutes a successful operatic performance was developed that year. I realized that I wanted to believe fully in the characters and the story and I wanted to be moved. Vocal shortcomings were always distracting, as was a "diva" performance of Mimì or the Countess, since I couldn't forget the *performer*. When the piece was over, I would get on my bicycle and ride back to the dorm, singing to myself phrases of what I had just heard and dreaming of someday sharing the stage with the wonderful artists I had seen that evening.

Professionally, I was growing quickly, but personally, I was miserable at times. It took me six months to gain enough comfort in the language so that I could communicate with other students and begin to socialize. Helpfully, Arleen sat me down shortly after I arrived and said, "Everything here is based on some form of one-upmanship. And if you can get comfortable with that, people aren't offended. Nobody gets angry, nobody holds a grudge, but assertiveness is respected." That at least gave me some sort of framework for what I was experiencing. My biggest triumph came at the end of the year when somebody cut in front of me at a vending machine and I cut back in front of him and said, "I was here first." To do all of this in a foreign language was doubly challenging. Germany taught me a great lesson, because while situations could often seem aggressive, nothing was personal. Once I understood that there was no emotion behind the attitude, it just became a different way of maneuvering through the day. I also learned to be genuinely grateful for the directness of my fellow students. If I had an off day singing, they would simply say, "You sound terrible today." At Juilliard, no one would have dreamt of offering so blunt an opinion, but they would have whispered it in the hallway after I left. There's a comfort in always knowing where you stand, and in Germany I knew where I stood, every minute, every note.

I've never been sure if sensitivity is a burden or a gift. The part of me that is moved to tears over a piece of music is the same part of me that can put that much feeling back into what I sing. On the other hand, when a nest of baby rabbits I was taking care of as a girl died, I was devastated beyond all reason. When a boy blew smoke in my face at a junior-high-school party, I thought I'd have to be carried out on a stretcher. In Germany, several things happened that sent me reeling. One was seeing an Iranian political protest poster in the hallway of my dorm, picturing a man being dismembered. I had a similar experience years later viewing the film *The Cook, the Thief, His Wife and Her Lover*. While I believe that extreme emotion is a reasonable response to extreme cruelty, I knew I had to toughen up if I was going to get through life, to find a way to stay vulnerable to certain things while at the same time growing more thick-skinned about life in general. All of my emotions sat too close to the skin, and I needed to rein them in. For me that was as much a physical process as learning how to connect through my registers.

Of course, there are some circumstances that would reduce almost anyone to a quivering bowl of Jell-O.

If I had been asked how I felt about Elisabeth Schwarzkopf before I took her master class, I would have said that a week's work with her was reason enough to spend a year in Germany. By now I had come to idolize her, and she only reinforced those feelings when she walked into the room that first day and spoke in three different languages to three different students inside of two minutes without missing a beat. It made a powerful first impression. Even by her very entrance, she epitomized everything I wanted to be: smart and glamorous and in command. She was the kind of person who brought the room to hushed attention just by walking into it. Everyone wanted to please her.

We worked with her in two long sessions, every day, for a week. Master classes are themselves a form of entertainment, conducted before an audience, which creates a very specific kind of dynamic. In our public, evening classes, Schwarzkopf chose to entertain her audience, but often at the expense of the students she was teaching. In my own case, one day I was the golden girl and the next I could do nothing right. I would sing two notes, and her hand would slice through the air to cut me off: "Nein, das ist es nicht."

I would attempt the two notes again, and she would shake her head. "Haben Sie nicht verstanden? Nochmals!"

My shoulders were drawing up toward my neck, my breath tightening. The other students looked away from me, relieved that for a moment I was the object of her attention. I tried again, and this time she was right: I sounded awful.

I was young, probably too young, and certainly not a finished singer. I'm sure she worked much better with performers who were ready for her, who were more confident in what they were doing. I wanted desperately to please her. I would have sung balanced on my nose if she had asked me. Yet even in the worst moments when she would interrupt me to sing a note or a phrase herself, I would think, *Oh, my God, it's her! It's* her *voice! It's that silvery tone!*

Fortunately, she was also imparting a lot of information. Her interpretive advice was brilliant and gave me more of a foundation for understanding how to use language in lieder. Further, I had always concentrated on making a healthy sound, but she was the first person who ever said to me, "You are responsible for the sound you make, the actual tone quality and whether or not it is beautiful." It was a powerful statement coming from her, since her own sound was so strangely manufactured, which is the very quality in her voice that I have come to develop a taste for over the years. She was the one who encouraged me to find a sound that was beautiful. Until then, my sound had often been criticized as too bright, even strident.

Ultimately, it was one vocal concept she imparted that added another important piece to the puzzle of my voice. She introduced me to the idea of *covering*. Nearly all tenors and baritones cover if they want to maneuver well into the top. For women, it's optional. In covering, as a singer moves up through the high passaggio, the transition area, she changes the very direction of the flow of air. Her use of resonance transforms the sound from a forward-placed, bright one that is entirely open to an almost *oh* or *ooh* position, directed toward the soft palate. The basic forward direction of the sound is never abandoned; a "domed" quality is added just above the passaggio. This gives the tone a covered sound, as if the singer has just taken a bright tone and put a lid on it. High notes can then bloom without pressure, as opposed to being harsh or spread.

As negative as the Schwarzkopf master-class experience seemed to me at the time, I look back on it now and can appreciate the two-year-long technical search she sent me on. Without it, and another six months at Juilliard fine-tuning my voice, I don't know how I would ever have found security at the top of my range. And what's a soprano without high notes? Schwarzkopf also established the very model of what a great Strauss singer is today, changing the focus from cantabile expression to declamatory expression, and emphasizing text over music. It sounds like something Strauss himself might have written an opera about.

My week with Schwarzkopf contributed to the development of my own philosophy about the purpose and benefit of master classes. The student who takes part in them has a very short exposure to the teacher, who is often an idol, which gives each criticism or bit of praise heightened importance. While useful information can be imparted, there is never a follow-up session to see if these concepts have been correctly assimilated. Today, in my own master classes, I try to be generally diagnostic, always with the disclaimer that the student should discuss my ideas with his own teacher. I am also conscious of including the student in any "jokes," so that no one feels as if he is being ridiculed. I enjoy entertaining the audience, but I never do so by undermining a student's budding confidence in a very difficult art.

Several different talents contribute to making a great teacher. Diagnostic skill is the first and most complex. Analyzing a voice and discerning why it isn't functioning freely, beautifully, and artistically are like trying to dissect a snowflake. Each instrument is entirely different from all the others, because each mind and each body that produce it are different. Because the instrument itself can't even be seen, one can only guess at the underlying faults by reading signals of tension, hearing fine gradations in use of resonance, and unlocking inhibitions and creativity in each young mind. The second major requirement is the ability to prescribe solutions for whatever these vocal issues are. If a singer cannot, say, descrescendo without the tone's cutting out, or if she cannot sing above the staff at all, a teacher must have at hand the relevant exercises, images, and physiological explanations that might address the problem. And the solutions for one singer may not work for another. Among the important realizations I had in my own days in the practice room was that if one route to any one phrase didn't work after days of trying, then the exact opposite route should at least be explored, as well as every alternative in between, as counterintuitive as that often seemed.

I sometimes think it's a miracle that anyone learns how to sing well, given the complexity of the instrument. It's not surprising, for example, that most great singers do not become great teachers. Some will openly admit that they haven't a clue how to explain what they do, and some can explain *only* that, without being able to apply it to other voices. The greatest barrier between the teacher and student is the involuntary muscles that produce the voice, muscles that have to be coaxed into fine coordination so that they can produce an even, beautiful sound extending through a singer's full range. But another hurdle to overcome is terminology. It can take six months to develop a common language between teacher and student. What does she really mean when she says she wants me to have "higher resonance"? What does anyone mean by "more support"? Someone can tell you that you need to relax, but relax where? Relax *what*? Oh, and now you want more energy at the same time? When I feel energized I also feel tense. How am I supposed to reconcile those demands?

A third requirement is the interpersonal factor. A teacher needs to be able to read her students. She has to be able to know who is sensitive and who is thick-skinned, who is bullheaded and who is stubborn. She has to teach differently for different personalities and for different stages of development. She must also have a keen sense of how she is being perceived. If she is so aggressively negative with a young student that he begins to shrink into a little ball at the side of the piano, singing smaller and smaller, and worse and worse, then the teacher should have the sensitivity to know that her approach isn't working. She's going to have to try another approach, which may simply mean being encouraging on that particular day. Some teachers have achieved enormous success by doing nothing more than stroking egos and holding hands.

And lest you think that the students are absolved of all responsibility, they face a challenge as well. Some of the greatest talents have the most fragile egos, unable to accept even the gentlest criticism and explaining away every fault. Needless to say, these singers don't go very far. The student's job is to stay open-minded, to quell the knee-jerk defensiveness we all possess in the face of suggestions for improvement, and to maintain patience when faced with a process that is often slow, confusing, and frustrating. On top of all that, the student must possess an unerring intuition about whether the instruction fits his particular needs. If not, he must be able to risk the necessary confrontation and move on to another teacher. Many young talents enter a studio, only to emerge three or four years later singing worse than when they began. A singer colleague of mine who had more drive and energy than I ever dreamt of having, not to mention tremendous vocal ability and intelligence, just didn't have the right intuition about what sort of teaching would benefit her most. She gave up after ten frustrating years, several teachers, and an enormous expenditure of money and hope. If singing were easy, that would never happen. Perhaps it's not intuition that guides a student but luck, or most likely a combination of both. Why did I have the good fortune over a period of ten years to keep finding the right keys to the doors, while my colleague failed? Although I used to joke that if I wasn't born with a particular vocal flaw, I would do my best to seek it out and try it on for size, eventually I found my way. Ultimately, it's the student who has to stand alone in the practice room and explore, using her creativity and imagination to flesh out the teacher's suggestions. In the end, singing isn't a science, but a highly cultivated, almost perverse use of our natural voices, and it requires persistence.

Sitting in my hotel room at two a.m. after a recital and perhaps a CD signing in which a hundred fresh young faces waited to meet me, after flipping through the 169 cable channels at least five times to wind down, I often wonder just what will become of those bright talents when their dreams of a life on the stage aren't realized. A conservatory director recently related to me the story of a young New York City taxi driver whom he complimented on the music she was playing on the radio. After he introduced himself, she burst into tears and said, "I'm a Juilliard graduate, and this is the only work I can get with my degree!" He rightly commented to me that her talents and top-flight education would have been put to better use helping our dwindling audiences grow, so that she could indeed at some future time have a chance to perform. One major study observed that in recent years, we have done a magnificent job of turning out fabulously trained performers with no place to play. More encouraging news is that employment options and a real strategy for developing the arts are becoming part of many conservatory curricula. My young singer friend eventually moved to Colorado Springs and started her own music school, using her vitality and drive to produce a new generation of starry-eyed musicians and, more important, providing a wonderful service to her community and, just perhaps, a new audience for the future.

CHAPTER FOUR

· M E N T O R S ·

*H*AVING FINISHED my Fulbright year, I tried to stay on in Germany and auditioned for *La Traviata* at the Staatstheater am Gärtnerplatz in Munich. I couldn't quite sing Violetta, but in my typical fashion, I rolled up my sleeves and tried out for everything. This time, no matter how hard I worked I couldn't get hired anywhere. One morning I was just about to head for the train to audition for a small opera company in Bern, Switzerland, when they called and canceled, leaving me standing with the phone in one hand and my ticket in the other. At another audition for a small theater in the far north of Germany, the intendant said, "I'm terribly sorry, but your G is wrong! You need to fix your G. Don't even *think* about having a career until you fix that pitch!" That was certainly the most original complaint I had ever received.

Starting out as an opera singer, you have two ways of establishing a career: one is to get management directly and begin the audition process, and the other is to get exposure through winning competitions. Managers were not beating down my door, so I entered as many competitions as I could. During my time in Germany I had two incredibly fortunate opportunities. First, I was chosen by Eastman to represent the United States in a competition in Chile. I went to Viña del Mar, which is on the ocean, not too far from Santiago, where I lived in a hotel for a month and seemed to have one extraordinary experience after another. I was chased by Gypsies in the park and later befriended an American astronomer and his Chilean wife, who lived at the top of a cliff that hung directly over the Pacific. The other international competitors and I all ate together at my hotel every night, and we had a ball, even surviving an earthquake, which hit during one poor tenor's audition. I often wondered if that prompted him to move on to another career or if he is the reigning Pavarotti of his country. I performed to the best of my abilities and won second prize.

I was, in fact, the greatest second-prize winner of all time. More than Manon or the Marschallin, the Underdog has always been my favorite role. I loved the comfort of being number two—just high enough to make me feel validated but not so high that I felt the air getting thin. Being number two was a powerful incentive to keep me continually working and striving. I'm so goal oriented that I don't know how my career would have turned out if I had found real success at such an early age. I felt as if the jury was saying to me, "You have promise," rather than "You're ready to have a career."

Not long after that, I was asked to represent Juilliard in South Africa. I had a lot of doubts about going there during apartheid, but I wanted to see things for myself. I lived in Johannesburg for a month with an Afrikaner family while I sang in Pretoria. There was political struggle and unrest in the country, yet at the same time it was an absolute paradise of physical beauty. The trip broadened my experience in a way that makes me believe strongly that all young people should travel if they possibly can. In South Africa I had the opportunity to reprise my role as the Underdog, coming in second to Marion Moore, an African-American soprano. Her victory made an enormous statement, and I was grateful that I was there to see her win. It was a rare meeting of music and politics.

Even though I relished second place, I was not above taking some pleasure in a win. I finally landed first prize in a competition in Verviers, Belgium, at the end of my Fulbright stay. Rodney Gilfry, the wonderful American baritone, and I were there together, staying with a family who didn't speak a word of English, and between the two of us we managed about three sentences of French. Rodney was hysterically funny, and for the two weeks we were there I never stopped laughing, which I've always thought was the reason I won. We saw one contestant faint dead away two phrases into her aria and wondered how much of a deterrent this would be to her, like the tenor who suffered the earthquake in Chile. Years later Rodney and I premiered Stanley and Blanche in André Previn's *A Streetcar Named Desire;* he still makes me laugh.

I went on to sing in several competitions in Germany, but I never got very far, which once again proves the theory that my greatest victories were often in losing. If I had won first prize in a major competition in Germany, I most likely would have stayed in the German system. Looking back, I'm sure my voice would not have withstood the rigors of a *Fest,* or fixed contract, with demands to sing many different roles, sometimes back-to-back, because my technique simply wasn't secure enough. The German network of theaters functions quite differently from those in the United States and the rest of Europe in that it is somewhat insular. Unless one is fortunate enough to break out, one rarely has an international career. The trade-off is a civil servant's security, great benefits, and the only place in the opera world where a singer can practice his art full-time, and in one country. It is a great foundation for raising children and a fulfilling home life.

During my Fulbright, I sang in the Munich competition, which is a high-flying operation with television coverage, contracts, and prize money. I made it, I believe, to the third round. The following year I went back and was released in the first round. The only one as disappointed in my performance as I was, was my pianist, who said, "You know, Renée, just go. Don't do this anymore, just go work."

Although I didn't realize it at the time, a big part of my problem wasn't *how* I was singing but *what* I was singing. I was still being far too ambitious about the arias I chose. There was no such thing as a career adviser back then, so I didn't have anyone guiding me on how I should be presenting myself. I thought I would impress people by performing extremely difficult music, so I sang Lulu's aria by Alban Berg, the first-act scena from *La Traviata,* Constanze's arias, and other music that was simply beyond me vocally at that time—not to mention obscure Wolf lieder. I feared I would fail to attract any notice if I sang simple pieces, but really, that couldn't have been further from the truth. If I had sung a soubrette aria—say, "Deh, vieni, non tardar" from *Le Nozze di Figaro*—and shown that I had mastered it, just presented the sound of my voice, then I think things would have come together for me much sooner. Still, I'm glad success didn't come quickly, because I really couldn't count on my high notes yet, and sooner or later anyone who hired me was going to find that out. It took a few more years of struggle before I could approach a high note without a creeping sense of panic. Was it going to come out this time, squawk, or abandon me altogether?

Since there was nothing left for me in Germany, I came back to New York for another semester at Juilliard. By now I was completely confused. Of the many vocal souvenirs I'd brought home with me, one was Schwarzkopf's covering, a technique Beverley didn't believe in and wouldn't teach. She was adamant that I give up the concept altogether, which sent me into a complete crisis. Being someone who likes to take polls, I was forever going up to people and saying, "Okay, covering sounds like this"—then I'd sing them a line—"and not covering sounds like this"—and I'd sing the same line again. "Which one do you prefer?" It was all about sound, tone, and projection: What's more beautiful? What works better? Ultimately, I realized that Beverley didn't mind covering per se, but had been urging me to avoid it because she didn't want me to *over*cover. It all goes back to teachers' and students' finding a way to communicate about the voice. It's a bit like talking about God: you almost have to talk around it, because there is no exact language for the thing itself. And the lack of an exact language is always going to cause a great deal of misunderstanding. The frustrating thing is that while I'm perfectly capable of making a decision by myself on most subjects, I can't remove my ears from my body and place them in the back of the room for a vocal check. What we hear while we're singing just isn't true, so we are always dependent on someone we trust to take the role of our "outside ears."

In fact I was obviously overdoing the covering, because when I came back to New York everyone kept saying to me, "What happened to your voice?"

"What happened to your voice?" is not a question a singer wants to hear.

What had happened was that not only was I working in a repertoire I couldn't master, but I was now trying to make beautiful sounds that were more suited to lieder in a small room than to opera. The result was that my voice had shrunk and moved to the back of my throat. Now I had a lot of work ahead of me to undo all the work I'd been doing. The confusing part was that this new sound I was making was lovely in my own ear, in my mind's ear, so I didn't believe Beverley when she told me that I should stop singing this way.

Along with this confusion came a fresh wave of stage fright, since I now felt unsure of every note. I sang in a master class at Juilliard that fall and broke down in tears, saying, "I just can't do this!" Fortunately, Jan DeGaetani was passing through town the same day, and after I finished bemoaning my fate she said, "I never won any competitions. Nobody ever handed me anything." In short, she gave me a brisk slap and told me to get to work, which was exactly what I needed. She also mentioned that it looked as though I had tension in the muscles in my chest. That one comment sent me on another exploration of physical tension, which later provided another piece of the puzzle, as I tried to understand how I could possibly survive my choral singing job.

In the end, I could see that what I had learned wasn't wrong, but that I had simply taken it to an extreme. My task now was to incorporate a brighter, healthier, more open style of singing. Taking a vague vocal concept from another singer is a little bit like sinking your life's savings into a stock tip you overhear at a cocktail party: even if there's a momentary boom, chances are it's not going to be the thing that sustains you into old age. Such is the potential danger of master classes, which can begin to seem like smoke-and-mirrors once the "idol" has boarded the plane a few hours later. You finally have to learn to pull all the different kinds of teaching and training and coaching together on your own, so that your voice and body and technique form a sound that is consistent and solid. It sounds simple enough, but it took me forever to achieve. Still, I wouldn't want to be someone who did everything right from day one, because then I wouldn't have any experience with correcting small changes in vocal production myself. I would have liked it if things had come together a little bit more easily, a little faster, but I also know it could have gone the other way and taken me five years longer than it did. After all this effort, I'm confident now that I know what I'm doing and I have the tools to maintain my voice.

Even though this was a time in my life when a lot of things were going wrong, the most important thing was suddenly right: Beverley and I were now in a state of perfect communication. Ever since I'd come back from Germany, we'd been growing closer, and our relationship only continued to get better for the rest of her life. It turned out that she had been taking a lot of prescription drugs for minor ailments in the years before I left for Germany and she had no tolerance for them. She must have had one particularly horrible day while I was away, because she flushed every last pill down the toilet and went to a new doctor, John Postley, who told her she couldn't take anything from then on, not even an aspirin; and it turned out to be exactly the advice she needed. She was a different person, energized and excited by the world again. In her eighties she was learning new things every day. She was obsessed with learning more about the voice, singing, and physiology. She loved doctors, and I suspect to a great degree they came to replace her husband. Besides, she was especially fond of

Dr. Postley and the famous Dr. Wilbur Gould, ENT to the stars. She stayed in close contact with them not because she was ill—she was rarely ill again until the very end of her life—but it was because she wanted to talk to them about the body. She was constantly inspired and would come up with ingenious new exercises. I would ask, "How did you think of that?" and she would tell me, "I don't think of it. It just comes. It flows through me." It was the richest time in our working relationship, which at times could also be oddly reminiscent of that of Eliza Doolittle and Henry Higgins. She wasn't just working on my voice; she was working on *me*. She taught me how to walk and pick out dresses for auditions, how to stand, how to write a proper thank-you note, how to say no in a way that was kind but firm. I used to think, if only I'd known her in my jazz club days, she could have taught me the fine art of stage patter.

We eventually became so attuned to each other that I could call her up from some foreign country and say, "You know, I'm having trouble with this note. Can I sing it to you over the phone?" and she always knew how to fix it. When I was especially nervous, she wrote me notes and e-mails that kept me on track.

Dear One:

Have you got a heating pad or hot-water bottle and a nice big bathtub that can be filled with warm water? Not too hot, just warmer than body heat. Now get into bed and put the heating pad on your neck and shoulders. Also, when you get into the tub of warm water, take a towel and wring it out of quite hot water and put it across your shoulders and then lie in the tub for at least twenty minutes counting from a hundred down. Don't rub yourself, just pat dry and then put some moisturizer on and GO TO BED TRYING NOT TO WAKE UP AND SEE IF YOU AREN'T PHYSICALLY RELAXED. I BELIEVE MUSCLES TENSE UP TO MATCH ONE'S OWN INNER AND MENTAL TENSION.

First, you KNOW HOW TO SING and telling yourself that will

remind yourself how much you do know and how well you use that knowledge. There is NOTHING IN THIS PARTICULAR OPERA THAT YOU CAN'T HANDLE. That is the first thing to remind yourself of, and you have people around you that know it, too!!! Every one of your coworkers loves and respects you and will be helpful without their being aware of your tensions. I believe everyone at your level gets tense as they remember their responsibility. Try to snap your fingers at the so-called difficulties. They are there but you have handled much greater difficulties and come through with flying colors.

I love you and believe in you all the way and now try to accept the way it is with being way up there!!!

Prayers and belief.
Always and always and always,
Beverley

One of the many gifts I got from Beverley, along with an enormous amount of comfort and love, was my top, my high notes. She taught me how to open the back of my mouth. When I came to her I was leaving virtually no space in the back of my mouth when I sang high notes, so in essence there was not enough room for them. It's not enough merely to open your mouth by creating space between your upper and lower front teeth; the jaw must literally unhinge. What works best for me is a square position that runs from the opening of the mouth to the back of the throat—not a long, vertical oblong, but a more horizontal placement. Different singers use different openings. Sam Ramey's long, narrow position has certainly worked well for him, but for my bone structure that approach would never enable me to move into my higher register. I tried it—and everything else, for that matter.

I also had enough tongue tension to choke on, and I regularly did. My tongue wanted to fall back, basically inhibiting the larynx from hanging freely and thus strangling my high notes, sometimes creating a gargling sound, sometimes cutting them off altogether. It wasn't pretty. Beverley would have me place a honey drop in the center indentation near the front of the tongue to tame its unruly wandering back and down. Not wanting to choke on the foreign object, the back of the tongue rises slightly and stays forward. One has to keep the tongue relaxed and ungrooved as well, resting softly behind the front of the bottom teeth. With the honey drop, the only scales that can be performed are on an *ah* vowel, as any other vowel would indeed put one in danger of choking. Then I had to learn how to lift my soft palate. Using hard *k* and *g* exercises helped it to gain flexibility, and even plugging my nose as I moved up into the top of my range was useful. Every time I had a cold, I sang better, since this blockage somehow helped me to relax the palate into position.

Covering came back into play when I picked up the "Song to the Moon" from Dvořák's *Rusalka* again. This aria not only gave me so much of my success then and now but taught me how to sing the "money" note, a soprano's B-flat. It was that blessed B-flat sung on an *e* vowel that led me to find the exact right combination of a square opening in the back of my mouth and a relaxed, low mental image of pitch. When I'm singing well, two and a half octaves feel like five pitches. There is absolutely no sense of an up-and-down direction, but only a forward one, which is led and never pushed. My top feels as if I'm not hitting high notes at all, but still singing comfortably in my middle range.

None of these concepts on its own creates good high notes. I had to coordinate them all, while never losing the forward direction of my sound. (Holding a pencil between my teeth while singing on an *e* vowel helped reestablish the correct position if I got too far back in resonance.) The subtle interplay of all of these ideas with the body can ultimately produce a sound that is completely natural. Once I managed to figure all this out, listeners would tell me how fortunate I was to be born singing so easily. The first few times I heard this comment, I was frustrated, wanting my hard work to be acknowledged, but eventually I realized that this was the very compliment I should welcome, as it meant that everything was working properly and that the seams weren't showing.

I helped the search for the high notes along by incorporating some of the more finely tuned breath concepts I had been working on. I watched countless videos of singers and learned an incredible amount by studying how they used their mouths, how they held their chests, how they would take a breath. Watching Dietrich Fischer-Dieskau, live, in a series of concerts at Carnegie Hall helped me to understand further the importance of chest expansion. He looked like a pigeon when he sang late in his career, with his chest puffed up to the extreme. From watching videos, I came to realize that all the great singers of that generation sang with very big, high chests. I don't think that I ever supported properly until I figured that out. Tapes of the old *Bell Telephone Hour* program from the sixties, or in fact of any compilation of singers, should be a requirement for every vocal department in every music school in the country. I had the chance to watch Birgit Nilsson, Leontyne Price, Anna Moffo, Joan Sutherland, and all of the other wonderful singers of that era. Because they were all singing in television studios, I could really view them close up. So much can be gained from watching other singers, seeing what they do and what they don't do, seeing how they look when they breathe, how wide they open their mouths for a high note.

Another of the missing pieces of the voice puzzle came from an unlikely source: my job singing in churches. Choir singing is deathly difficult for a soprano, because choir directors are always telling us to blend, which requires mostly soft, high passaggio singing. I would die whenever I attempted this, for I was strangling, thinking I was never going to be able to sustain it. *If the choirmaster's so interested in soft singing, then why don't we just drop out altogether? In fact, why doesn't he just get rid of three of us sopranos?* It felt impossible and frustrating to constantly have to hold back. But what I had been trying so hard to understand about support in school I finally understood when I was in church. I made the connection between intercostal expansion—the expansion of the muscles between the ribs—and the relatively high chest position I had observed in all of the great singers I'd been watching. I kept my shoulders relaxed, as well as my back, trapezius, and neck. I remembered what Jan had said about tension, and when I began to experiment with an even fuller expansion of my chest when I took a breath, I suddenly felt as if I had no neck. It seemed as if the distance between my chin and my chest was growing shorter and shorter, and that my neck was spreading out and in a sense dissolving into my shoulders. As a result, I never needed to reach my chin up for a pitch again. The other key was making sure I didn't sing with any pressure in the voice. I realized that I had been singing with a high larynx for years. Every time I finished practicing, my speaking voice would be up an octave, and that's a sure sign that tension exists somewhere it shouldn't. Soon I was singing comfortably in the passaggio, and for long stretches—something I would need for a lot of the Mozart repertoire I eventually specialized in, not to mention Strauss's *Daphne,* which involves extreme singing at its most intense. It's so important that a young singer—and really, anyone at any stage of her career—remain open-minded, for you never know where you're going to learn your lessons.

Once I got a taste for singing softer, I was adamant about learning how to sing softly. I was in awe of Montserrat Caballé, who was famous for her pianissimo. She seemed to be able to use that skill at will, anytime, in any place, and in any piece. It was a spectacularly beautiful sound. Some would criticize it as an effect, but I loved it nonetheless. With Beverley's help, I began to find this space, which involved two concepts. First, I learned to aim the sound mentally into the two slight indentations on either side of the nostrils. The result is not at all a nasal sound, but this technique aids in focusing the use of resonance and in lifting the soft palate. I still use this concept often, particularly in extended passaggio and pianissimo singing. Second, I imagined leading the tone rather than pushing it. It was helpful to visualize this process with images like serving the tone to the audience on a platter, pulling taffy with a phrase, or extending spaghetti out of my forehead to the back of the hall. (Food-related images work well with singers, of course.) The best exercise for practicing these ideas is the *messa di voce*—which begins very softly on one tone, crescendos to a forte as loudly as is comfortable, and then scales down to pianissimo again— moving evenly up and down the chromatic half-steps on a scale. This is a painstaking and slow process, but it can teach all there is to know about dynamic control.

There are many pieces involved in assembling the puzzle of the voice, and no one teacher can provide everything that is needed. I can still trace the origins of all the key elements of my own voice: the foundation from my mother and then Pat Misslin, the most important pieces and a solid understanding of technique from Beverley, the contributions from Schwarzkopf, from Jan DeGaetani, and from choral singing. These were all crucial components, but there were also dozens of smaller lessons from other coaches and teachers along the way, and I brought them all together in incremental stages. I still discover something new with every engagement. Today, it often involves learning how to incorporate new repertoire and how to manage the voice from day to day, when stress, fear and other emotions, hormones, acoustics, colds and other health issues, diet, and the interpersonal dynamic of a cast and conductor can all have an effect on my singing.

I look back at myself at six, sixteen, and twenty-six, and I reflect on how much of my identity was tied to my relationships with my teachers. I never stopped being a good student, for I genuinely like to learn and I have always been eager to please. Even after I left Juilliard and began to make my way in the world, I still worked with Beverley, and I always kept my eye out for other people who had something to offer. I found a whole new crop of mentors when I was a young adult, and I found them in a group of women some might regard as a highly unlikely source of sisterly support: other sopranos.

Sopranos are burdened with a stereotype that is rivaled perhaps only by librarians and mothers-in-law: we are, as a group, invariably labeled divas and prima donnas, though neither term had a negative connotation in its original usage. We are selfish, high maintenance, and hugely demanding. We drink only Swedish spring water without ice from a Lalique glass that has been chilled to exactly sixty-seven degrees; if it is sixty-eight degrees, we simply will not perform. We call our managers from the backs of our limousines so that they can call our drivers and ask them to adjust the air-conditioning. We wear scarves copiously, and preferably Hermès, Gucci, or Loro Piana. We speak in high voices, à la Julia Child, in a "continental" nonaccent; or we don't speak at all, but write on little personalized pads; or if we're terribly modern, we type on our tiny laptops or personal organizers, which are also cell phones, iPods, Palm Pilots, and digital cameras. We travel with an entourage of assistants, so we needn't actually speak with a hotel receptionist or flight attendant (what a waste of the five thousand utterances we may have left), a dresser, hairdresser, and, as I recently observed of a very famous tenor, a personal hat maker. Before performances we eat only carbs, avoiding apples and any gas-inducing vegetable, or we eat only protein, and apples to combat phlegm. We never consume an acid-producing tomato sauce or spicy food, and we wouldn't dream of eating past seven p.m. for fear of causing the dreaded reflux (I'm crossing myself ten times in both the Western and Russian ways just thinking about it). We drink lactose-free, low-sodium, soy-based, and decaf everything. We don't drink alcohol before a performance, since it dries the throat. We instruct our secretaries to call ahead and make sure our hotel rooms have not one but two humidifiers running at least twenty-four hours in advance of our arrival. We have not touched our own luggage since we graduated from high school, lest we stress the trapezius. We wear spike heels and have our hair teased, straightened, colored (an absolute three-color minimum), and cut to within an inch of its life for rehearsals. Some of us wouldn't feel dressed without false eyelashes, while others won't allow anyone in the theater to actually look at them. We're not very collegial, especially within our own voice type—i.e., with the competition. Did I miss a stereotype? Trust me, I've heard them all, even though I've seen little to support these images. I much more often encounter a group of generous women who are happy to share what they know.

The first in my own career was Renata Scotto, who kindly gave me a private lesson in Beverley's apartment in advance of Scotto's master class at Juilliard. She laid the music out in front of me and told me to read what was on the page, to do that and nothing else. "Just sing what the composer asked you to sing," she instructed. Because Scotto is famous for being a brilliant singing actress, I had thought she would care more about the theatrical values than musical ones, but I was wrong. She has enormous integrity and intelligence. During a conversation at the end of the lesson, she said, "Have children." I was young at the time, and that was a subject I hadn't even begun to think about. She told me that after she had had her son, she approached singing from a much healthier perspective. "I don't live or die on the stage every night," she explained. "I have more than that in my life."

When I met Joan Sutherland, I actually was pregnant with my first child. (Good student that I am, I had taken Scotto's advice.) I was singing in Geneva—my debut in *Così fan tutte*—and my manager, Merle Hubbard, drove me up to the mountain chalet where Sutherland lives with her husband, the conductor Richard Bonynge. It was for me, as it would be for anyone who loves opera, a dream come true. The Bonynges' living room was painted a dark hunter green, and every inch of its walls was covered with drawings or needlepoint. The entire house was full of needlepoint, which was Sutherland's hobby between acts, while traveling, and while waiting around at rehearsals. Bonynge was an avid collector, and he had stacks upon stacks of original manuscripts and scores, including first editions of obscure Massenet operas that he brought out to show us. I had a chance to gingerly ask Joan Sutherland a few questions about singing, and what I most wanted to know about was her extreme high notes. How had she managed to sing them? She told me she aimed them directionally, not just out of the front but more toward the back of her head as she climbed into the stratosphere. She also said she loved not singing anymore; her grandchildren were the greatest joy in her life. "Absolutely have children, and don't worry about when. Years after the last engagement, a beautiful child will be loved, and the engagement will be completely forgotten." It was her most impassioned piece of advice.

Marilyn Horne has been a great friend ever since we sang together in John Corigliano's *The Ghosts of Versailles*. I love her no-nonsense, down-to-earth style. She knows what she thinks and she'll always tell you. One day during rehearsals, I took her aside and told her that someone had asked me about singing Norma. She stared directly at me and said, "OOOOOH, no, you don't! I'll tell you right now that role would be a terrible mistake for you." And of course, she was exactly right at the time. I had asked Joan Sutherland about it, too. "It's not that there is anything on the page that is so difficult," she explained. "It's just that the role is incredibly long. One has to have an enormous amount of stamina to get through it." Fortunately, though I have tended to consistently work too much and have been known to spread myself too thin, I've always been naturally disinclined to take on anything that has the potential to harm my voice.

Marilyn has also been a real mentor to me, advising me about repertoire. She suggested that we do an album together, for which we rehearsed, but after both of us became ill during two different scheduled recording periods, the record company gave up on us. She's always been so generous whenever I've called on her, as has Frederica von Stade, who helped me through a difficult personal time. Singers don't get together just to talk about music, after all.

When I think of the remarkable singers I've met in my life, the one who took my breath away was Leontyne Price. She had said to a mutual friend not long ago, "Tell Renée I would like to meet with her," and so I went down to her home in Greenwich Village, a house that once belonged to the first mayor of New York.

Though I was paying my first visit to her home, it was not the first time I had met Miss Price. When I was ten years old, my mother took me to see her in a song recital at the Eastman Theatre. After the performance, we stood in a long line that wound up a narrow staircase, all of us wanting to pay our respects to her backstage. I listened to my mother talking to another music teacher about Miss Price's technique, how her neck stayed soft and showed no signs of strain when she sang, and they agreed that this was something of a miracle, considering the power of her voice. This conversation, the hushed and serious discussion of her voice, was indelibly etched in my memory. I nodded slowly in agreement, feeling as if I had just been allowed into some exclusive club. When we got close enough to see her, I watched as she signed programs and greeted fans, one after another; but when my turn came, she smiled hugely and took my hand. I told her I wanted to be just like her, even though I didn't understand precisely what that meant at the time. I doubt I even meant that I wanted to sing like her; I simply wanted to have her beauty and power and presence. She wrote out my name across my program—"To Dear Renée"—and then signed her own name close to mine with a flourish. I walked down the staircase pressing it to my heart.

Of course, I told her none of this when we met again. I am old enough myself to know how often a soprano hears "You've been my role model since I was ten years old." None of us likes to be reminded of our relationship to time. "Die Zeit, die ist ein sonderbar Ding," to quote the Marschallin in *Der Rosenkavalier*. I simply shook her hand as I had done the first time and told her what an honor it was to meet her.

When I walked in the door, the first things I noticed were nineteen Grammys displayed on a table in the living room. I could only think,

If I work for the rest of my life I will never achieve anything like this. Miss Price was surprisingly petite and still very beautiful, and she paced the room while she spoke. "It's funny the way people talk about the voice as if it is a separate entity, like it's another being separate from us," she said. "It's not." She had put the needs of her voice first for her entire life, and as long as her voice was in top condition, she was fine. Her voice was her comfort, and she had lived for the gift she had received.

She stopped her pacing for a moment, looked at me firmly, and said, "I called you because of what you're going through right now. I thought you might need some advice. You're experiencing the noise."

"The noise?" I asked.

"The noise, the hype, the demands that are being made on you from all corners." She talked about people literally crowding around me, wanting this and demanding that.

"Miss Price," I asked, "would you mind if I took notes?" I was in school again, but she was more preacher than teacher, so impassioned was her speech. She nodded her head and I began to write.

"You have to learn to tune out all of the noise and focus on one thing."

I looked up at her, and she tapped an index finger against her throat. "This is all that matters. Because the minute this goes, they'll disappear so fast you won't even know what happened."

And of course she was right. It was a moment of complete clarity.

"I feel intuitively that you are in a place right now where you need to hear these things. You're confused and torn by the decisions your success is forcing you to make. The priority is to stay focused here." She pointed to her throat again.

She said she wanted to be helpful because she thought we had some similarities. We were both what she called "three-prong singers," which meant that we sang not just opera but recitals with piano and concerts with orchestra. She spoke of the strength she had developed when she faced tremendous racism at the beginning of her career. When she first toured with the Met, she was not allowed to stay at the same hotels as the rest of the singers and was forbidden to enter the theater by the same doors. Time after time she made her debut in houses where no black artist had ever sung before. But she always took the high road and maintained her dignity, over time developing a self-protective persona.

She had had a career of extraordinary longevity, touring and singing into her seventies, but she had handled herself with tenderness and care. She never went to the theater, never went to hear other singers, explaining that she preferred to avoid the drafts created by air-conditioning. She had little interest in the business outside of her own career. After she retired from the operatic stage, she sang recitals and premiered the music of American composers, giving back to the profession, which adored her. She would sing a recital program that wasn't especially strenuous or long, but then would return to the stage and sing six demanding arias back-to-back as encores—a feat I couldn't imagine having the stamina to accomplish even now. Whenever people ask me about my favorite voices, hers is always the first one that springs to mind. I used to joke that I was hoping for her high C in my next life.

When I was leaving, I stood at the door and held her hand. I felt as if I was touching someone who was a sacred part of musical history. I thought of how one day I would say to my grandchildren, "I once held the hand of Leontyne Price."

"I can't begin to thank you for being so generous," I said.

"I can tell you this, I can be generous with you because I can still sing all of my roles." She looked at me hard. "And I can still sing them in their original keys!" In short, she wanted me to know that if there was ever an occasion for us to be in competition, she could go head-to-head with me any day.

And there wasn't a doubt in my mind that she would win—over me, over any of us—every single time.

CHAPTER FIVE

·SUCCESS·

*P*ICTURE THE EDUCATION of an opera singer as a beautiful country—say, England—full of museums and concert halls, palaces and rose gardens, where people can study and learn and grow. Now picture a career as a successful opera star as another country—say, France—and imagine it as being full of culture and couture, Champagne and the Eiffel Tower, where the power of a single voice is lauded and adored. Now picture the English Channel separating those two countries, with its icy gray waters and choppy waves. Having completed my stay at Juilliard in 1987, I found myself stranded on the English side with no boat, no plane, and no Chunnel, trying to figure out how to get across.

I had loved my student days, and between college, graduate school, the postgraduate program at Juilliard, and the Fulbright grant in Germany, I had hung on to them for as long as possible. I was accustomed to living in a world where people told me what they expected of me and I worked hard to meet those expectations. But so little of what I learned seemed to have any bearing on this new period of my life. For competitions or apprenticeships, I would go into an audition room and sing for a group of people. In return they would look at me, unimpressed, and tell me no. They didn't invite me to try again, or ask me what I could sing that might better reveal my talents. They wouldn't even tell me what I was doing wrong. It was simply "Thank you," and then the next soprano would come in and take her shot at it.

For potential engagements, the catch-22 was that it was very hard to get an audition if you didn't have a manager, and it was almost impossible to get a manager unless you'd won an audition. Beverley, as usual, paved the way by introducing me to a friend of hers, Merle Hubbard from the Herbert Breslin Agency. I sang for him at Beverley's, and while he was very encouraging, he didn't sign me. He promised to stay in touch, and I was back to auditioning for summer apprenticeships, competitions, and studio programs.

For all the progress I had made with my voice and with languages, style, and musicianship over the years, I had advanced very little in my auditioning skills. I was fine on the stage once the part was mine and I could concentrate on working out its nuances, but in auditions I inevitably felt insecure. Everything about me had the air of an apology. I continued to believe that it was my job to impress people, to dazzle them with my bold choices, so I persisted in singing pieces that were beyond my technique. I auditioned with lyric and dramatic coloratura arias such as "Qui la voce" from *I Puritani*, when I should have been singing something like Musetta's Waltz. Alternatively, I would select pieces that were perfect for my voice, but not perfect for an audition. I still refused to part with Anne Trulove's "No word from Tom," for example, which at that time seemed simply too long to hold a jury's interest. While a student at the Aspen Music Festival, I had the opportunity to audition for August Everding, the great Munich intendant. Feeling very much in the know about the German theater system and its devotion to new and difficult music, I figured I had a leg up on everyone else there by choosing the Stravinsky aria. Mr. Everding, however, leaned over to the audition assistant and asked, "Why on earth is she wasting my time with this awful piece?" The faster you can go in there and show them what you're made of, the happier they're going to be. If there's some other aspect of your voice they want to hear, they'll ask.

Choosing repertoire is a critical part of a great presentation. Some juries will want to hear only the most popular pieces, which give them a standard by which to judge you. Other, more experienced judges will throw your biography in the trash if you force them to listen to yet another Juliette's Waltz. They would be interested instead to hear one of the two never-sung short arias from *Thaïs*. It is often difficult to second-guess any jury, but for an audition like the regional Met finals, tried-and-true might be safer. For a large company or studio program, which typically has a jury that auditions hundreds of singers every year, something off the beaten track might be refreshing to tired ears. If nothing else, you would be presenting yourself as an inquisitive and thoughtful musician. Since five arias are often requested, a mixture of both might be the most solid choice.

Since there was no such reference book as *The Soprano's Handbook for Landing a Spot at the Met*, I had no choice but to keep dusting myself off and trying again. At one point, an acquaintance asked me to audition for a competition with which she was involved. I was excited because it was clear that she was familiar with my talent and would put in a good word for me. It was a three-round competition, and after I sang the first round I felt that I had done my best, but I was immediately passed over. It was too much. I went to my sister's apartment in abject despair.

"You can't *invite* someone to sing and then kick them out in the first round!" I complained. "I hadn't even planned to go to the audition. They pulled me in just to squash me!"

"You just had an off day," Rachelle said.

"When am I going to face up to the truth? I have to stop doing this. I have to get a job. I have to get going with my life. How many people have to tell me they don't want me before I start to get the message?"

"Renée, you have the talent, and you've worked so hard. You know that."

But I felt that I couldn't stand the rejection anymore; I was wearing down.

Rachelle put her arms around me and then took me out for a cup of coffee. Over the course of an hour she very gently talked me down from the ledge on which I was so precariously perched.

• • •

There are some things that a book can teach you, and others you figure out just by virtue of showing up over and over again. Through the latter method I finally learned to use my acting ability when making a presentation. I still might not have felt completely confident, but then again, I hadn't felt like a coquette when I was rehearsing the role of Musetta. If I was a good enough actress to fake sexual confidence, then I surely could fake self-confidence as well. Simply losing the self-consciousness that was immediately apparent in my presentation was difficult, if not impossible, because I knew I was being scrutinized—which is, after all, the whole point of being in an audition. So I pretended. I learned to enter the room with a warm smile, to introduce my pieces without mumbling, to suppress the apologetic body language and nervous twitches and shuffling feet. Naturally, my being at ease put the jury at ease as well. Although I was still having a hard time grasping the fact that they didn't actually want or expect me to fail, I learned not to stare the judges down or sing directly to them, as they probably weren't eager to feel my adrenaline-crazed eyes pinning them to the back wall. If I was performing a declamatory piece that required contact with the audience, I would include them, but if it was an interior piece or a dialogue with another character, I found I was better off picking a focus that was just over their heads or to the right or the left of them.

It is always critical in an audition to tell whatever story you have to tell, to enact your dramatic scene and let that process take the place of vocal self-consciousness and whatever terror you're feeling. Staying connected to the text can help you avoid the following inner dialogue:

Watch me tense up as I lead up to the phrase with the high B.
Yup, I've stopped acting altogether, my fists are clenched and my legs are shaking, but wasn't that a good turn of phrase there? And how about that pianissimo?

Darn! While patting myself on the back about nailing that last pitch,
I lost my concentration, and that long decrescendo that was going
so well just ended in a machine-gun stutter.

And while worrying about its ending badly, I forgot to prepare for the
top phrase, and now it's too late.

I'm trying not to grimace, but I can't help it.

The extra tension provided, thank you very much, *by my nerves has*
just caused me to blow the top B-flat, and at the same time my pe-
ripheral vision just saw my right arm rise in perfect Frankenstein
fashion, seemingly unattached to the rest of my body, as the per-
fect visual accompaniment to this perfect disaster.

I can see the disappointment on your faces.

You were hoping you could choose me and pay lip service to the other
two hundred sopranos waiting outside the door.

Once, my accompanist got lost on the last page of music after a cut, and despite a bit of fumbling to find his place, he finally simply stopped playing. I kept on going and reached up for the high E-flat at the end, but without piano support, I was so distracted that my top note, which would have been difficult in the best of situations, was quite simply a scream. The two judges immediately hunched over, shoulders shaking, pretending to write furiously in the hopes of disguising their laughter—not that I could blame them.

The sad Murphy's Law of auditioning dictated that at exactly the moment when I became good at it, I no longer needed to be, for I was finally getting hired without submitting to this difficult and some-times humiliating process. Try to make the experience your friend far sooner than I did. I've given enough master classes by now to know that the thing that really distinguishes an individual, voice and singing aside, is Personality with a capital *P*. Charisma. Touch me, move me, take me out of this stuffy little room with its fluorescent lights and dropped ceiling, its linoleum floor and badly tuned upright piano. I want to hold Rodolfo's hand while he tenderly explains his life, all the while seducing me—er, I mean, Mimì. That kind of conviction and engagement will win the audition and, later, the audience.

In the end, I felt things really started to turn around for me when I began auditioning with the "Song to the Moon" from *Rusalka*. It wasn't a widely known aria yet, but it was perfectly suited to my temperament and voice. It was Merle Hubbard—who, true to his word, did continue to check in with me from time to time—who had suggested that I sing it. Not only had I learned to sing it in English at Potsdam with Pat, but I later studied it in Czech while at Eastman. My friend Charles Nelson Reilly sent me a Dorothy Maynor recording of the aria and told me about her extraordinary career. Maynor was a wonderful African-American soprano who was never invited to sing opera on any of the major stages, and so made a concert niche for herself in much the same way Marian Anderson had. She provided a wonderful service to music lovers by recording unusual and obscure repertoire, which she sang with a voice of unparalleled sweetness. Charles always maintained that it should have been her recording of the aria in the film *Driving Miss Daisy*, because she deserved the recognition and because her recording actually coincided with the period of the film. Once I picked up the aria again, it felt as if I were slipping my hand inside a glove. This coincided with the period in which the aria's final B-flat, because of the approach to the note and the vowel involved, enabled me to crack the problem of how to sing above the staff. The ease with which I performed the piece gave me confidence, and this confidence in turn helped me to embark on the beginning of my career.

Dear Richard Bado, my friend and accompanist from Eastman who had played for me at my disastrous first audition for the Met competition, was at that time working for the Houston Grand Opera. He suggested I audition for its young artists program and promised to give me a good character reference and perhaps pave the way for me if he could. Once I passed the first round in New York, I was flown to Houston for the finals, where David Gockley, still the acclaimed general director; Scott Heumann, the artistic administrator; and the composer Carlisle Floyd made up the jury. The audition was set up as a competition for a place in the studio program, which I won, but at the end they took me aside and said, "We really think you're beyond the studio level. We're going to keep you in mind for a main-stage role."

Beyond the studio level? I hadn't come close to being accepted by any of the studio programs, and now I was beyond them? I felt as if I had been toiling away trying to get a spot in the secretarial pool and was now being handed the keys to the executive washroom. I floated back to New York on a cloud—though still without any work.

More good news came quickly after that. I won the Metropolitan Opera competition a few months later in a year when the other winners included Ben Heppner, my friend Susan Graham, and Heidi Grant Murphy. A week later, I won the George London Prize. Fortunately, grants from the Shoshana Foundation, the Sullivan Foundation, and the Musicians Emergency Fund had been supporting me with the money I desperately needed to pay for voice lessons and coachings in preparation for this sudden rash of wins. Nothing succeeds like success. I finally had my arias worked out, my confidence in place; and when Merle Hubbard signed me, I then had a manager as well. Drenched, frozen, exhausted, and completely exhilarated, I was pulling myself out of the English Channel and onto the glorious shore of France.

In all my years as a student, I had been undermined by a very negative inner voice, a little nattering in my ear that said, "Don't do that. . . . Don't do this. . . . That's awful. . . . What a horrible sound! . . . You're grabbing. . . . You're holding. . . . Your breath is tight. . . . Your tongue has gone back. . . . Your palate is down. . . . The top is spread. . . . Relax your shoulders!" I carried inside me a running monologue of nagging complaints that wore me down as effectively as any rejection from an opera house ever did, and so I made a very conscious effort to rid myself of it. I read books like *The Soprano on Her Head, Zen and the Art of Archery*, and *Performance Anxiety*, and I came to the conclusion that it was as essential for me to work on my attitude as it was to work on my voice. I decided that I was going to start repeating mantras to myself, to fill my head full of positive thoughts to counteract the infinite loop of negativity I was feeding into my subconscious. I would ride the subway between Queens, where I was then living, and Manhattan, saying to myself, "I *will* win the Met competition. I *will* win the Met competition. No, I *am* winning the Met competition." I found that if I gave myself a list of positive tasks to concentrate on during a performance or an audition, I would have something to think about other than the success or failure of the aria at hand. Without those tasks, fears would start to creep in. I always did better when my mind was occupied. I would think, *Tonight my job is to keep the back of my neck open, relaxed, and free. I will find more space in the back of my mouth for my high notes while easing up on my breath pressure, so that I'm not forcing them out. I will review the text carefully before the performance, so that when I go out it will be fresher and clearer and delineated with more detail. I will keep my visual focus simpler and not become distracted by the audience.* With every performance I tried to come up with something new, something positive to focus on, instead of something negative to worry about. I still use this technique when singing multiple performances of the same piece, and for exactly the same reason.

Unless someone is universally lauded as the talent of the century at the age of twenty-three and it's obvious to everyone that she is going straight to the top, what a singer needs more than anything else to get a career going is one brave impresario who is willing to take a chance and put his or her stamp of approval on her. Because it is an impresario's job to discover talent, it would seem that this should happen regularly, but somehow it doesn't. What they're looking for is someone with buzz. Buzz is critical to a young singer's career, but it always comes down to who is willing to start it. Who wants to risk being wrong? For me, it was David Gockley and Scott Heumann who gave me my first, unequivocal, important vote of confidence. Based on my Houston studio audition, Scott hired me to sing a concert of bel canto scenes in Omaha, Nebraska. A duet from Donizetti's rare *Maria Padilla* was so successful that I was hired back to sing the entire opera. This experience solidified my love of the bel canto repertoire, which I would pursue further with Eve Queler in New York. We sadly lost Scott Heumann soon after to AIDS. Speight Jenkins, of the Seattle Opera, was also one of the few impresarios to take a chance on unknowns. Based on our Metropolitan National Council Auditions wins, he brought Susan Graham, Ben Heppner, and me to Seattle for a production of my beloved *Rusalka* in 1990. If Speight had bet his life savings on those three young singers' having stellar futures, he probably could have retired. This is the joy of discovering young talent, for the casting directors in whose hands our potential lies, and for the audiences and aficionados alike. For the three of us, it was simply wonderful to have a real live engagement.

Shortly thereafter, and true to their word, I got a phone call from the people at the Houston Grand Opera saying they'd had a cancellation in the role of the Countess in *Le Nozze di Figaro,* and could I be ready to sing the part in two weeks? This, I knew, would be the single biggest turning point in my professional career. I threw myself into learning the role, spending hour after hour trying to perfect the pronunciation of each word. The Italian recitatives are among the most difficult aspects of singing a Mozart opera. These declamatory sections, accompanied by harpsichord and cello alone, which are half-sung, half-spoken dialogue between the arias, move the story forward and require an exhaustive understanding of the language. It was a huge amount of work, but I loved it and felt as if I were in school again. Finally, I wasn't trying out for the part; I *had* the part, and now I could settle down into the work of it, which was the place I felt most comfortable.

Houston was presenting Göran Järvefelt's Drottningholm production of *Figaro*, which remains one of my favorites among the many I've appeared in. Unlike most productions, which focus on Figaro and Susanna, this one centered on the Countess as its driving force. Small wonder that I found it so appealing. I was onstage with Thomas Allen and Susanne Mentzer, among others. The standards of the cast were so high that it seemed as if I'd moved from the wading pool to the ocean overnight. Tom Allen, especially, is such a brilliant actor that I literally felt as if I were on fire when I had a scene with him. You can study in the classroom forever, but to rehearse on the stage with a great actor is the fastest way to refine your own skills overnight. His delivery of recitative is among the finest and most imaginative I have ever heard. It was Tom who suggested that I might add to my list of positive tasks a change in the way I presented the character, just to keep performances fresh. He made his Count Almaviva a seducer one night and an abuser the next. Just to react to him while staying in character and managing to get through my lines without stumbling took every bit of training, talent, and courage that I had.

Christoph Eschenbach, the new music director of the Houston Symphony, was also making his operatic debut in Houston conducting our *Figaro* production. Christoph took me under his wing and worked with me every day, a practice that is, unfortunately, highly unusual in today's opera houses. Conductors rarely have the time to help young singers now, or the desire to do so. It's not that they aren't generous—as a group, conductors, and other musicians tend to be very generous people—but there are simply never enough hours in the day, and the tradition of conductors' learning their craft as repetiteurs, or musical coaches, in the theater is gone. So when Christoph gave so freely of his time and talent, we formed a deep and lasting bond. He gave me inspiration, which is what great conductors can offer to singers, and in turn, I trusted him. He urged me to push myself to greater heights, to take risks, to sing and express music in ways I wouldn't have been brave enough to manage on my own.

This was especially true for my performance of "Dove sono," the cornerstone of the role of the Countess, and the aria that really launched my career. It was at once my signature piece and my personal cross to bear. It is terrifying because it is so sustained and exposed, and because its tessitura (or median range) lies consistently in the passaggio, which makes it uncomfortable to sing. Add to that the fact that there are virtually no interludes in which to rest muscles that are beginning to tighten, leading to the vocal equivalent of repetitive stress syndrome. Oddly enough, I never had any problems with the Countess's other great aria, "Porgi amor," which, though equally exposed, moves more and doesn't lie quite so unrelentingly in one place. What Christoph had me do with "Dove sono" was to sing the aria slowly, and then sing the repeat, or da capo, even slower and very softly. The risk in that interpretation was that my voice would give way altogether or falter, and I was prolonging the very elements of the aria that intimidated me in the first place. But in singing, as with many things, it's the risks that always bring about enormous gains.

The production was a huge success. I was paid approximately $12,000 for the entire run, which was a staggering amount of money considering that $300 a week was the most I'd ever earned before that. I was launched, I was rich, and I was incredibly happy. I went home to New York and made plans to get married.

Within a couple of months of my moving to New York to study at Juilliard, I had started dating Rick Ross, a young actor working as the orchestra manager on the production staff. But it wasn't until I moved away to Germany for the Fulbright the following year that we really became close. He wrote me beautiful letters every day, filled with stories and affection. He explained that he wrote to me so often because when he had been in the army stationed in Korea, he hadn't received much mail from home, and he wanted to make sure I didn't feel the same isolation.

Rick was wonderful for me in so many ways, the greatest of which was his unflagging support. I believed in his art, and he believed in mine. I see other women who struggle with their partners' being envious or wanting them to work less or to stay home more. What Rick gave me was total independence and limitless encouragement to pursue my dreams at full speed, an environment that men have traditionally expected from their partners but which professional women are very fortunate to ever find. Rick never set up any sort of contest between my love for him and my love for my work, but was always there, encouraging me. He understood that I had to travel, just as I understood that he needed to stay in New York and audition. Rick helped my ups and downs by being a sympathetic ear and continually reinforcing the message that I really didn't need to go through life taking every setback so seriously, which ultimately helped me recuperate from a disappointment or a bad review that much more quickly. He taught me to take a level approach to life and not allow myself to be blown around by my emotions as much. It was also just comforting to have him there. It's easier to go out on the road when you know someone is waiting for you to come home. Besides, he's a saint for surviving my most neurotic singing years. Once on a blisteringly hot and humid New York City August night, when the temperature in our tiny railroad flat had probably reached 105 degrees, I leaned over and said, "Honey, could you please turn the fan off? It's drying my throat."

So now, in a matter of months, I had a husband, a manager, and a serious role with a major opera company to my credit. The years of hard work and disappointment were finally bearing rewards.

Merle was able to use the success of the engagement in Houston to launch my career, and we ultimately had a very successful six years together. He had tremendous confidence in me, certainly more than I had in myself, and felt that I should simply skip the regional level and sing in major houses. I was still inclined to work my way up through the ranks and learn what I could along the way, convinced that I would gain valuable experience by taking things step by step. Merle, however, would announce, "Let's have you audition for the Paris Opera!" And I would think, *Oh, no, I'm not ready for that*. But he believed I was ready for everything and pulled me along accordingly. I also benefited from his representation of Carol Vaness, because I was able to piggyback onto the many Mozart engagements that she was too busy to accept. Carol was in great demand, and companies could occasionally be persuaded to at least consider a newcomer when the star they'd hoped for wasn't available. Merle gave me the same basic speech he had given her a few years earlier: "You will be fortunate to follow in Carol's footsteps, just as she followed in Mirella Freni's footsteps by taking over engagements Mirella wasn't available to accept." Merle felt that his responsibility at the time was simply to make it possible for me to make a living singing, so I could hone my skills onstage instead of in a practice room while temping.

After I auditioned for the Royal Opera in London, a note came back to Merle that said, "We like her very much because she doesn't sound American." My Slavic ancestry had proven to be a real benefit because my wide, open face and the color of my voice made me distinctive. Oddly enough, a drama teacher at Potsdam had made a similar observation when I was an undergraduate, remarking, "You'll look great onstage because you have a big face." I wasn't exactly insulted, but I didn't take it as a compliment, either. I realize now that larger faces do look better from a distance, in the same way that larger people generally look better onstage in period costumes. The Royal Opera's reaction also made me realize for the first time that my citizenship might prove to be something of a detriment in my career. Americans who want to perform in Europe face a cultural and vocal uphill battle. We're considered good students, very professional and often technically sound; but though there are droves of us to choose from, a European singer is almost always going to be the first choice of a European company—and often, of an American company as well. That preference is understandable, as singers who are native speakers of the languages operas are composed in sound more natural singing them. Also, at that time Americans were regarded as being somewhat bland and as having voices that often seemed indistinguishable. Once I understood this, I knew I'd simply have to focus harder on languages and to attain fluency in as many as possible.

My next audition was for Hugues Gall, the intendant of the Geneva Opera. The company had asked for several arias, and so I sang "Dove sono," Rusalka's aria, Micaëla's aria from *Carmen*, and Pamina's "Ach, ich fühl's." Gall and his artistic administrator sat in the audience and whispered loudly to each other the entire time I sang, which, needless to say, made me wretchedly uncomfortable and convinced me that they weren't even listening. I kept thinking, *They must hate every note of this*. At the end of the audition, Gall stood up and asked rather formally, "May I see you in my office, please?" And I thought, *Well, at least that's polite, he's going to take me aside and thank me for coming all this way and reject me in private. It's a nice touch*. When I went into his office and took a seat, however, he proceeded to offer me five roles. It was the beginning of my European career.

Hugues Gall has a place in my heart next to Christoph Eschenbach, because they both made a point of looking after my career. With Christoph, it was the repertoire. I debuted my Strauss roles, some Mozart repertoire, and Strauss's *Vier Letzte Lieder* with him. Hugues tried to interest other important intendants in me, but often they said, "No, she may be fine for you, but not for our theater." One of the tremendous satisfactions involved in fostering young talent is that you later can say, "Renée Fleming? Oh, yes, I saw that she was the one right from the start." In exchange, both men have my undying loyalty.

One of the many opera houses that was convinced that I wasn't yet that interesting was the Metropolitan. Even after I'd won the Met competition, Merle was told, "She has pitch problems." Being considered "special" is a hugely important asset for a singer. A soprano can have a perfect technique, but she has to have something more than that, something ephemeral that makes her voice memorable. I sang at Chautauqua when I was very young, and the soprano Frances Yeend and her husband, the vocal coach Jim Benner, told me then that my voice was unique. They then patiently explained that this was an element that was absolutely necessary for real success. I'm sure the concept went right over my head then. All these years later, that was exactly what I needed my voice to be: an instantly recognizable sound. In the Lyric Opera of Chicago's opinion, I was "a B singer, not an A singer. Not for this house." Which is all to say that although I'd had some significant breakthroughs I hadn't arrived yet. In a way, these rejections were almost more disappointing than those earlier in my career, because now I really did feel that I was doing things right.

Still, there was plenty to be happy about. Covent Garden cast me as Dircé in the French version of Cherubini's *Médée*, and I made my debut in Geneva as Fiordiligi in *Così fan tutte*. The New York City Opera hired me to sing Mimì in *La Bohème*, the first of only two times I have performed that role, and I won the Debut Artist of the Year award, sponsored by the generous philanthropists Rita and Herb Gold, who had helped me with a Shoshana Foundation grant earlier at Juilliard. The most important competition win—and vote of confidence—came a year later with the Richard Tucker Prize. At that time it was an award for which one auditioned; today it is bestowed upon a deserving young singer by committee. It carried with it a $25,000 prize, which enabled me to focus entirely on music (and, I hoped, would free me from worrying about how I was going to pay the rent). It also came with a telecast, which introduced me to a much larger public: my real debutante ball. I sang regionally from time to time, but it didn't always go especially well. Once I got a scathing review after an engagement in California, during which the general director came backstage at intermission and asked me if I was marking (meaning "half-singing" to save my voice). I wasn't, but clearly I was doing something very wrong. I was probably listening to myself too much or singing in what I thought was a more artistic manner, but whatever the reason, my voice wasn't projecting that night. I was discouraged by both the response and the review, but when I told the story to Beverley, she just said, "Listen, you have to be more generous with yourself, because even though you're singing professionally, you're still learning. You have a lot of ground to cover and you're going to have to do it on the job with other people scrutinizing you."

My Paris Opera debut, in *Figaro*, was on Christmas Eve in 1990. The gleaming new Opéra Bastille presented another opportunity to sing with an organization that had an illustrious history of presenting great artists and operatic premieres. It was humbling to be there, and in Paris, which I came to adore and now refer to as my second home. I rehearsed the beautiful Giorgio Strehler production until the arrival of Lucia Popp, who was to sing the first five performances, after which I would finish the run. Hers was among the voices I truly loved—pure, spinning, and seemingly effortless—and once again I was privileged to witness a great artist's generosity. Rather than scrutinizing the competition and behaving accordingly, she immediately invited me to lunch. She spoke of things I honestly couldn't fathom then, for she was in love and felt that as she had already worked hard and had paid her dues, it was her time to enjoy life and revel in her relationship. I'm sure that as I listened to her I had a look of total incomprehension on my face, since I was at that time so desperate to be where she was, in demand as a great artist and recording star, and I couldn't imagine wanting to wish that away. I didn't know then that she was terminally ill, and indeed, I'm not completely sure that she herself imagined that she would be gone just a few short years later.

The Metropolitan finally came through with a cover contract for the Countess in 1991. One morning at ten a.m., the word came that I would be going on for an indisposed Felicity Lott, whom I was understudying. It was one of those phone calls, like the one from Erica Gastelli when I got into Juilliard. Rick and I were living in a railroad flat, and I ran up and down the hallway shouting with joy. I made a few calls and tried to pull together all the friends and family I could to be in the audience and share this momentous occasion with me.

The Met's *Figaro* was Jean-Pierre Ponnelle's 1986 production, already a classic. I remember making my entrance feeling calm and prepared, and within minutes I was joined by Samuel Ramey and Frederica von Stade, two artists for whom I had tremendous admiration and two people I had never actually been introduced to before. And now there I was, singing with them on the stage of the Met! It was one of the many, many times in my life I felt grateful to Mozart.

I had never chosen to become a Mozart specialist but felt, rather, that Mozart had chosen me. With performances of the Countess, I had already laid a relatively complete foundation for an international operatic career. It was unusual and fortunate that I could achieve it so quickly, for there are many examples of great singers, such as Dietrich Fischer-Dieskau, who never appeared at the Met, while very few artists manage to sing in all of these places, preferring instead to focus on only two or three markets. However, as Merle had to remind me, getting hired is easy. Getting hired *back* is the goal! It was my good fortune that the Countess was so difficult to cast, as the role requires a pure and consistent tone, perfect pitch, style, quality, and nerves of steel, because the singing is so exposed. I was young enough and hungry enough to embrace these opportunities enthusiastically. If someone had laid out all the facts for me before I started, I would have passed on the Countess and been much happier singing Mimì all over the world, as Mimì is an easier role. But the Countess taught me how to sing, and in that respect, Mozart kept me in the role of the good student long after I had left school. By the time I was called upon to make my Met debut, I was as comfortable being the Countess as I was in my own skin.

In 1992, while I was pregnant with our first daughter, Amelia, I left New York for three months for engagements in England, at Glyndebourne and the Royal Opera. Though I was relieved that my career had taken off, I was under tremendous stress. I didn't want to be away from Rick for so long a time, and I was anxious about all the work that faced me in my condition. As I was changing planes in Europe, the flight attendant took my carry-on bag but I was so sad that I didn't think to get a claim check from her, and in this case the bag contained everything that was important to me, including the paperwork for the mortgage and the co-op application for an apartment we were hoping to buy in anticipation of the baby. The suitcase vanished. Every day I went back to the airline office to plead, but no one could find it, until, after a two-week-long detour to Saudi Arabia (where all stylish luggage longs to go, I suppose), it made its way to England and then, miraculously, to Glyndebourne, unharmed.

Before the luggage was returned, I started to bleed in my fifth month of pregnancy. I was completely alone in an apartment fifteen miles outside the town of Lewes in the middle of nowhere. I used to think it was a good thing to cut myself off from people before an engagement because I would get more work done, studying scores and practicing in the evenings, or, in this case, answering the year's worth of mail I'd brought with me, but now I know there is such a thing as too much isolation.

The Glyndebourne administration found a general practitioner who made house calls, a service that's still possible to find in rural England. He ordered me to lie down and not move, put my feet up, and stay in a horizontal position for five days, or I'd lose the baby. That meant no cooking, nothing but quick trips to the bathroom and then back to bed. The festival staff was remarkably gracious, sending someone to bring food and visit me every day. The experience would have been awful enough if I'd been in New York with Rick, home in my own bed, but to be so alone with the terror of perhaps losing my baby was nearly unbearable. I didn't have the money to talk on the phone all day to my family and friends, so I just had to wait it out.

In the end, we two bounced back, and I wound up performing until a few weeks before Amelia's birth. The beauty of singing while pregnant is that the baby provides the support that the abdominal wall usually has to work much harder to offer. With pregnancy comes the lovely, buoyant pillow of a womb for the diaphragm to press against, which makes singing wonderfully easy up until the last few months, when there's simply no more room for breath. However, as long as I was breathing intercostally, with the most horizontal opening of the rib cage possible and an open chest and back, I could get through everything by simply breathing more often than usual.

The real challenge was singing again after I had the baby, but I didn't have the luxury of time to regain the supportive abdominal strength I needed. I would have to do it on the job. When Amelia was a month old, I took her to Dallas to sing my first Tatyana in *Eugene Onegin*. Memorizing an opera in Russian is difficult under the best of circumstances, but now it seemed virtually impossible, since like every other new mother I had given up sleeping through the night. This was the time when I discovered that having an infant and memory are mutually exclusive, and in my case I also had no ability to concentrate for long periods of time, which is another essential component in memorization. The Russian conductor and largely Russian cast were understanding, and it was with this engagement that I began to forge a life on the road with young children in tow.

After a quick trip back to New York, Amelia, my new nanny (a young singer), and I were off to Milan, where I made my La Scala debut as Donna Elvira in *Don Giovanni*. I was just learning how to travel with everything I needed: baby food, formula, diapers, a stroller, and soon a portable high chair, a jumper, and a walker. It was a true exercise in packing ingenuity to travel to a foreign country and set up shop with a baby for six weeks. Beverley used to call me the earth mother with a core of steel, and I think that pretty much described it.

I didn't have an especially enjoyable time at La Scala, due in large part to the house's tradition of the Sala Gialla, the Yellow Salon. The Sala was a conference room in the theater where rehearsals were held. At that time, all of La Scala's productions were double-cast, and ultimately there would be an A cast and a B cast. Normally, opera companies have understudies, or if a singer cancels, another singer is flown in at the last minute. When an opera is double-cast, the configuration is set and contracted long before anyone arrives. But at La Scala, Riccardo Muti, the house's music director, would host rehearsals with both casts, at which everyone would get up and perform his part, in effect a sing-off, as Muti alternated between the two casts. There were the people who were clearly the big stars, and then the rest of us, who were jockeying for a position on the A team. Unfortunately, I was one of the youngsters, in a brilliant group that included Thomas Allen, Carol Vaness, Cecilia Bartoli, Vinson Cole, and the late Gösta Winbergh. Despite the tension that the circumstances created, I was thrilled by Muti's talent. He was incredibly charismatic, and the sounds he could wrest from the orchestra were inspired.

At the very last rehearsal, I received a call from the artistic administrator, who said, "Maestro is concerned about you. He doesn't want you to be booed and so he's thinking you shouldn't sing opening night." In fact, I had already been informed that I *was* singing opening night, and, more to the point, I had been rehearsing with the first cast. I thought the situation through quickly and replied, "That's okay, really, but I'm going to leave now. It's better if I just go home to New York." A great deal of back pedaling followed, and he promised that the maestro would call me. Muti did phone me and said the same thing, and again I said that this was demoralizing and that I would prefer just to get on the next plane. I had enough of a sense of myself by now to know that I probably wouldn't embarrass the theater by singing Donna Elvira. I was part of an ensemble, and I knew the other artists in the cast and felt comfortable with them. In the end, they agreed to give me opening night, and I wasn't booed. I did, however, slip on the stage and tumble backward within seconds of my first entrance. Fortunately, the Leporello was quick on his feet and managed to catch me, but I should have known right then where things were headed. American audiences love an underdog. If I'd tripped on my opening night at the Met they probably would have signed me to a lifetime contract merely because I was brave enough to pull myself together and go on. But European audiences are a bit less tolerant. When you slip in Italy, the audience thinks, *Is this the best they could find?*

In 1993, I sang the title role in Rossini's *Armida* at the Rossini Festival in Pesaro, Italy. Even though I had debuted in several Mozart productions in Europe, this was the moment the door finally opened for me there. It was a wonderful engagement; I was living in the beautiful town where Rossini had composed, and I was eating fresh fish and pushing my darling towheaded cherub in the stroller down to the beach every day to cries of "Che bella bambina!" The *Armida* had an especially imaginative production by Luca Ronconi, with striking costumes and wigs. (One cannot underestimate the contribution a good costume makes to how one feels in a role.) My character was made to look like a cross between Marilyn Monroe and Judy Jetson, complete with a futuristically swirled platinum-blond wig. I was particularly amused when Ildebrando d'Arcangelo, a young Italian bass, wore a mask molded from my features and a copy of my costume, and from the theater, my husband couldn't tell us apart. I'm not sure which of us felt less flattered. At the final performance, the audience rained rose petals down on the stage—a dreamlike conclusion to a perfect run. I love the complete immersion in the work of a single composer that a festival allows. Whether Rossini in Pesaro, Wagner in Bayreuth, or Mozart in Salzburg, festivals appeal to the musicologist in me and give me the luxury of time to create an in-depth interpretation.

One of my favorite things about the work I do is that it presents so many opportunities to grow. Sometimes, in a case like the Rossini Festival, that happens because of the circumstances in which I get to sing. At other times, I learn things about myself by exploring the character I'm portraying, as we all have a little of the Countess in us somewhere. And of course there is always something to be learned from the music itself. But perhaps the best education for a natural-born student is through a mentor, and in Sir Georg Solti I found both a wonderful teacher and a valued colleague.

Solti had cast another soprano as Fiordiligi in *Così fan tutte*, but the role was too heavy for her and at the last minute she wisely stepped down. As had happened so many times before in my career, I benefited from someone else's cancellation and my own ability to step up to the plate on short notice. Decca's senior vice president of artists and repertoire, Evans Mirageas, had recommended me to Solti because he had faced a similar problem two summers before, when an unexpected vacancy came up in the role of Ilia in *Idomeneo* and he had summoned me to Tanglewood. He knew I worked well under pressure.

When Solti called me, I was singing my first Desdemona in *Otello* at the Met, with Valery Gergiev conducting. I was in the second cast, and the Met generously released me from my final performances. I was grateful at the time, but even more grateful later when I realized how important the *Così* performances would be to me. I got off the plane to London at two o'clock in the morning, my time, went directly to Solti's studio at nine a.m., and sang through the entire opera—not the kind of thing singers normally do, but now and then it's good to know you can rise to the occasion. I was immediately struck by Solti's intensity—not to mention the record thirty-two Grammys lining the windows of his studio. I felt inspired just being in his presence.

We worked for three solid hours, there in the sun-drenched studio overlooking the lovely garden of his house, and Solti's commanding presence and musicianship—not to mention the much-needed coffee sent down by his beautiful and supportive wife, Valerie—soon made jet lag a distant memory. And so began another of the central relationships in my career. My recording contract came about in large part because of Solti's excitement about my voice, which he was to christen "double crème" in Paris, when we reopened the Paris Opera's Palais Garnier in *Don Giovanni* after a long renovation—a nickname that has stayed with me to this day.

*B*Y 1995 I was taking on new roles at the insane pace of five to eight a year, and there was even one period in which I was scheduled to sing ten new roles in fourteen months. I had become a great procrastinator when it came to learning operas, not because I was lazy but because my schedule demanded that I learn one role after another in quick succession. Ultimately, the adrenaline of working under pressure became addictive and created a work habit that I still find tough to break. (My former manager Matthew Epstein's pet name for me is Mother Courage.) When I was pregnant with our second daughter, Sage, I was engaged to sing my first Marschallin in *Der Rosenkavalier* with Christoph Eschenbach in Houston. In this case I was really backed up and had to learn the Marschallin in two weeks, so that I could arrive in Houston and be onstage for a dress rehearsal the same day, since a previously scheduled Vienna engagement curtailed my availability. As I started to study the score, I was thinking it wouldn't be impossibly daunting. After all, the Marschallin doesn't sing at all in act 2, and makes her third-act entrance only toward the end of the opera, and of course I already knew the trio from concert performances.

Unfortunately, I didn't take into account how difficult act 1 was, how wordy, how conversational, how *long*. There was so much singing, and it was all so chromatic and rhythmically challenging. It was hard enough for me to understand it on the page, much less read it and memorize it. While in Vienna I had rented one of Plácido Domingo's apartments, and if I close my eyes right now I can still see the wallpaper, the pictures on the walls, the piano, everything. The entire apartment is etched in my mind forever, because I ended up sitting in a chair all day, studying the score, sunup to sundown. By the time I got to Houston I knew it cold, and in this way began my love affair with one of the greatest characters ever created for a soprano. Strauss, anything in Russian or Czech—those parts are graven in my memory forever. Even roles that I haven't sung very often over the course of my career I could sing again tomorrow, if they required painstaking attention the first time around. I appeared in Benjamin Britten's *The Turn of the Screw* once as a student and then had to sing it again several years later on one day's notice. I was surprised to find that I could conjure it up again in twenty-four hours. Repeating operas also helps to establish them in my memory. Not only could I still sing all three soprano roles in *Don Giovanni* (though I'd need a little warning to brush up on Zerlina), I could probably sing Leporello and Giovanni as well. If you perform in an opera often enough, everybody's roles become familiar.

Sage was born in August 1995, and again I sang until late in my pregnancy. I was engaged to open the Met in *Otello* with Plácido Domingo, which was an exciting opportunity, both for singing with him in his signature role and for opening the season, so two and a half weeks after she was born I pushed myself to begin rehearsals. Opening night came two weeks after that, and somehow I managed. I lived only five blocks away from the Met, which was enormously helpful, and rehearsals were not strenuous, given that we all knew the production, but the performances certainly were. Being in New York with Rick and my family there to help me made things much easier than having to scoop up the baby and run to Dallas, the way I did after Amelia was born. It also helped that I wasn't learning a new role in Russian. But mostly it worked because I was young and energetic and had a very strong will.

Having children has been an incredible gift to me. Only time will

tell if my daughters will feel equally fortunate, but so far they seem
to be happy, well-adjusted girls. It was easy when they were very
young, because I simply packed them up and took them with me on
the road. In the days when my schedule consisted almost entirely of
opera, we'd simply travel to a new city and set up camp in an apartment, staying in the same place for a month or two. The girls thought
of home as being wherever I, their current nanny, and their respective
toys and paraphernalia were, and they didn't seem to mind that it
wasn't a stationary place. Rick would visit, and when we returned to
New York he would largely take over the nuts and bolts of care so as
to have his time with them as well. It truly was the perfect existence. I
had everything I wanted without the pain and guilt of leaving my
children. I kept this up for as long as I could, even moving the girls
to schools in Houston and Chicago for longer opera engagements.
Amelia actually extended her kindergarten year in Paris, and two
years later, both girls attended the bilingual school. Because the Paris
school year lasts until the middle of July, it meant some extra weeks
of work for them, but I wanted the girls to have as much exposure to
another language as possible.

Once Amelia entered the first grade and school became more demanding, I knew things had to change, as Rick and I both felt that the
girls needed a solid education combined with a stable social life—no
traveling tutors for us. Eventually, I switched over from what was almost entirely an opera schedule—which had me on the road for as
much as ten months out of a year—to a schedule that balanced operas with concerts. I made a general commitment to sing opera only
at the Met every season and in Europe in the summer, when the girls
can come with me, with very few exceptions. The rest of the season,
I take only short trips, typically three concerts in five days to a week,
as opposed to an opera engagement, which requires three to six
weeks' rehearsal before six to ten performances—a commitment of
up to two months. This system still presents a challenge, however,
because operas are planned five or six years in advance, making it

next to impossible to work around the school calendar and its treasured plays and dance recitals. Fortunately, concerts are scheduled much later than opera, so I sometimes have the flexibility to confirm a date just a year in advance. I feel tremendously fortunate to have both riches in my life: the satisfaction of a thrilling career combined with the sharing and unconditional love of a mother-daughter relationship. Amelia and Sage know without a doubt that they come first, but they can also see firsthand the joy I experience in my work. It was this same kind of personal satisfaction I observed in my own mother's life, and one that I hope my daughters will experience as well.

But even as I was managing the scheduling and the girls, I wasn't managing everything well. In the early part of 1998 Rick and I began to discuss divorce. Most people would look at us and assume that our marriage broke up because of my career, when in fact it was just the opposite. Rick and I had fallen in love when we were living in different countries, and while I was away so often we did very well. But once the girls were older and established, and I started staying home more with them, we were finally forced to confront the problems we had, which were not unlike the problems any other couple has. We'd grown apart.

Feeling initially relieved that a step had been taken, I was completely unprepared for the havoc this was about to wreak on my life and sense of well-being. We had already been leading largely independent lives and remained devoted parents, so I naively thought that our separation wouldn't really amount to too dramatic a change. My subconscious had other ideas, though, and was soon to knock me down—hard.

Professionally, 1998 began very promisingly. In January I sang a televised concert with Plácido Domingo, Daniel Barenboim, and the Chicago Symphony, followed a week later by Strauss and Mozart in Cleveland. Everywhere I went I sang with incredible ease, loving every second I was onstage. I felt that things were settled for the girls, who would be accompanying me for a long upcoming opera engagement in Chicago, and who had been accepted into two different French schools. Although Rick and I were beginning to map out our divorce, we were managing to put the girls' needs first and to work well together to take good care of them. I began to feel a tremendous sense of relief.

Then, while I was performing the Countess at the Lyric Opera of Chicago, I experienced some stage fright during "Dove sono." It caught me by surprise. That aria was never an easy piece, but it was certainly one with which I had had an enormous amount of experience. Suddenly I found myself growing nervous every time I heard the music coming up, and I couldn't seem to shake it. The aria proved to be difficult to perform for the entire run, and there were a couple of phrases in particular that I started to dread, tensing whenever I had to sing them. Opera singers are rightly terrified of fear, because by affecting our relaxation it undermines our breathing. I recognized that I had good reasons to be feeling stressed. Besides the divorce, I was facing three new roles back-to-back in the coming months: the title roles in *Arabella* and *Lucrezia Borgia,* and Blanche in the world premiere of André Previn's *A Streetcar Named Desire*. It made perfect sense that the pressure would show up somewhere. If it showed up in "Dove sono," well, at least I had identified the problem, gotten through it, and could move on to the next engagement.

I went to Houston and began the rehearsal period for *Arabella* with my beloved Christoph Eschenbach. I was glad to be starting a new opera, safe with my friend and with my art, my girls with me, away from home and the stress of the addition of lawyers to begin the process of separation. I didn't have any trouble learning the role this time, but I had an incredible amount of physical tension in my shoulder muscles and neck—tension that grew so strong that I began to wonder if, by the time opening night came around, I'd even be able to get through the performance. Somehow I managed to calm myself down and find a great masseuse, who worked on me as if with a hammer and chisel, and I survived this beautiful but demanding role.

From Houston, I went on to La Scala for Donizetti's *Lucrezia Borgia*. I felt physically better, and with the love and support of the girls and my visiting family, I was able to put my previous experience in *Don Giovanni* behind me and think of this as a fresh start. I did have a slight run-in with the conductor, Gianluigi Gelmetti, over decorations and cadenzas that I wanted to add to the piece, to all of which he was patently opposed. They were beautiful and all stylistically correct, since Philip Gossett, a superb musicologist who specializes in nineteenth-century Italian opera, and with whom I had collaborated ever since singing *Armida* in Pesaro, had written them. Although Gossett's scholarship is greatly respected, Gelmetti insisted, "We are in Muti's house and so we will follow Muti's strictures," which meant to sing what was on the page only. Gelmetti, who was advancing in age, was making his own La Scala debut with this performance and was probably fearful of doing anything that might cause Muti any displeasure. After some discussion, I gave in on almost everything, with the exception of one particularly dramatic cadenza in the final scene that I lobbied to keep. Finally Gelmetti agreed, and I was pleased that we'd managed the whole issue in the spirit of civility and compromise. The final dress rehearsal was perfect, the chorus and orchestra were supportive, and we had an excellent cast. I thought that everything was going to turn out beautifully, which is a tribute to my particularly American naïveté.

The first piece of troublesome news on opening night was that the tenor had canceled. I think he knew there was trouble brewing and had been advised to distance himself from it. Fortunately for me, my friend Marcello Giordani had been scheduled for the second cast. We had worked together often in the past, and I was relieved to be sharing the evening with my friend. At the end of my first aria, just as I finished the last note, I heard a loud thud, and when I looked down I saw that the conductor had disappeared. There was a gasp from the audience. Gelmetti had collapsed, and Marcello and I continued standing in our places, peering into the pit, not even sure if he was alive, though at that moment I feared the worst. Eventually the curtain came down, and we learned that he had only fainted. After fifteen minutes he pulled himself together, and we resumed, though it was all downhill from there. At the end of my first big duet with Marcello there was some scattered booing, but I felt remarkably unscathed by it. It really wasn't until the much-discussed cadenza at the end of my final scene that all havoc broke loose and the serious booing began.

Now, just to set the record straight, the protagonists in this drama were a very small group of men, probably fewer than ten, who were sitting in the very top reaches of the theater. Rachelle and several friends who were there witnessed it all from the audience. Fortunately, those of us on the stage are very limited in what we can hear clearly in the house, and if I'm actually singing I can hear almost nothing at all besides the sound of my own voice, which in this case was a blessing. So I am relying on others' reports when I say that many audience members in the orchestra section and other areas in the house began screaming at the catcallers, warning them in no uncertain terms to stop the disruption. Nevertheless, the screaming and booing continued throughout the final scene, which is Lucrezia's scene entirely, as she realizes she's just poisoned her own son by mistake (one of opera's more ludicrous plots). I kept my focus and stayed with the music. Thankfully the force of what had happened didn't hit me until it was over. And then I began to shake, and I shook for days.

When the curtain went down, Gelmetti turned to the auditorium and shrugged his shoulders as if to say, "Well, it wasn't my fault," and then left us to face the audience on our own. The cast bowed together with me in solidarity. Naive to the end, I called the clinic to which Gelmetti was admitted and inquired about his health. He wrote me a telling letter that said simply, "Your Lucrezia is very special."

"Special" is not a compliment in the Italian language. At its very best it implies ambivalence, and at its worst it implies no ambivalence whatsoever.

I managed to stay and sing two further performances, rather than the five I was scheduled for. There was virtually no booing after opening night, and the critics and journalists were sympathetic, criticizing the *loggionisti* for ruining the performance and, further, for frightening away top-flight singers. After the fiasco in which Pavarotti was booed in *Don Carlo* and swore never to return to La Scala, one is now likely to encounter an obscure Gluck opera being staged there alongside the riskier cornerstones of traditional fare. I never did find out the true reason for my own clash with the claque—whether they were paid by someone to contest me, whether they were honoring the memory of Maria Callas or Leyla Gencer, or whether it was simply a nationalistic slur. (Anti-Americanism was rampant that summer because, earlier in the year, a U.S. Marine jet had sliced through a ski-lift gondola cable in the Italian Alps.) A live radio broadcast of *Lucrezia* exists, so anyone curious enough can decide for himself if indeed this was a conspiracy or simply a spontaneous response to my performance.

I did find the courage to return to La Scala six months later for a recital. One of my Robert Mitchum–style uncles said, "You're a Fleming. Of course you'll go back." Leyla Gencer herself sent me flowers and told me not to worry about it, that the whole affair meant nothing. "That happened to me all the time," she said. "If you're used to the culture, it isn't so bad." But I wasn't used to the culture. If I wasn't the thin-skinned girl I had been in my youth, this still was a decidedly unpleasant experience.

When I returned to the Met, Renata Scotto stopped me in the hall and congratulated me on joining that long and illustrious list of performers who had been booed at La Scala. It turns out that singers save up their own La Scala horror stories and swap them like baseball cards. "Fiorenza Cossotto got booed. She was singing Orfeo beautifully, and they booed her. Why on earth would they contest someone singing Orfeo?" Renata mentioned Luciano and then told me that after it happened to her, she never went back. "You can sing recitals, but forget about the opera," she said, giving me a kiss on the cheek before she left.

Even Mirella Freni was kind enough to tell me how she had been badly booed (I love the fact that there are even *degrees* of being booed) when singing Violetta at La Scala. It was a debut in the role for her, a fairly early engagement, and she undoubtedly sang it beautifully. "I was scheduled to sing *Bohème* right after that, and I thought it was impossible. Still, the conductor told me I had to get right back up on that horse. I resisted. I said no, I couldn't do it, but he said there was no other way." She somehow got her courage up to sing another famous Italian opera a month later and she had an enormous success with it. If they gave medals for valor and bravery in opera, Mirella Freni would get one studded with diamonds and rubies for that.

Even with all the invaluable words of encouragement from other sopranos, the stress of that year had accumulated until I felt as if I was in some sort of vise and the whole world was squeezing in. It was affecting me physically to the extent that I never knew if I was going to be able to sing from day to day. Any exposed pitch in my middle voice had become terrifying and unreliable, making me feel as if I had just woken from a dream and found myself naked onstage. Still, my fears were all internal, an anxiety I was feeling rather than displaying, until a chamber music concert at the Ravinia Festival. I was performing before a small audience in a place where I felt very comfortable, and Christoph was the pianist, which is a rare luxury for me. There should have been no pressure in this engagement, but when I got to the middle of Schubert's "The Shepherd on the Rock," I suddenly suffered a paralyzing attack of stage fright. Nothing had happened to precipitate it, nothing had changed, but without warning, my throat closed up entirely. I was miserable, and for the next couple of days I sat in my hotel room thinking, *You know, you're just going to have to give up singing*. I had some very high-profile engagements coming up, including the world premiere of *A Streetcar Named Desire*, followed by a new production of *Le Nozze di Figaro* at the Met, and I couldn't decide whether it would be more humiliating to cancel or to go through with them in my uncertain state.

Why not quit now? After all, I had had a wonderful career. I had already accomplished more than most singers could ever dream of. I had certainly accomplished more than *I* had ever dreamed of. What profession was worth enduring this level of stress? I could find myself a nice teaching job somewhere in the Midwest, raise my girls, and call it a day. I would get all the details of my new future worked out in my head and then would suffer another crushing wave of anxiety that was both physiological and psychological, leaving my hands shaking and my teeth chattering. I had no idea what was happening to me; I knew only that I was in a state of abject misery. I remember sitting at the window of the dining room of my house a few weeks later, looking at the ancient trees and praying that this would stop.

I had always been such a positive, can-do sort of person that this pain felt incredibly debilitating, though of course it would have been debilitating to anyone. I couldn't function. The simplest things, like getting dressed or making breakfast for the girls, felt nearly impossible and required all the fragile will I could muster.

In the middle of my dark night of the soul, *60 Minutes* was filming a piece on my glamorous life as an opera singer. The program's staff followed me around for about six months, during which I somehow managed to keep my state of mind from them. I remember one particular morning when they had come to the house to tape, and I pulled my publicist, Mary Lou Falcone, aside and said, "Look, I cannot do this." I was shaking. I was, as I used to say back then when things were especially bad, going into the tunnel. It was as if everything was happening at some great distance from me. Once I went into the tunnel, it became very difficult for me to focus on what people were saying. It was a symptom of panic, which didn't happen often or last for long, but when it came over me it was terrifying. Mary

Lou, who has been a constant rock for me, looked me dead in the eye with the calm firmness I would have received from Beverley had she been there, and said, "Of course you can do this." She fixed me up, and sent me out to meet the cameras.

Through this entire period, I never stopped, I never backed out, and I never canceled. I give much of the credit for my ability to continue to the people who worked with me and to my friends and family, who looked out for me. I often think that if I had stopped at this point, it really would have been the end of my career, for I might never have found a way to get going again. The remarkable thing is that I can look at that *60 Minutes* tape now and see that no one would have suspected that I had been in the bathroom only five minutes earlier, looking in the mirror and saying, "I can't do this . . . I can't do this."

Through all of this, my girls were the only ones who could lift me out of the fog. They would come home from school with the pictures they'd drawn and their books and all their stories and kisses, and I would simply melt into them. I knew who I was whenever my girls were with me. I was their mother and I loved them.

While I had experienced stage fright before, it had never followed me off the stage. By the time I began rehearsals for *Streetcar* every interview was excruciating. In the past I had always joked, "You want the soprano to talk about herself? Be sure to cut me off after two hours so I can get to my next interview." But now all I was thinking was, *How do I form an intelligent sentence? How can I control this intense anxiety?* Every minute that I was talking about my work, I wanted to crawl out of my skin.

Oddly enough, the very thing I would have thought would send me careening over the edge turned out to be my saving grace, and that was playing Blanche DuBois. There were days when I really did question my sanity, when I wondered if I was ever going to be well again, and the character of Blanche, with her darkness and fears, gave me a place to pour all of my own. I also, blessedly, had André Previn, in whom I could really confide, to work with. He was consistently reassuring and had a deeply calming influence on me.

In fact, everyone involved in that production was stellar. The director, Colin Graham, through his quiet organization somehow managed to assemble this piece of enormous musical and theatrical complexity in only three weeks. Thankfully, the role of Blanche fit me like a glove, so there were no vocal obstacles to overcome. André had been open to several changes in tessitura, adding glamour to what were initially middle-voiced passages on my behalf, and generally being wonderfully collaborative throughout the process—which is one of the satisfactions of working with a living composer. All I had to do was focus on holding myself together for the run of performances.

By this point my stage fright was a full-blown reality. Fortunately, though, through this period and any other time I've had it since, most of my misery comes in advance of actually having to go onstage. I wake up in the night drenched in sweat and walk around consumed with terror at the thought of having to perform, but once I take the stage, something in my brain kicks in and says, *Okay, she's suffered enough. We'll back off and let her perform now.* It's a strange phenomenon, but one that enabled me to continue. The alternative—that I would feel fine offstage and completely freeze up once I got on—was far worse. I thought so often about the story of Laurence Olivier's having to stop in the middle of a play because he simply couldn't continue. That was what I kept dreading would happen, and over and over again I pictured myself staring at the audience, frozen, until I finally had to say, "I'm sorry, I can't," and find a way to walk off with some semblance of dignity.

Just before beginning *Streetcar* rehearsals, I went to see my internist, Dr. Postley, in New York and said to him, only half joking, "Please just tell me I have a brain tumor." I was shaking so much that I had begun to think there had to be something physically wrong with me. He said that it was probably just anxiety (just!) and that he knew the perfect person to help me, Dr. Ellen Hollander, a psychiatrist whose specialties included success conflict. I spoke to her every day on the phone during the time I was in San Francisco, feeling as if my connection to singing and performing, not to mention my equilibrium, was hanging by a single thread of spider's silk. Dr. Hollander was very helpful in pulling me through the crisis, explaining that many factors can trigger a success conflict. She told me about an actress who had achieved overnight success and then walked away from it. Throughout her life she said it was the right choice for her and she never looked back. I think I would have said the same thing had I jumped the tracks, given it all up, and become a teacher, and I have no doubt that I would have been happy doing so. I would have looked back on the life I'd led and reflected, "Well, it was perfectly fine, but you couldn't pay me to do that now." Think of Barbra Streisand, who left the stage for more than twenty-five years, Olivier for seven, and Carly Simon; in our own world, Carlos Kleiber, Glenn Gould, and Rosa Ponselle left the stage at relatively young ages.

The psychiatrist explained my fears in general terms as a result of the subconscious mind more or less saying: "You've gone too far. You weren't supposed to step away from the pack. You've strayed from your roots. You are by your nature an underdog, the second-place winner, and you shouldn't be here on top." This syndrome is by no means limited to successful individuals. It can affect a waitress who's just gotten a job in the best hotel as easily as it can the president of the country. Think of the number of overnight successes in performing, for example, who soon sabotage their careers with drugs or alcohol, or even commit suicide. It's an entirely relative operation and, in many ways, not rational. It was no accident that this came over me at the same time I was getting divorced, which proved to be more than my psyche could handle. Divorce is terribly painful on its own, but to then add the possibility of losing my identity as a singer, losing my career, was really too painful.

Every cell in my body was screaming, *No! I cannot do this!*

Stage fright makes you feel as if you will die if you go out on the stage. In such a situation, the positive effect of an excellent therapist cannot be underestimated. There were too many issues in my life and my mind's response to them that I just didn't understand. Guidance in these areas can be critically helpful when you start pushing yourself out past the places where you're naturally comfortable, especially when you have a tendency toward self-sabotage anyway. As a woman, in particular, I feel I wasn't socialized for success. Number two, the first runner-up, gazing adoringly at the winner, had always been my favorite role.

When it came time to go back to New York and sing the Countess, I was actually more panicked than I had been in San Francisco. In *Streetcar,* I had been afraid of the stage, but because the music had been written for me I was completely comfortable in it. Even though there was no role I had sung more often than the Countess, it never stopped being a challenge, with "Dove sono" still inspiring nothing but nerves. I could feel myself moving back into the tunnel. On opening night, just before the curtain went up on act 2, I was backstage waiting to go on and started wondering if there was some graceful way I could slip out of the theater without anyone's noticing. Then Beverley Johnson came back to my dressing room. Staring at me with those piercing blue eyes, she held my hand tightly and said, "You *will* do this. You *will* go out there and sing." She knew exactly what I was feeling, but wouldn't let me turn away from her. It was as if she were pouring herself into me, giving me every ounce of her strength and will. Even to this day I can see her piercing eyes at that moment, and the memory gives me strength. She had so much authority in my life, and genuinely understood the depth of my struggle. After she left me, in the remaining minute before my first entrance, I began to feel confident that I wouldn't be alone anymore. It was then that I felt the vise begin to loosen around my chest and slip away. This is not to say that I never knew fear again; but the horrible, paralyzing darkness gradually broke around me over the course of the next eight months, until finally I could see. I could sing.

And when I went out on the stage that night, who should join me at the end of "Porgi amor" but my six-year-old daughter, Amelia. Jonathan Miller, who directed the production, had asked me if Amelia could play the invented character of the Count and Countess's daughter. Automatically I had said no; it felt exploitative. But then he reminded me that the performance would be televised, and mentioned what a wonderful memento it would be to have this tape of the two of us together. I said I would ask Amelia how she felt about it, and she was thrilled. So there she was, my gorgeous, golden-haired girl, holding my hand on the stage of the Met with total confidence during one of the potential turning points of my life. In the finale, the entire cast assembles to sing a joyous chorus that tells the moral of the story. There we were singing when suddenly I heard a very high little voice belting right along with the rest of us. Amelia? For a second I was a little embarrassed, because I realized that no one had told her not to join in. But since everyone else was singing, why would she be quiet? She didn't know the words, but she was faking them well enough. She sang out at the top of her lungs, and I felt more joy in that moment than I remembered feeling in a very long time. I had sung that piece a hundred times before, but tonight was Amelia's debut, and we were together, hand in hand before the world, healthy, glad, and whole.

CHAPTER SEVEN

·BUSINESS·

*F*OR ALL THE INVALUABLE lessons I learned about being an opera singer while I was in school—whether chest resonance, languages, style, or how to sing above the staff—no one had ever sat me down and told me to make sure my airfare was covered when I sang in foreign countries. No one said a word about bookings, interviews, or cancellation policies. In short, no one explained anything about how the business works. People don't naturally think of business as being a concern of artists, least of all the artists themselves. We're supposed to be like birds: natural, free, trilling our songs on a flowering branch whenever the mood strikes us, living off seeds. But this is the modern world, and even the most profoundly artistic of souls has to pay her taxes on time. For that reason and many others, it is essential that young singers familiarize themselves with the business aspects of their work. No one just walks onto the stage of the Met when she feels like it and launches into an aria, no matter how heavenly her voice is. Scheduling is just one of the many requirements of the job.

The offers were pouring in at an alarming rate now, and I felt ill equipped to decide between them. My budding international recital career also needed the attention of a full-time booking staff, so after six years together and a wonderful start, Merle Hubbard and I parted company. He had by now left the Breslin agency and started his own fledgling company, at exactly the point when I felt I needed the support of a large office. So I signed with Matthew Epstein at Columbia Artists Management Incorporated, or CAMI, as it is better known.

Merle, who loves to say that I am the single most ambitious singer he has ever known, gave me a final, generous gift: an introduction to publicist Mary Lou Falcone. Mary Lou didn't have any singers on the client list of her boutique agency, which handled several instrumentalists and almost all of the major orchestras in the Western world with a staff of two. I was tremendously fortunate that she took me on, owing perhaps in part to my relationship with the late Arleen Augér, who, like Lucia Popp, had succumbed to cancer at an early age. Arleen had been a friend and a client, and I met Mary Lou when I sang at Arleen's New York City memorial.

Mary Lou and Matthew quickly set up a team to oversee my career, consisting of the two of them and the various executives of my new record company, Decca. I can remember meetings at which I sat for hours just listening to them, a student again, as I realized that I still had an enormous amount to learn about the business I was in. Matthew and Mary Lou were both extremely experienced and successful in running the careers of musicians. One of their first goals for me involved my recital debut at Carnegie Hall, two years in the future, which they were determined to sell out. Mary Lou has a real brilliance for and strong opinions about pacing—when to have an article written and where to have it appear—and she knew which opportunities should be passed on to avoid overexposure. Often, it's important not to pursue too much press before an event, which raises expectations to a level that's impossible to satisfy. A seasoned publicist has the ability to build things slowly and steadily and to see exactly what needs to be done. The notion of turning down publicity—or anything, for that matter—was a new one to me, and it seemed totally illogical at first. "You're not going to be hyped," Mary Lou would say. "We're going to concentrate on a steady upward trajectory."

I panicked and felt sure that other singers would pass me by, leaving me in the dry, dull dust; but she held firm, and over time I came to see the logic of her arguments. Too many singers are overly praised in advance of their appearances, before they have time to develop, and then, in turn, are unfairly vilified later in a wave of backlash. Years of training and professionalism could easily be undone by too many magazine articles in which I would come across more like a young starlet than a serious artist. I certainly had no history and no experience to guide me through these potential pitfalls.

Matthew wanted to help me establish focus in my schedule and in my repertoire choices. He suggested that I specialize more in Mozart, Strauss, and Handel, and probably would have been pleased if I had given up the Italian repertoire altogether. I saw his point and agreed that I needed to narrow my interests, but I wasn't willing to give up the Slavic repertoire, or new music, or my beloved French composers— and really, I wasn't going to give up the Italians completely, either. Bel canto was one of my great passions. Getting me to limit my repertoire was a task akin to turning a ship around while it's going full speed ahead. I knew I needed to cut back, for maintaining a high quality of artistic interpretation is nearly impossible when there's so much music to learn. At some point it becomes a question of survival. I knew I had to stop trying to be all things to all people. After years of confusion on this subject, I finally decided to limit my repertoire, but *not* to become a specialist, and looked to the careers of singers such as Victoria de los Angeles, Lotte Lehmann, and Eleanor Steber as templates. My taste, and my penchant for musical exploration, simply did not allow me to call myself a Mozart/Strauss specialist exclusively.

When Matthew left CAMI to become the artistic director of the Lyric Opera of Chicago just a few short years after he began to manage my career, I was pleased for him while at the same time feeling disappointment for myself. His strength and conviction as a manager had taught me so much about staying focused on the larger picture and making a long-range plan, or even a complete career plan, for

that matter. He stressed batting instead of fielding—actually pro-
actively deciding what I wanted to do, rather than just considering
the offers as they came in. He has been one of the strongest impresarios in the industry, whether as a manager or as the artistic director of
one of the world's most important theaters. His presence at a performance can propel the audience into a frenzy, since he shouts bravos
freely and resonantly throughout. For a live operatic recording of
mine we actually chose a take from a performance that he attended,
because his presence in the hall so clearly added to the excitement of
the night. Most important, he is the most passionate person I have ever
met in the business. We weren't always in agreement in regard to the
direction I should take, since I eventually absorbed a great deal and
had a few ideas of my own, but I still appreciate his advice and care.

Matthew suggested I work with Alec Treuhaft at CAMI, and after
meetings, consideration, and my usual polling, I did. Alec has fully
embraced my need to stay home with my daughters as much as humanly possible, and has therefore managed to greatly reduce my operatic commitments while increasing those for recitals and concerts.
He is thoughtful, has enormous integrity, is highly respected, and
speaks softly but carries . . . well, you know. An opera production requires a time commitment of a minimum of four weeks and as much
as eight weeks, and at best I'd probably find myself in the same six
cities year after year. Recitals and concerts allow me to perform in as
many as thirty cities a year, for audiences who wouldn't otherwise
hear me, while still spending much more time at home. Alec left
CAMI not long after I joined his list, and he moved to IMG, where I
have been with him ever since. Alec's job isn't always easy where I'm
concerned. He has to apply firm pressure now and then to get me to
stick to the program, and in that respect reminds me of how Leontyne Price told me to tune out the noise and concentrate on my
throat: "You won't gain anything by trying to please everybody."

In regard to work, my theme song in that period was very definitely "I'm Just a Girl Who Can't Say No." Although I never found turning down inappropriate repertoire to be difficult, merely keeping control of an overwhelming schedule was next to impossible for me. The problem lies in the different rates at which the scheduling is done. What looks perfectly manageable five years in advance—which is when opera engagements are fixed—can begin to look rather crowded two years in advance, as I neglected to account for the last-minute press interviews, the television appearances, the children's horse shows, concerts, and illnesses, and my own friends and family.

One of the great assets of being with a professional management company is its international booking departments, which can efficiently organize a worldwide tour. Alec, who is my worldwide manager, is based in New York and is responsible for the overview of all of my scheduling and specifically for dates in the United States. Peter Wiggins, my longtime manager based in Paris, takes care of most of Europe, and there are additional tour managers based at IMG in London for larger concerts and appearances worldwide. They receive or suggest the offers and present them to me through Alec, and I decide on them based on a consideration of my schedule and whether or not the engagement is either artistically interesting or important—such as an appearance with a major company or conductor, or one that offers an opportunity for exposure. My management negotiates the contract, which for opera will usually include a round-trip flight but no housing, and until very recently for concerts, neither. The management receives as commission a percentage of the fee, which is split with the European management if the engagement takes place on the Continent. Alec also negotiates my recording contracts, which include royalties, an advance on royalties, and a per diem during recording sessions. Only recently I received my first small royalty payment after eight years with Decca, which means that it took that long for my recordings actually to be in the black.

It sometimes seems as if it's a full-time job to maintain communication among my managers, Decca, and the various marketing and publicity teams. Between coordinating my opera and recital calendar, making and promoting recordings, and supporting my engagements in new cities with press interviews, I often feel as if I'm the chairman of the board of Renée Fleming, Inc. In some respects it *is* a company we're talking about, and all of the salient marketing principles apply.

Hearing me bemoan the media's glass ceiling in regard to classical music a year ago, a close friend introduced me to the veteran Hollywood impresario Sandy Gallin. He observed that although I may have accomplished a great deal in the world of classical music, the public at large probably knows very little about that achievement. "In addition to the work you've already done," he told me, "what you need is someone who will have the clout to get you on television." Sandy introduced me to Pat Kingsley of PMK, the powerful Hollywood publicist, who graciously agreed to help, and is generating opportunities to reach a wider audience through television appearances and other media outlets that are not usually receptive to opera singers.

These days, it sometimes feels as if I spend more of my time on the logistics of singing than I do on the art and performance of it. I go over every detail of every travel schedule, interview, recording, repertoire choice, and program (now that I'm performing less opera, programming has become an enormously time-consuming job), to the point that I often feel as if I'm planning a military campaign rather than a tour. I once knew a woman who kept a diary of all the dinner parties she gave: what food was served, what wine, the guest list and who sat next to whom, what she wore, what was discussed, the plates, the linens, the music that was played. That amount of minutiae is not too far removed from what I have to keep up with in my career. I have to remember what I've sung in New York so as not to repeat myself there too often. Gone are the days in the Potsdam jazz club when I could belt out the same songs every weekend and only have to worry about whether or not my jokes were fresh. I keep track of which gowns I wore at venues all across the world, because, believe me, my Parisian fans would notice if I came onstage in last year's dress.

At the heart of it all is my schedule of singing engagements. The practice of planning operas five years in advance began in response to the frenzy created by Luciano Pavarotti and Plácido Domingo. Their appearances could sell out an entire season in subscriptions, so the competition to sign them up became fierce. Individual orchestral concerts can be discussed as early as three years in advance but aren't generally contracted until approximately eighteen months to a year before. In general, it takes less time than that to schedule recital tours with either orchestra or piano. Ideally, a new recording will also be supported by a tour, or by related performances, but the timing of this is difficult, given the way a calendar can fill up before the recording is even finished. To the performance schedule, I then have to add personal and business demands, because singing is only a part of the overall picture. Interviews are planned in support of tours and engagements, which can require an entire day devoted to press, one interview after another; photo shoots are scheduled, events are attended, and I still have to get up at seven a.m. to accompany my daughter to the school-bus stop.

In scheduling I also need to think carefully about how different roles will be juxtaposed. Extreme changes in styles of singing aren't recommended for vocal longevity, as they can fatigue and stress the muscles and weigh negatively on nerves and technique. One of the factors cited to explain the early decline of Maria Callas is that she sang Verdi, bel canto, and even Wagner roles back-to-back. Fortunately, I have never really been asked to sing "everything." Sir Georg Solti suggested Isolde, Leonore in *Fidelio,* and Leonora in *La Forza del Destino* during our three years of work, but I knew that he simply felt that he wanted to hear a voice he loved in whatever he was conducting. Alternatively, some mixture of opera, concerts, and recitals, as long as there are a few days in between for turnaround, does my voice good. Too much consecutive Mozart can have me singing in too controlled a fashion, fearful of singing out, while too much singing at the opposite extreme of my repertoire can make it more difficult for me to sing softly and with refinement. While I have always felt compelled to sing the greatest variety of music possible, I have been careful to keep it all within appropriate vocal parameters.

Planning and programming a recording is a collaborative effort involving Decca, my management, and myself and is a surprisingly arduous process, as it involves deciding not only what repertoire, but when and with whom. In a perfect world, I could choose a repertoire that suited my voice, that I adored, that extended from the popular to the unknown; the repertoire would already have been performed and layered; and the quality of the conductor and orchestra, or the pianist, would be on the highest level. Obviously, this isn't a perfect world. When I recorded Strauss's *Vier Letzte Lieder* with Christoph Eschenbach and the Houston Symphony, I had never sung this cornerstone of the soprano concert repertoire, a piece that already boasted many wonderful recordings. Using twenty-four different interpretations—some commercially recorded and some pirated performances—I tried to come to terms with the recorded history of the piece. Fortunately, since it had been premiered in 1950, this was possible, beginning with the great Norwegian dramatic soprano Kirsten Flagstad, who sang the first performance. Armed with that knowledge, I then began to forge my own interpretation, to make the piece my own, without the experience of performances. An interpretation exists because of what we find between the notes, and it is the only way for us, other than by timbre, to make ourselves distinctive. A brilliant execution of any phrase is only the beginning. Can something fresh be said with it? Can something personal be expressed? We dream that one day our talent, intelligence, and inspiration can take us from being a singer to the exalted station of artist.

In past times, a Jon Vickers could record his first *Otello*, as he did for RCA, before ever having performed the role onstage, and still have a chance to record it again, fifteen years later, and film it, too. More recently Plácido Domingo has made three recordings and several video versions of *Otello*. Nowadays, it is unrealistic to think that singers will have that many opportunities to record even their most central roles. So, the decision to make a particular recording, and at a particular point in a singer's career, has to be very carefully weighed. Fortunately, there are a few advantages to this situation. Because I don't have time to discover my limitations through the medium of performances, I tend to take more risks, especially with a conductor like Christoph, who doesn't hesitate to test the limits. There is also a freshness in performing pieces for the first time that never quite returns as more depth is added to interpretations. This is one reason that I enjoy mixing some new works into my recorded repertoire as well as in recital programming. In actually choosing the repertoire, I hail from the school of pedantic research, so in the case of my recent Handel CD I needed to explore every suitable aria I could get my hands on. I never want to run the risk of accidentally passing over some lesser-known jewel because I wasn't willing to take the time to dig through piles of manuscripts. Beginning with a list of music I already know, I often end up rejecting most of these original choices because I get so excited about new discoveries. Next, I had to decide what the focus of the recording should be: Italian arias? Secular or sacred? Mixed baroque repertoire, or only George Frideric himself? I'm aided in this process by the record company, its marketing staff, my management, and ideally the expertise of a musicologist. Polling is still one of my favorite tools, and I conduct it among my own professional advisers, friends, and parents.

Recital programming is arduous to say the least. Jean-Yves Thibaudet and I spent countless hours reading through stacks of song literature to come up with our program for the recording *Night Songs*. We started without a clear-cut concept and through trial and error eventually realized that we were gravitating toward music of the late nineteenth and early twentieth centuries. I wanted to be sure that Jean-Yves was pianistically challenged enough to warrant his collaboration, while also choosing pieces that suited me well. I approach every recording as if it could be my last one, which makes the selection process into a nail-biting frenzy. This same obsessive attention goes into the programming of my recital tours. My goal is to please most of the people some of the time: a balance of well-known gems, a few obscure discoveries, virtuosic display, and more intimate fare. It is difficult to second-guess the public's wishes for an evening of song, but I try to consider the differences among audiences in Sydney, Zurich, and Kansas City, without repeating previous repertoire choices.

During one of my first recital engagements, the presenter bemoaned recitalists' loss of regard for the audience, prompting a quick decline in attendance and interest in the art form. He spoke of an earlier recital in which Jerome Hines had brought his costumes and sung complete opera scenes for an audience that might otherwise never have heard him perform live in his greatest roles. I took what the presenter said very much to heart and have ever since paid close attention to the public, reminding myself that we are first and foremost entertainers. Why should someone leave the comfort of his home, computer, and television if not to be moved, enlightened, and inspired, rather than lectured? I was a student during the period of declining interest that the presenter mentioned, and I remember being bored by recitals in which the most obscure—and therefore uninteresting—repertoire of single composers filled the recital halls in New York, when I had never even heard any of the best repertoire by these composers performed by great artists. I would have been so thrilled to hear just one "Erlkönig." Still, stretching horizons and challenging the audience is an important consideration. One all-American world premiere concert I gave prompted hate mail, but I made sure the next program contained favorite arias. My program with Jean-

Yves was time-specific, but it also introduced relatively unknown repertoire to an audience with already brimming CD collections.

My daughters, of course, take precedence on any calendar I may be drawing up to help organize my life. School pageants, homework, doctor's appointments, birthday parties, heart-to-heart talks, and solving disputes occupy my time as they would any mother's. I now make sure I travel for only short periods, and I try to be someplace interesting where they can join me over school holidays. The girls delight in having a second home in Paris, where we often spend a month in the summer. Paris is an absolute playground for children, and we have been exploring some of its hidden delights. The Jardin des Plantes and Angelina's hot chocolate are a must on every visit. I want them to enjoy and benefit from being the daughters of an over-scheduled opera singer. They have already traveled the world and are at home in many of the capitals of Europe and the United States. They have also toured Japan and Australia with me. To see the world through a child's eyes is as great a gift to me as it is to them. These are adaptable, unflappable, independent children, much to my great fortune and pleasure.

Of course, I can't manage any of this alone. I have help on every front, from scheduling my Met engagements to packing a suitcase, and I always maintain that I'm nothing without a great nanny. But I don't turn a blind eye to any corner of my life. It is my life, after all, my career, and the ultimate responsibility for making sure that everything stays on track is mine, as difficult as that sometimes seems.

For all the traveling I do, I still have a moment when I fill out the landing card at the airport and feel uncertain. What do I put down as my profession: Singer? Opera singer? Musician? Artist? Diva? Prima donna? If I'm landing in France for the summer, am I a *cantatrice*? A *chanteuse*? An *artiste lyrique*? I'm not sure I know the correct answer myself, which is some form of existential confusion. On career day in high schools, the halls are full of doctors and firefighters and engineers, but chances are that few students are discussing the career possibilities of becoming an opera singer.

I have always wanted to understand what my professional place in the world is, and to do so has taken me years of putting together snippets of advice and wisdom, and slowly coercing people in my own management and record companies to share real information with me. I am a musician, and primarily a classical musician, and as such I believe that it is my responsibility to understand both the mechanics of the business itself and the changing role of classical music on contemporary culture. If your preferred image of me is as an artist above the fray, incapable of sullying her delicate mind with facts, figures, and marketing terminology, by all means please skip this section.

While a new album of Strauss scenes is never going to have Madonna looking nervously over her shoulder, recorded classical music does have a significant audience; and unlike most forms of popular music, it can be marketed worldwide without the language barrier that limits the careers of many pop singers. As recently as the 1950s, classical recordings represented 25 percent of all albums sold in the United States. While we are not likely to see these levels again soon, classical music does hold its own, representing 3 percent of the U.S. market and 3.2 percent of the worldwide market, which translates into total annual sales of just under a billion dollars. To put it into perspective, however, as of 2003, 37 percent of all recorded music worldwide is sold in the United States, so even a 3 percent share of this, the world's largest music market, is significant.

While we've been allowed to remain fairly rarefied for most of history, classical musicians are now as subject to marketing principles as any other performers. We have to think about the percentages our records sell, as well as the demographics of our audience. We are now a brand, and every brand vies for the attention of the nineteen- to thirty-nine-year-old disposable-income buyer, although the AARP set, the over-fifty demographic, which is largely ignored, has 35 million members with a larger overall income. (In the rest of the record industry, they're even targeting the purchasing power of thirteen- to sixteen-year-olds.) What's more, older people are more likely to be operagoers. We have to be willing to explore how to sell to both groups if we plan to stay alive in the business. Most people today have had less exposure to classical music than their parents and grandparents, who grew up believing that classical music, like serious literature, was "good for you." Husbands get dragged to concerts by wives, or the boss brings along a handful of executives courtesy of a corporate sponsorship program, but that isn't enough. We need to spread the passion for music that makes some people such enthusiastic concert- and operagoers.

There's no arguing the fact that a night at the opera can be expensive, but we do pay equivalent amounts for other forms of entertainment. Fifty-yard-line seats at a football game, or front-row Knicks tickets for a family of four—once you add in the Cokes, hot dogs, and Cracker Jack—aren't going to be cheap. Broadway tickets are often one hundred dollars apiece now, and can reach dizzying heights beyond that if the show is hot and sold out. Yet while seats for a Pavarotti performance may have approached the three-hundred-dollar mark, they also went as low as ten dollars for standing room.

Sometimes all people need to rethink their position is a little incentive. The Handel and Haydn Society in Boston was able to increase its top-price ticket sales 20 percent by throwing in free parking. Some companies are adding packages with restaurants and offering a free drink at intermission. None of these measures diminishes the music; they merely say, "If you make an effort, we'll make an effort." Because of the nature of the art form, opera companies have been able to take the lead in marketing and advertising: they recognize that they have drama to sell. Opera can be marketed as something that's sexy and hip, and no longer just for the canary fanciers. Orchestras are finally starting to catch up with this idea. Still, it can be a hard sell when you have a young audience that grew up without any sort of musical education that reached farther back than the Grateful Dead. Singing in choirs and studying piano and other instruments were once normal parts of a child's upbringing, aided by amateur groups, churches, and schools. These programs planted the seeds for a love of serious music that bloomed in adulthood. What we're finding now is often a case of no seed, no bloom.

The problem isn't only one of getting people into opera houses and concert halls. It's also figuring out how to sell records. More people are listening to classical music than ever before, but most of them are doing it via the radio. Anyone wanting to hear my recent performances as Arabella, as Imogene in *Il Pirata,* or as Violetta in *La Traviata* would have been far more likely to encounter them on a live radio broadcast than through any other means. Part of that is simply a matter of price—CDs are expensive to make and expensive to sell—but part of it is also a matter of saturation. After all, how many recordings of Beethoven's Ninth Symphony does a person actually need?

Not only is the industry badly in need of paying audiences and CD sales, but there are also gifts to be solicited to keep the opera and symphony alive. No one expects to be asked to make a donation for the upkeep of Britney Spears, but classical music is forced to reach out to patrons for support. In the 1950s and '60s, charitable giving primarily benefited cultural institutions, as governments in Europe and America were more attentive to social concerns. But as public funds have been slashed on all fronts, the public is understandably much more likely to give its discretionary dollars to hospices, homeless shelters, and educational causes rather than the arts. The one partial exception is the construction of performance spaces, which involves tangible realities like bricks, mortar, and donors' plaques, as opposed to an abstraction like the annual operating budget. As a general rule, people like to build things but are much less comfortable about being asked to sustain them.

On every front there have been shifts in our cultural tastes in music including the newfound popularity given to the composers of film soundtracks, a genre I had firsthand experience with when Howard Shore asked me to sing on the soundtrack of the third film in the *Lord of the Rings* trilogy, *The Return of the King*. When I first met Howard he said, "I'd love to have you to do this; however, I want to explain to you that we have a vocal concept and a musical concept that you might not want to fulfill." He told me that he was looking for a medieval sound and that my singing would have to have a very pure, chantlike quality (words I expected to hear from William Christie!). I listened to the previous soundtracks and understood exactly what he was looking for, so I said, "I would love to try." I recorded five three- to four-hour sessions for what ultimately became about ten minutes' worth of music in the film.

I was amazed by how different recording techniques are for a film score than, say, a collection of Strauss scenes. When we record classical music in the studio the process is not very far from a live performance, with just enough orchestra time to get through a piece two or possibly three times and then patch in a minimum number of corrections. In any three-hour orchestral recording session, fifteen minutes of usable music is about what is expected. Perfection isn't even an option, since the finances of recording with an orchestra simply don't allow for much repetition. It turned out that the people making movies from J. R. R. Tolkien novels did have endless time for perfect results, however, and could afford the London Symphony for months of work, thirty or forty sessions for a single film—an unimaginable luxury in the classical music world. Add to that the discussion of the proper pronunciation of Elvish, and I can definitely say that this was a unique experience.

To get the degree of perfection in the singing that they wanted, I had to imagine beyond what a boy soprano could contribute. The producer asked me to take every ounce of expression out of my voice in order to make the cleanest sound possible, saying, "Remember, no vibrato, no connecting between tones, no dynamics." Then he said, "Good, now could you add a little bit of emotion?" He lost me there, because to achieve the sound he wanted I had eliminated all the standard devices to express emotion: vibrato, portamento, legato, and dynamics. Without any access to those tools, I didn't have the faintest idea of how to create something beyond the pitches.

Amazingly to me, the final result sounds much richer and warmer than it did when I was singing it, and my short selections are incorporated into the film in a beautifully seamless way. I left that experience feeling a tremendous sense of respect for people who work in film. They have remarkable patience and stamina, given that the hours they put in are endless—or in this case, not just hours but years. Barely a month later, I recorded a disc of Handel arias and found to my delight that the experience of fine-tuning my ears to hear the tiniest change in vibrato and dynamics lent itself perfectly to the baroque style. A fortuitous side benefit to taking on the music of the Elves!

Many people think the answer to the salvation of classical music is to tap into the obsession with celebrity, to find artists who can make the industry seem less *classical*. Others predict that what has been called "the cult of celebrity" is a sure path to ruin. I myself have spent most of the past ten years confused about the whole subject, and to make matters worse, my recording career began during one of the most difficult transitions the industry has ever faced. Just where do I fit into the larger picture of our culture?

The demand for Enrico Caruso's recordings single-handedly changed the phonograph from a curiosity to a commercial enterprise. Caruso dominated the musical world, and while he was always an opera singer first and foremost, he was equally beloved for his Neapolitan song repertoire, which sold as well as his aria recordings. All of his recordings are still in print, something that can be said of few recording artists.

Thanks in large part to Caruso, opera singers became such celebrities in the early twentieth century that they were even sought out for silent-film roles. In Europe, the great beauty Lina Cavalieri made a film of *Manon Lescaut,* and in America, Geraldine Farrar did an incredibly popular version of *Carmen,* which is still screened to this day. This is particularly ironic in light of the fact that the biographical films made about opera singers in the second half of the twentieth century featured nonsinging actresses whose singing was dubbed.

Once sound came to the movies, singers were everywhere. Grace Moore, Jeanette MacDonald and Nelson Eddy, and Mario Lanza all could be considered crossover artists, as they were well-trained performers who brought popular songs and light and core classics to a larger audience. And even though Deanna Durbin never had an opera career, she managed to sing (and sing well) at least one aria in each of the twenty-two musical films she made before retiring at the age of thirty. During the height of her fame in the 1930s and '40s, she became the highest-paid woman in America, and in some years the biggest-selling female box-office star. All while singing arias!

Today, "crossover" has become the golden word of the age. Crossover is based, in fact, on the model used for the development of pop artists. It is a lesson taken directly from the recent pages of star development, where bands are constructed out of pretty faces with an ability to dance in sync. Their recordings do not generally travel internationally, and some of the groups are actually paid a salary rather than a royalty, allowing the company to reap great profits if the band takes off; or, alternatively, an enormous amount is spent on promotion and development. The image is decidedly far more important than the content, enhanced with arrangements of classical tunes or original material, light shows, costumes, and choreography. Crossover is definitely finding an audience, and an enormous audience at that.

It was the staggering sales of Andrea Bocelli's CD *Romanza* that spawned a series of successful CDs by people who are generally referred to as opera singers without actually having the requisite training or stage career. Most could also never be heard without amplification, not necessarily because their voices are small, but because they haven't had the years of development and knowledge of projection and the craft of singing. Furthermore, higher voices have a juvenile purity of sound and not the ripe, warm tone of a true operatic voice. The smart ones will either use their overnight success as a launching pad for a career in television or film, or will find a way to develop as musicians and change with the times, as some pop idols can.

Ironically, the success of crossover repertoire for these performers means that young artists who are pursuing a traditional classical career face choices that were not there just a few years ago. Young musicians want to sell their extraordinary gifts to the major labels, but when they get no response, they hire professional photographers to shoot them draped across the top of a piano or around a cello in tight clothes. Then the labels start to be interested.

In today's market, classical recordings, at least at the major labels, are also being held to the same standards as pop. There are fewer releases, enormous expectations for sales, more money spent on promotion, and shorter contracts, with artists no longer being signed for the duration of their careers. But classical music isn't pop, and its numbers really can't be run the same way. It used to be expected that a classical recording would recoup its investment in seven years, and that was an investment companies were willing to make. But by 1999, it seemed that classical recordings were being held to the same standards as those of U2: the investment had to be made back in one year. Most operas cost at least $250,000 to record; Solti's *Die Frau ohne Schatten* cost a million including all marketing expenditures and company overhead. My recording of *Rusalka* cost around $300,000 and has sold forty thousand units to date. It will have to sell seventy-five thousand to earn back its cost. Yes, these recordings may stay in the red for a long time; but in truth, even staying in the black is no longer enough. The only thing that counts for the shareholders of the largest companies is a huge profit.

Fortunately, huge does happen every now and then. In recent years, classical artists such as Yo-Yo Ma and Joshua Bell have even made it onto the *Billboard* pop charts. And the phenomenon of Pavarotti, Domingo, and Carreras, the Three Tenors, flew—eventually to the tune of twelve million copies. Their success, however, ultimately served to mask an overall malaise in classical recording. Thanks to the seventeen million units they sold, the bottom line for classical record sales looked very bright on average, but if anyone bothered to examine individually some of the other recordings, it was easy to see there were huge losses. In the end, the Three Tenors' legacy was primarily an extraordinary string of spin-offs: Three Mo' Tenors, the Three Scottish Tenors, the Three American Tenors, the Three Irish Tenors, the Three Countertenors, the Three Broadway Divas, Three Men and a Tenor, the Three Phantoms, the Three Sopranos, the Opera Babes, Ten Australian Tenors, and the Three Finnish Basses. It seems that all the music industry took away from the experience was that three seemed to be a very palatable number for the buying public.

Studio executives suddenly turned their attention to their classical divisions and had the idea that all of their projects should live up to these results. Executives who were considered "old-fashioned" were asked to step down and were replaced by mostly young, marketing-driven managers. But the forces that were driving the sales of the Three Tenors had little to do with classical music. Their success was a phenomenon: a confluence of stars, the connection to the World Cup, well-established artists performing at the peak of their careers, and a great human-interest story. In the long run, this spike in popularity did little if anything to tarnish the seriousness with which Pavarotti, Domingo, and Carreras were taken as opera singers. They were firmly established by the time the recording was made, and each had a substantial body of work. Even some aficionados were thrilled to hear Plácido sing Macduff in a Three Tenors concert in Los Angeles or José sing the tenor aria from *Le Cid*. Where else would they be able to hear that?

Some have criticized the Three Tenors phenomenon and other exceptional classical music events as bad for the classical music industry, in that they accustomed major artists and the labels themselves to unsustainably high advances and royalties, while rewarding record companies with unrealistically high profits. This may be an unnecessarily negative view. No singer I know, myself included, would ever turn down an opportunity to preserve the legacy of a career in the opera house simply because she's not being paid Three Tenor–size royalties. Yes, singing is how we make our living. But sometimes it really is a labor of love, and for most of us, the artistic satisfaction of a challenging role is far more alluring than a big fee. If not, why would we have become classical musicians in the first place?

If I wanted to capitalize on my commercial potential entirely, I would sing only the most popular classical arias, not in their original forms, but arranged stylistically to fit everything from techno to Hollywood film music. I would sing even less opera, and then only Italian opera and not the lesser-known Strauss and French rarities that I adore. I would tour only my recordings in pursuit of ever larger sales, rather than performing world premieres and the concert repertoire of Strauss, Berg, and Schoenberg. I am not at all against adding visual elements to a performance, whether through image and fashion or through lighting or perhaps film. In fact, I would welcome opportunities in the future to bring, say, the imagination of a Pina Bausch production to a musical performance, but never at the expense of the integrity of the music.

The most important point to be made about mass audience events that sometimes feature opera singers, whether the Olympics or televised celebrations such as the Kennedy Center Honors, has to be this: that somewhere out in the audience, whether on a grassy hillside viewing a big-screen monitor or at home watching his own television, will be someone hearing opera for the first time—possibly even hearing classical music for the first time. That alone has to make it worthwhile for artists to continue—in appropriate settings, with musical integrity—to try to expand the audience for their music. If we failed to do that, we would be, and should be, criticized even more strongly, as our audience, at least in the Western world, shrinks away.

•   •   •

My own recording career got its big boost after I stepped into the role of Fiordiligi for Sir Georg Solti. He suggested to his label's new vice president of artists and repertoire, Evans Mirageas (who, along with Bettie Buccheri, a pianist for the Chicago Symphony, had recommended me for the engagement in the first place), that I be signed up as an exclusive artist for Decca. Evans asked my London manager, Tom Graham, if I had a recording contract and was told with emphasis, "Not yet." That contract came into being over the course of two telephone conversations between Evans and Tom, but the actual signing took much longer. RCA and Decca were both interested in me, and I was in the enviable position of having to choose between the two. I went with Decca.

Having an exclusive recording contract with a record label is a delicate arrangement. Often the payoff doesn't come until the second or third recording. No one wants to make a supreme effort and investment in an artist's early recordings, only to see the artist taking the benefits of that promotion and support to another label. Fortunately for me, the senior management at Decca and its parent, Universal Classics, and I were ultimately in total agreement on this point. I believe that I'm now seen as one of the label's core artists, who has continuing long-term sales potential. In turn, I've learned that besides recording, my contribution is in the promotion of my recordings, which includes seeking out the kind of celebrity that goes beyond the classical audience. Of the group of people who are available to purchase a classical recording—that is, those who have been exposed to classical music before—5 percent will probably purchase one of my recordings. The next 15 percent who like classical music will purchase something if it catches their attention, and the next 25 percent will purchase the Three Tenors, Andrea Bocelli, or popular classics such as the Beethoven Ninth. The remaining people simply won't buy classical music; it isn't going to happen.

Therefore, it's necessary to invest in publicity, even if it means that I spend my own money, trying to take myself above the usual level attained by core classical artists. The only way I'll reach that other 25 percent of potential buyers is to appear on, say, the *Late Show with David Letterman* or perform at such events as the lighting of the Christmas tree at Rockefeller Center. I take advantage of the opportunities that come my way. If I don't maintain my sales, I can't continue to record, and recording is the only chance I have to reach that larger audience and to keep my art alive after I've stopped performing. It's also something I genuinely enjoy. What a luxury to spend a week in the studio focused solely on the music, with no uncomfortable costumes, no worrying about the public or the critics, no wondering if I'll forget the text, or how the lighting is—just an unadulterated collaboration with musicians and composers I admire.

My performing career and my recording career dovetail and reinforce each other. It's been a slow and steady climb, but at least it's always been a climb. Making recordings enables me to communicate with people, many more people than would ever have the chance to hear me sing. I'm not sure I have a definitive answer for why that is important to me, but it is. Perhaps it's wanting to re-create the wonder I felt when hearing recordings as a young singer and hoping that someday I would sound just like them. Perhaps it's just part and parcel of my personality, the need to continually strive and improve, which seems such an integral part of my being. Or perhaps it's simply the excitement of continuing to grow.

There are ominous signs about the future of classical music. The record companies are facing threats from piracy and unauthorized downloading. It's important for those of us who have achieved success to speak out for the choristers and violinists, and beginning artists who won't have work at all if the piracy continues. I asked Christopher Roberts, president of Universal Classics and Jazz, if I could interview him about technology and the future of the recording industry for this chapter. He has been the only continuing thread throughout my relationship with Decca, and it was his support some years back that helped turn the company in my favor. So many dire predictions abound right now about the future of recording: studio recordings will cease to exist altogether; the large labels will collapse and only small and budget labels will survive the illegal download-ing and piracy crisis; operas will be available only on live recordings and DVDs or will be streamed live via the Internet around the world.

Chris explained that the recording industry has historically been driven by new technology, from wax to the electronic microphone, from the 78 to the long-playing record, and most recently the develop-ment of digital recording and the compact disc. I joined the company at the end of an enormous wave of sales, as the public scurried to replace their LPs with the smaller, indestructible disc with digital quality. The future savior of the market appears to be the Internet, the beauty of which is that it offers unlimited choice. Traditionally, recordings are kept in or eliminated from each label's catalog based on their ability to earn more than their basic upkeep. Imagine, though, a digital catalog available on the Internet that includes every available recording ever made. As Chris explained, though, before a piece can appear on iTunes, it has to be compressed in digital format. That's an initial expense at a time when people are skeptical about undertaking expenses without be-ing assured of the future. At Universal, one thousand out of four thou-sand tracks are on iTunes. The acceptance of this technology is still in its early stages, but Chris predicts it will grow within five years. China especially may prove to be an enormous market, given its public's ap-preciation for, knowledge of, and awareness of classical music, and its huge media outlets. The downside of the technology is piracy. Chris doesn't see retail sales disappearing altogether, even though they are shrinking and are certainly under pressure. Anything but a hit-driven CD is being replaced with DVDs, in general, and that applies to classi-cal, jazz, new age, and soundtracks as well. The same choice offered in the area of recorded music can also exist in the domain of perfor-mances. Imagine tuning into a recital in Tokyo just by turning on your computer. Most radio lovers have already discovered this feature on the

Web for music alone, and it's just a matter of time before the picture follows.

The music itself will never disappear. Beethoven still makes people cheer, Richard Strauss can thrill, and Mozart can even develop young minds. It's our responsibility to learn how to speak to an audience that is less informed about music, to give it a reason to want to come and see us instead of going to the movies. For me and for the rest of the industry, it's going to take hard work and a lot of creative thinking. But then, thinking creatively is our business.

CHAPTER EIGHT

·LONGEVITY·

My BELOVED Beverley Johnson died in January of 2001, after suffering from a serious illness the year before. In some ways those long months helped me and the tenor Anthony Dean Griffey to prepare for what was to come. Tony was like a surrogate son to Beverley, and we both took shifts at the hospital. Mary Lou Falcone came to visit and wisely counseled me to ready myself for losing not only my friend but my teacher. Yet it was even more than that: I was losing my touchstone.

"Maybe one imagines that people expect more of us than they really do," she wrote to me in 1999. "I think, by and large, your public has come to love you and they are happy just hearing your voice, just as it is. So I wish I could help you believe that it is there for you to call on. You have nurtured it and been good to it, so it won't let you down. I know for sure that this is true. I get so awkward when I try to tell you how much I respect what you have accomplished and what you are doing."

Amazingly, Beverley remained active right up until the end of her life. She gave me a lesson on December 23, a day I still remember so clearly, as she lay on the couch and just listened to me sing, and in her deep blue eyes there was so much wonderful joy, so much strength. Singing meant more to Beverley than to anyone else I've ever known. I brought the girls by the next day to wish her a merry Christmas Eve, and she was visibly tired. She clearly hadn't been well, and a few days later I checked her into Columbia Presbyterian hospital. I told her I would pick her up to take her there, but she insisted on meeting me at the hospital. This was a woman who didn't want anyone doing anything for her. She couldn't stand having a nurse in her home and didn't want to be taken care of, for she just couldn't bear to be weak. She was going to live her life to the fullest, and when she couldn't do it her way anymore, that would be it. When I got to the hospital I found her sitting in a wheelchair in the waiting room, looking terribly small, a scarf wrapped around her head. "I'm coming here to die," she said to me sadly.

Her last three weeks were especially painful for me, not only because it was clear that she was dying but because in those final days she pushed me away. I was rehearsing a *Live from Lincoln Center* telecast at the time, and in retrospect, given Beverley's condition, I wonder if I should just have canceled it. But it was imminent, and everyone was relying on me to come through. Every day I would leave rehearsals and go straight to the hospital on my way home to Connecticut, and though at times I'd arrive as late as two o'clock in the morning Beverley was usually awake. She would look at me for a second and then stare up at the ceiling. "Oh, Miss Fleming is here. Miss Fleming has come for a visit," she would say, for she spoke of me only in the third person then. She was so angry at me, or maybe it wasn't directed at me so much as at her awareness that she was dying. I would sit by her bed in the middle of the night and try to talk to her, and sometimes I would be quiet and touch her hand. I felt how strongly she wanted to live, to stay and to help me through *Traviata*, to help Tony through Britten's Serenade for Tenor, Horn, and Strings, a piece her husband, Hardesty Johnson, had premiered in America. She wanted to remain involved in our lives, and we wanted the same.

In mid-January I had to make a trip to Europe. Yet again, I was following the old dictates of "should": I should go to London, and I should meet my obligations instead of staying close by. Two days after I left, she died of pneumonia. Tony called and told me she was very peaceful in the end. She was taking a great deal of pain medication by then, for she had cancer, though we hadn't known. We hadn't known, either, that she was ninety-six. I was scheduled to sing the Verdi Requiem that night but called my manager in London and said, "I'm sorry—this is just impossible."

"You have to do it," he told me. "It's a live telecast, and we don't have anyone to replace you."

I learned that night that it's possible to set aside whatever else is going on in my life and play the part. I have no memory of that concert; it was as if I were not even present, and yet so many people have come up to me since then and told me how moved they were by the performance, how much it had meant to them.

It took me a long time to get over Beverley's feelings toward me when she died, as I struggled with missing her and tearing myself up over everything I could have done differently. A friend told me his mother had done the same thing to him, and that sometimes people push away the very ones they love the most because they can't bear to leave them. Whether or not that was the case with Beverley, it was a comforting explanation of why things went so badly between us during that last month. Beverley had been such an extraordinary influence in my life, believing in me when I was going nowhere, and giving me a clear perspective when life seemed to pull me in a hundred different directions. She had helped me find my voice, teaching me how to shape it, how to expand it, and how to coax it back when part of it got away from me. She provided me with a consistent thread through so many inconsistent times. I felt at once grateful for ever having found her in the first place and, at the same time, heartbroken to have lost her.

There have certainly been moments when my voice has failed me, when it has seemed capricious and unreliable. But there have been other times, like the night of Beverley's death, when my voice has been a true friend, carrying me rather than my carrying it. The fragility of the voice is in many instances due to its being tied so strongly to the mind. Dealing with vocal problems is not always as straightforward an issue as simply dealing with a technical shortcoming, for confidence and trust also come into play. Trust has everything to do with my ability to go onstage certain that when my mind tells my voice to do something, it's going to happen. It's hearing a phrase in the mind's ear and then knowing the body can reproduce that phrase a split second later. Without that trust—without taking it for granted that I can sing the notes fast enough or execute a particularly high passage or produce a diminuendo in the score—I really have nothing. Without confidence, my body's muscles would just get in the way of expression, leaving me subject to clutching, grabbing and holding, and other faults that singers try so hard to eradicate.

If I have to hold a note for a very long time, I imagine it as moving and spinning, for the note has to have life. In a way, a singer actually refreshes a note with every beat that it's held. Once the hammer hits the string in a piano, there's no way to retrieve the tone. There's absolutely nothing the greatest pianist in the world can do to keep that sound from dying away. That's the nature of the instrument. Like any wind instrument, however, the voice can sustain a tone as long as the breath stays actively engaged. As soon as any sort of holding occurs as the result of muscular tension, it reveals itself as a glitch in the sound. Sometimes it's a pitch problem (the note will go flat or sharp) and other times it's a problem in the tone quality (the vibrato will slow down or speed up, and the note will lose its beauty and evenness). When any such problems develop, the secret to a long-lasting career is to stop singing for a while. It's a tough decision to make when you have a mortgage to pay, or you don't feel as if you can disappoint an audience, or you don't want to lose a part in a particular production. Still, no matter how high-profile the performance, its benefits have to be weighed against the longevity of the voice. Keeping the voice in as healthy condition as possible for as long as possible is a concern that hangs over a singer's head every day of his or her career.

Of course, taking care to protect one's voice will not always be met with understanding and support from opera houses and concert halls. Generally speaking, a singer will begin to suffer professionally after more than a few cancellations, and only a great artist will be indulged in frequent absences. Someone like Teresa Stratas, for example, who always explained that her health was fragile, was such a brilliant singing actress that the companies would hire her at any cost, knowing she could not always be reliably counted on to appear. Pavarotti likewise became prone to last-minute cancellations and was almost inevitably forgiven. With a voice like that, how could he *not* be?

My own experience in canceling performances due to illness was always at the Metropolitan Opera. The first was opening night of Britten's *Peter Grimes,* when whatever infection had been brewing finally camped out directly on my vocal cords. Unfortunately, my symptoms worsened just as I was getting into my costume, wig, and makeup backstage, which meant that my understudy was doing the same, since by then we all knew that I might not make it. The Met representative came into my dressing room five minutes before curtain and tried to encourage me to go on, since I hadn't yet been able to decide firmly not to. Just for a scene, for the audience, he pleaded. I continued to vocalize, and fortunately for me, a coach standing directly behind him risked her job and shook her head no, based on what she heard. I had the good sense to listen to her advice. We never know if singing on a cold or a throat infection will be our last performance, so prudence is rewarded with a future. Still, it is devastating to any singer to sit in her dressing room in tears, removing her makeup and getting ready to go home as the performance continues without her.

My second Met cancellation came more recently, during the production of Bellini's *Il Pirata*—the very opera toward which I felt the greatest sense of obligation.

The way things normally work at the Met, the artistic administrator calls a singer's management and says, "We're casting these ten operas over the coming seasons and we'd like to consider your client for these roles." That is, repertoire is chosen first, and the casts subsequently. But on one occasion I was asked to come in for a meeting with the general manager, Joseph Volpe, so I knew something important was up. When I sang at the Met, I always had the sense of being a cog in a large machine, and never lost sight of the fact that it's an honor to sing there. At this particular meeting, Joe said to me, "Here's the list of things we'd like to see you do, but we also want to know what opera you would be interested in singing." This was an enormous change in protocol; I was being offered the luxury of choice. Joe Volpe's reputation is based primarily on his gruff exterior; but to me he has always been a caring mentor, helping me with personal problems as well as the production at hand. I once totaled my twelve-year-old BMW at Broadway and Seventy-ninth Street (it takes real talent to total a car in the middle of Manhattan) and Joe sent a car for me for the rest of the run of the production, for both rehearsals and performances. When I finally had an opportunity to thank him for his thoughtfulness, he said, smiling, "It's not for you, it's for me. We need you in one piece." He most recently, and without my knowledge, assigned security to my postperformance exits from the Met, after I received an alarmingly threatening hand-delivered letter at the stage door. It wasn't until a friend asked "Why are these men following you?" that I realized it.

Our relationship only continued to grow stronger over the years, and now he was offering me a remarkable opportunity. As I sat in his office thinking of a role I would like to perform at the Met, I knew it would be something from the bel canto repertoire. I did some research and learned that Bellini's *Il Pirata* had never been performed at the Met, and I liked the idea of challenging the audience as much as myself. I am still my father's daughter, after all.

The problem, of course, was that since *Il Pirata* was obscure, and since I was the one who had chosen it, I felt a special responsibility to make it a success, both for the audience and for the house. Seven performances were scheduled, and I canceled two of them. My daughters and I were living in a tall Victorian house in Connecticut at the time, and I had already been having some trouble with my throat when one afternoon I was calling upstairs to Sage. When she didn't appear quickly enough to suit me, I did what any normal mother would do: I called out her name again, and *loudly*. At that moment I felt a strange little pinch and thought, *Oh, no . . .*

I went to my ENT, Dr. Slavit, who after examining me said, "I could shoot you full of cortisone and you could go onstage, but if you care about the big picture or even the rest of this run, and your longevity, don't do it—don't sing." When I asked him to explain what was wrong with my "cords," he said, "For the record, it's the vocal fold that actually vibrates to produce the sound—the inner membrane or tissue which looks as if it's been folded. The actual vocal *cord* is the back third of the entire membrane. In toto, you have muscle surrounded by mucosa, which vibrates and creates the sound, attached to cartilage, and there's a tiny area of swelling on one side." In all the years I'd been going to him, he had never told me to cancel any performance, and whenever I had been concerned about a particular problem, he put me at ease, saying, "Oh, come on. You'll be fine." In this case he called Joe Volpe personally and said, "She cannot sing." Even worse than my disappointment was the fact that when I went back I never gained complete confidence in the role again. Because of the injury, I felt as if I was being too careful, which created its own set of problems. You don't really protect your voice by undersinging or holding back. It's a little bit like whispering when you have laryngitis: in the end, it only does more damage. Beverley had always been so good about shaking me out of that habit. I'd complain, "It doesn't feel right," and she'd reply, "You're undersinging, dear. You're worried. Stop that. Just sing." She had an uncanny ability to discern subtle differences in my voice and call me on them, and once she gave me permission to sing out, things would click and fall back into place again.

Success is a wonderful thing—until highly anticipated performances have to be canceled. Not only was I worried about my voice, I felt as if I had a giant spotlight focused on me. Still, no matter what obligations await, it's better to stop. Otherwise, small problems have a bad habit of becoming large ones. It's easy to begin a downward spiral as a result of the bad habits and confusion formed by singing when ill, so that when your health finally does come back, you find you've lost your confidence. The voice can be a terribly fragile instrument. Someone once repeated to me in hushed tones regarding a well-known tenor, "He sang on a cold and could never trust his voice again." This kind of statement can leave even the stoutest bass waking up in the middle of the night in a cold sweat. Have these voices actually been harmed, with damage done to the vocal cords or the tendons surrounding them? Has the technique been thrown off, and is the problem reparable? Or was it just a loss of faith? It's rare that anybody has the precise answers to these questions. Every voice has a shelf life, and one has to be extremely careful of anything that might end a career mysteriously and prematurely.

Caring for a voice includes paying attention to aspects of physical health, the environment, mental fortitude, and, above all, a solid technique. As a Juilliard student, I was constantly ill, and even had back problems, until I happened to notice that they occurred only before major auditions—a case of self-sabotage, caught red-handed. When I asked the legendary Dr. Gould to have a look at my throat for the third time in one year, he suddenly took hold of my shoulder and said, "You're not sick. You're tense." That marked the beginning of a journey of self-exploration, which eventually would enable me to become one of the singers who rarely, if ever, got more than a generic cold. I've always considered the question of health to be one of mind over matter. Whether I imagine smiley little scrub brushes cleaning out the dirty bacteria or virus in my veins, or I simply tell my body in no uncertain terms that there's no time for a cold this week, whether it's making sure I am aware when tension threatens my health and well-being, or finding a way to ignore the common illnesses of my children and other loved ones, I manage to keep singing. Some are surprised to discover that, indeed, we are paid only if we sing. There are no sick days in opera. Otherwise, I live in moderation and try not to make any unusual allowances for my voice in speech, diet, or how I spend my day, with just a few exceptions: I avoid excessive air-conditioning and cold drafts on my head and ears, refrain from unnecessary speaking on performance days, and drink little or no alcohol, which dehydrates, the night before a performance. I can't imagine using up many precious hours of my life worrying about my throat in the third person.

The key factor, however, is decidedly technique. A solid technical grounding enables me to realign my voice and gently coax any hoarseness out of it on a daily basis, no matter what allergies are circulating, how tired I am, or whether I spent the day at Disneyland with my children.

Amazingly, in my generation of top singers, I'm considered conservative in the ways I protect my voice. Some of my colleagues have never even heard of the word "moderation" and blithely go on singing beautifully after playing eighteen holes of golf, in-line skating, and then spending a night on the town—*all* night. Because I push myself to the limit with multitasking and work, the one concession I do make is in taking care with *how* I use my voice, whether speaking or singing. Higher resonance and very little breath pressure can extend my stamina in rehearsals, and if I need to be heard, I speak high, and with as much mask resonance as I can. This tactic works especially well in a crowded restaurant—which, by the way, is one more thing I try to avoid. Who decided that louder is better in New York City restaurants? I can't even *hear* the person across the table half the time, let alone communicate with him.

Marking is another point of controversy. I learned an important lesson about marking—half-singing or singing down an octave so as to preserve the voice in rehearsals—during one of my very first engagements. My role was small, which gave me an excellent opportunity to observe how the more seasoned professionals prepared their roles in rehearsal. The opera was a rarity, and the two leads, to my disappointment, never sang out in rehearsal. Still, I assumed they knew exactly what they were doing to preserve their voices, and so I was shocked to find on opening night that neither had the stamina to survive his or her role. Vocal muscles have to be trained consistently for strength, flexibility, and stamina, just as an athlete's would. Alfredo Kraus said that one should be able to sing easily for six hours a day, although for me, two or three hours is usually the limit. Ideally, marking should be reserved for only the most extreme phrases, and for the most extreme kind of singing: high Cs or Wagnerian outbursts, for example. If these phrases are solid, one can afford to let them fly just every so often—but unfortunately, in my case those are usually the phrases that need the most practice. Although I find that sustaining high-tessitura passages, especially without interludes, isn't possible for any great length of time, less demanding singing certainly shouldn't be tiring at all. Unless I'm under the weather or genuinely tired, I try to avoid marking, as do many of my colleagues. If marking seems to be necessary for an artist, chances are something uncomfortable is occurring in his vocal production, which should immediately be attended to, as ignoring it promises only a career of worry about the voice.

Even with exemplary discipline, every singer faces a vocal crisis at some point in her career. Most of us have several. I needed to take a few weeks off and realign my voice after my debut as Eva in Wagner's *Die Meistersinger* at Bayreuth. I spent an exhilarating summer there—with Wolfgang Wagner himself directing and Daniel Barenboim in the pit—soaking in some of history's greatest repertoire in Wagner's very own theater. I adored the entire experience from start to finish, with my toddler and my infant girl happily in tow. In the second act the role is conversational and low, and I oversang, adamant that I be understood at all costs. Hindsight is, as usual, twenty-twenty, and it wasn't until I recorded Donna Anna directly afterward that I realized that something wasn't quite right. The role, which is demanding and high, felt much more difficult than it had several months earlier when I sang it in Paris. *Così* at the Met was to follow, and I decided to take a break and spend two weeks with Beverley so that we could unravel the tangle. Fortunately, we did, and fortunately, Mozart was again my teacher. Beverley and I used to joke that my coming to see her every so often was like a twice-yearly visit to the dentist—just making sure things were in place and still healthy. More recently, since her death, I've relied on Gerald Martin Moore, based in London, as my "outside ears" for difficult roles and recordings, as well as my sister, Rachelle, who knows me and my voice as well as anyone now.

As a beginner, I often pulled my senior colleagues aside and asked for coaching. During my San Francisco debut as the Countess, I asked Michel Sénéchal, the great French tenor, if he would work with me on Massenet's *Thaïs*. He graciously agreed, and gave me another important piece of the vocal puzzle when he said, "The danger with sopranos—in fact, mostly American sopranos—is that they tend to sing too thickly in the upper middle [the notes at and around the top line of the staff], and before you know it, the voice has aged, the top is gone, and a wobble is born. . . . The weight is too much, and the voice can't bloom in the top. It's a stone column, and not the sapling it should be." I developed my own idea of the voice as hourglass from this very conversation, and I have come to agree with him, having seen a number of voices come to grief in precisely this way.

Certainly, there comes a time in every career when the voice begins to decline and no technique, no amount of rest, and no teacher can turn it around. The natural aging of the voice, according to Dr. Slavit, is caused by the membranous tissue of the vocal cords changing and becoming less flexible. However, the same treatments that can rejuvenate the skin of our faces can potentially regenerate and nourish the lining tissue on the cords. Dr. Slavit is working now on a possible safe method that could in fact prolong our careers. Imagine, I might be performing with a walker someday!

If not, it has always been my goal to stop when I choose to and not when I have to. We should never sing past the point at which audiences begin to forget why they used to love us, or a new generation comes along and can't figure out what all the excitement was about. Of course, I might like to sing for another twenty years, or maybe longer. But if I have a good voice for just another twenty days, then I only hope I can be dignified enough to recognize that and step aside gracefully.

No one took a more gracious leave of the stage than the great German soprano Lotte Lehmann. She had given up most of her roles but continued to sing the Marschallin in *Der Rosenkavalier* into her late fifties. She wrote, "Whenever I sang it, I felt caught up in the sheer joy of it, swept away by its magic, the words and the music streaming out as though they were truly part of myself, created by me. And whenever I closed the door on Sophie and Oktavian to leave them to their bliss, I always felt as though I were closing a door upon part of my own life, taking leave with a smile. . . ." When she finally announced the end of her career, it came during a recital at New York's Town Hall, when she made a lovely little impromptu speech, cried a few tears, and then met nearly everyone in the audience backstage afterward. In her dressing room she said, "It is good that I do not want to wait for people to say: 'My God, when will Lotte Lehmann shut up!' "

One of the most often-repeated pieces of advice that's given to young singers is: "Never sing on your principal." It means just that: Never sing to the extreme, and be careful about singing to the outer dynamic reaches of your voice. A big component of longevity is choosing repertoire wisely. The most difficult word for a singer to learn is *no*—no to too much, too soon, too heavy, too dramatic, too mature, and to an orchestra that's too loud. But these are dangers that many singers find impossible to resist. A lyric soprano may so desperately want to sing *Madama Butterfly* that she tackles it before she's ready—and then wakes up one day and finds she no longer has a voice. I once wrote to Carlos Kleiber to ask about an offer I had received for a role that perhaps seemed too heavy. He wrote me back: "Don't even *think* of doing [it]. Don't give any reasons, just say *no!* Don't argue, don't apologize, just say *NO! N.O.*"It's a letter I should frame.

Just as some bemoaned the passing of the "Golden Age" of singing when I was a student at Juilliard, today the complaint is that there are no dramatic voices for the heavier Italian and German repertoires. What has emerged is a wealth of talent perfect for the baroque and Mozart repertoire, with the intelligence, musicality, and musicianship to bring this music to the forefront of opera today. I do not for a minute believe that the available pool of contemporary voices possesses significantly smaller instruments than those of singers of past generations, but rather that several changes have taken place in the way music is performed over the past sixty years that have affected how singers are perceived. Both the size of theaters and the pitch and quality of the instruments in modern orchestras have had an enormous effect on vocal requirements. The advent of recording has likewise shifted the priorities and expectations of both singers and audience. In the early part of the twentieth century, the highest priority beyond a beautiful voice was the ability to be understood. Onstage, everyone was expected to be perfectly clear in an operatic performance. There were no supertitles then, and operas were generally performed not in their original languages, as is customary today, but in the language of the audience. Granted, audiences had the leisure time and desire then to prepare themselves for an operatic performance by reading the libretto before attending. One of the reasons that diction was so clear earlier in operatic history was that voices in general were produced for brightness and sheen, rather than for warmth and roundness.

Bringing language to life in music and pronouncing phrases correctly are challenging enough for any singer, but for sopranos particularly, making sure the audience can hear the actual words is next to impossible. For us to be understood while singing above the staff is a little like trying to have an intelligible conversation while yawning.

(Try it.) The high voice used for singing lies far above the actual speaking voice, and the production of beautiful high tones—or, for that matter, even passable high tones—requires an enormous amount of space in the mouth, which doesn't lend itself well to the clear enunciation of either consonants or closed vowels, like *a* and *e*. My goal is to push the diction envelope as far as is humanly possible without compromising the quality of the sound or causing fatigue, both to be understood and because words color the line and give character to what would otherwise be a wash of legato sound.

I had to remind myself when I sang Eva in *Die Meistersinger* at Bayreuth that there were no "Wagnerian" singers when this music was composed. There were Mozart and Italianate singers, and it was their voices for which Wagner wrote. The opera house in Bayreuth was built precisely to house both his large orchestra, which was placed in a sunken and partially covered orchestra pit, and the beautiful voices it wrapped in rich sound. Since then, nearly every new theater that's been built has been larger—and in some cases, much larger—than the European theaters for which these operas were originally composed. Add to that improvements in technology, which have enhanced the sound of many of the orchestra's instruments, and the growing taste for a more brilliant string tone, and singers naturally have to be louder just to be heard. One of the most difficult elements of all is the raising of the basic tuning of the orchestra from the baroque 430 to 435 in the mid-nineteenth century, and then to 440 early in the twentieth century, and now to 444 in Vienna. This calibration had differed as much a tone and a half over time, which challenges singers enormously if a piece is already high, a fact I didn't fully understand until I sang Mozart and Handel with period instruments.

Another factor working against opera singers is that over the years taste in recordings has moved toward warmer, thicker tones for the voice in every repertoire, and that type of sound doesn't cut through orchestral textures as well as a brighter tone. It takes more volume, and therefore more breath pressure, to be heard when using a darker sound. The benefit of brightness in the voice is that it's the center, core, or *squillo* edge in a voice that enables it to project in a large hall over an orchestra. Unless the conductor and the orchestra have a disciplined sense of dynamics when accompanying singers, we wind up with the inner-ear problem again, believing we're not meeting expectations. As we can hear and feel the surge of sound behind us or under us, we become aware that we're not able to ride over it as easily as we should be able to, so we compensate by pushing and singing louder. Singers who succumb to this temptation soon lose their vocal sheen and beauty and burn out much more quickly. If I could wave a magic wand and effect any sort of change for singers today, it would be to address these balance issues. Dynamic markings should be read with an understanding of the context in which they were written and adjustments made to reflect the kind of orchestra and size of the hall, so that the human voice isn't expected to vault over this suddenly enormous hurdle. There is nothing exciting about a climactic solo passage when the singer's voice is covered by the orchestra. How can the audience feel the thrill the composer intended when the vocal line is buried at its richest and most powerful moment? An orchestra can actually build enormous tension through holding back, which doesn't mean it plays with less energy, but merely that it allows the voice the chance to trace an exciting arc and then joins it like a horse that has just been let into the race.

Given these requirements for more vocal heft, what opera singers need more than ever to survive is a proper understanding of stamina. Stamina is a measure of one's ability to sustain a very long performance—whether a recital, which, with encores, can last two and a half hours, or a Wagner opera, which can last five or more. One isn't singing every minute of that time, but nevertheless the effort is exhausting. The only thing I expect to feel at the end of a long performance is physically tired, but ideally never vocally tired. I say

"ideally" because in practice, it's not always possible. Length, tessitura, the dramatic components of a role, and physical conditions such
as allergies can all affect one's strength. The length of a piece alone
does not necessarily lead to stamina problems. The extended final
scene in *Capriccio*, for example, is manageable because the phrases are
broken up by orchestral interludes. In contrast, "Martern aller Arten"
from *Die Entführung aus dem Serail* is next to impossible because it's
high and unrelenting. *Daphne*'s major monologues would also test
just about anyone with their combination of dramatic writing and
high tessitura. Many Mozart arias present stamina issues, because
they have few if any interludes and therefore require long stretches
of uninterrupted singing in the passaggio.

Fortunately, stamina can be built up through training and repetition,
if it's done in a healthy way. Muscle memory is an important factor, because we have to depend on involuntary muscles and coax them in the
right direction. Singers must train just as an athlete would, with repetition just to the point of fatigue but not to that of injury. One of the best
ways to ensure stamina is not to sing too heavily, for adding weight to a
particularly long section will only lead to fatigue. At the same time, care
must be taken not to hold back when singing, as that creates the same
problem for different reasons. In these challenging sections of music I
try to make sure that I'm producing a relaxed, free sound. I'm also con-
centrating like mad to make sure that the muscles I don't need at any
given moment aren't involved. The trapezius, the neck, any tension in
my face, the way I hold my chin—all of those elements, when improp-
erly handled, can make a difficult piece an impossible one. If I feel my
jaw beginning to shake in a difficult passage, it's usually because I'm
putting too much breath pressure on the voice, and that's a sign to lay
off. It's only with a disciplined technique and a great deal of experience
that I can get through these roles without problems.

Picture me during the *Pirata* hiatus, sitting at home worrying
about these things. The worst part of it was that physically, I felt fine.
A spiking high fever or a sore throat would have been almost com-

forting, because at least I wouldn't have been second-guessing my decision. While I would have liked to go and hear my understudy sing and see the production from the house, realistically the only way I could have done so was with a black veil over my head. If you've called in sick at the Met, no one wants the surprise of seeing you chatting in the lobby. Just imagine trying to explain to the people who are staring at the cast-change sheet tucked into their programs that you are really feeling fine, but just can't sing.

Thanks to the enormous break I got at the Houston Grand Opera singing the Countess, I essentially got to skip the understudying portion of my career, with the large exception of my Met debut. The relationship between a scheduled artist and an understudy is at best a delicate one. The understudy obviously has to be present during rehearsals and performances to know exactly what she has to do if she is needed to step into a role, but ideally she can memorize the part without making the lead singer feel as if the Angel of Death is hovering over her, waiting to make a move. I have heard stories about understudies literally standing in the wings mouthing the words at the poor soprano while she sings. One soprano finally cracked under the pressure, insisting, "I don't want her here. I don't want to see her"— a fair enough request under the circumstances.

Of course, there have also been sopranos who have gotten rid of other sopranos because they didn't want any competition on the stage. There's very much a split between the kind of artist who wants to absolutely outshine everyone else, even at the cost of bringing down the level of the piece they're in, and the kind of artist who feels that the best performance is one in which everyone is performing at the highest level and working as an ensemble. A retired artist said to me once, "Every night onstage was a fight to the death for the audience's love, and by God, I was going to win it." Perhaps I should become more of a gladiator.

Being a newcomer is in many ways the loveliest time in anyone's career, because audiences and critics have a special fondness for novices, hoping to discover the next great talent. It is a pleasure to be the recipient of so much goodwill. At the same time, there comes a point in everyone's career where familiarity can breed at least a little bit of contempt. If it's a critic's task to find fault with singers, it's much easier to take a shot at someone who's established. I do read most of my reviews, bypassing only those that seem to be gratuitously hostile, but wait until the end of a run of performances before I look them over, because if they're particularly bad I can lose heart. I always have someone else read them for me first. Sometimes there's real validity in what's being written, and I try to discern common threads, either positive or negative. If I see that a particular criticism is being raised consistently from city to city, then I stop and take a look at that aspect of my performance and see if I can adjust it. In the end I'm not sure how much impact reviews have had on my career one way or the other, or any other performer's, for that matter. An artist who is in demand and who is singing well is not going to lose work simply because of a bad review.

Some years back, I was consistently criticized for a certain blandness, or for carrying vocal values above artistic ones, which was probably true, due to the difficulty of the repertoire I was singing and to the stage of my development. I took these comments to heart. Then the pendulum swung, and the complaining turned to my tendency toward interpreting with too much "artistry," or with too artful a use of text and phrasing. It's a matter of adjusting the bubble in the level again, finding the center.

I think there are very few people who truly don't care about what's being written about them. Most of us try to find a decent balance between paying too much attention to criticism and completely ignoring it. I have to remind myself continually that this is one of the few careers in which you work at night and read your performance evaluation in the newspaper the next morning. It takes some getting used to, and fortunately, thicker skin does start to build up over the years.

If you separated reviews into three categories, you would have those that come at the beginning of a career when critics are experiencing the thrill of discovery, harsher reviews once the real scrutiny begins, and then later, kind and nostalgic reviews, which come merely by virtue of having survived for so long. Everything changes, and sooner or later the day comes when a fresh new face will outshine you in a performance. There's a great joke about how opera management views the five stages of a singer's career:

"Who is Renée Fleming?"

"Get me Renée Fleming!"

"Get me the cheap Renée Fleming!"

"Get me the young Renée Fleming!"

"Who is Renée Fleming?"

I try to prepare myself step by step for each new direction in my own career. Recently Matthew Epstein told me that I had to change my attitude about my work, explaining, "You've got to move away from the striving and climbing place and understand that maintaining your position isn't drudgery. In fact, it's much more difficult than the climb." You must improve your skills constantly, to keep your audience and yourself interested in your repertoire and in the choices you make.

In trying to sort through this transition of sorts, I called Jim Loehr, sports psychologist to the stars. It turns out that all those encouraging words that tennis players need to hear when they're going into the finals at Wimbledon and that quarterbacks need to hear in the last quarter of the Super Bowl are the very ones that sopranos need to hear as well. The goal is to help performers in all fields achieve their peak under extraordinary pressure. He left me with some fascinating new ways of approaching this issue, though I have never been able to think of them without imagining myself standing on the fifty-yard

line, shouting them out to a man in a coach's uniform with a whistle
hanging around his neck.

*The longer you are successful, the more some people are going to want
to find dirt and see you struggle. They hover like vultures. This is a
very different feeling from the one that you had on the way up, when
people were excited and were rooting for you. It requires more tough-
ness to stay at the top. The pressure you are feeling is absolutely
normal.*

Isn't it easy to imagine all these things being said to a fourteen-
year-old girl in tennis whites?

*You want to go out there, push the envelope, and do something you've
never done before. Be proactive instead of defending something. If your
goal is simply to hold your own, you're dead. Do this because it's a gift,
a joy. You love it and you want to get better until your last breath. The
biggest mistake that people make is that everyone wants a piece of them
and they wind up resentful and angry, because they don't know how to
say no [an idea that sounds very much like Leontyne's "noise"]. Some
sabotage themselves just to get a break. Decide how much time you need
to heal, get balance, and recover. Everyone in your position needs to deal
with these issues.*

It was a helpful experience, which made me stop and consider
what I really wanted to accomplish. In short, I want to grow artistically.

If I have come to realize that I am ambitious, I still occasionally
feel uncomfortable acknowledging it. Ambition still too often has a
negative connotation, implying that you have to step on other people
to make sure you're the first one to get through the door. My own
sense of ambition is that it is very much an inward motivator. In a
sense, it's less about seeing how high up I can vault than about seeing

how deeply I can explore my potential. How can I find a truer interpretation of a role? How much more depth and light and emotion can I find in my own voice? How much can I feel when I'm singing a piece, and how much can I in turn make the audience feel? Ambition for me is about the willingness to work, the ability to mine my own soul fearlessly. At the end of my career, I want to know in my heart that I did everything I was capable of doing, that I succeeded in singing in a way that not even I had imagined was possible.

CHAPTER NINE

·IMAGE·

*W*HEN IT COMES to interpretation in opera, my primary goal is to make the audience forget that I'm singing. The basis for this is a technique that is so solid I can, for the most part, put technique out of my mind. Of course, it can never be completely ignored. There are always a few places in every performance when I have to really think about what I'm doing, whether it involves how to approach a certain pitch or how to execute a particularly difficult phrase. Stepping into a role should be like getting into a car: you no longer have to be conscious of how to drive at this point, but only of where you're going. I expect it's the same kind of experience for an athlete—in that case, it's the concept of going into the zone. There is a kind of suspension of thinking involved, as though there is so much inspiration and ease that it feels as if you're channeling the music rather than singing it. Reaching that place allows me, in a sense, to step out of the music's way and leave my mind free to discover new shadings in the role that I might have missed in the past.

When I spin out a long phrase, for example, I give that phrase a shape in my mind, which then travels out into the air. If it could be seen, it would appear as the silhouette of a mountain range. The shape would not so much trace the melody as the dramatic direction of the phrase. Where is its high point? Where is its most dramatic moment? Does the phrase vary dynamically, or is it steady? I make some of these decisions in rehearsal, while others are left to a moment of inspiration. But all of the choices go together to create what I hope will be a perfect moment in the performance, something that is both unique and ephemeral.

Part of the work done in a role is fine-tuning my approach to the text, making sure I can be understood and pronouncing the words as authentically as possible. Then there's the musical work: where I take a breath; the shape of the phrase; should it be sung legato, which means that the notes are strung together seamlessly, or are there different articulations in the bar that would require staccato, marcato, a tied note, or stresses? Although these are fine points that are usually spelled out very specifically on the page by the composer, it's surprising how much discipline it takes to actually study a score so carefully that all these little details are attended to, and unfortunately, memorizing them takes twice as long. However time-consuming, this process adds depth to a performance, and anything less can result in an interpretation that is bland and not necessarily true to the composer's intentions. A wonderful conductor will also use rehearsal time not only to encourage us to enrich our own performances, but to collaborate with the rest of the cast and the orchestra in presenting a unified whole. James Levine has just this kind of musical intelligence in spades, which is one of the reasons he is such an extraordinary conductor.

Only once all of these musical elements are in place do we begin work with a stage director, who presents his concept of this opera, both visually and dramatically. Most directors will begin by blocking each scene—meaning, for example, that Figaro sits upstage center on the bed for the first phrase of a recitative, and then Susanna crosses downstage left of him to cradle Cherubino in her arms for her response. Blocking gives us a frame-by-frame template for movement. This is the least enjoyable part of the work for me. I prefer to get through the nuts and bolts of blocking as quickly as possible, because what follows is the joy of interaction and collaboration with my colleagues. We play off one another the same way actors in the theater do, except that our pitches and rhythms are fixed by the music. This limits our freedom when it comes to delivering a line, but it also helps to ground us in the scene. We are left to interpret by means of how we use and emphasize the text, and by our dynamic shaping or bending of each phrase. We can obviously inflect a good deal expressively with our faces and bodies as well.

A good director will use this preparation time to motivate and build character, but in a revival, which might have only two days of rehearsals, we are fortunate if we know which doors to enter and exit from. My favorite *Rosenkavalier* performance was at Covent Garden, with the Royal Opera. We had only two weeks to prepare and were left rather to our own devices, once we had the geography of the stage down. This had to be one of the most detailed performances of that opera I've ever taken part in, because each performance had an element of freedom and improvisation to it, which kept us all on our toes. It worked in this case because we were an ensemble of performers who had already sung together in at least four other *Rosenkavalier* productions.

Even if our singing is at the point of complete confidence (and let's be honest, how often is that the case?), there are still plenty of other things to worry about in a performance. Beyond the challenges that any stage actor would face, we have to be sure we can be heard over an orchestra and sometimes a very large chorus as well, and without amplification. Considering how large theaters can be—four thousand at the Met, for example—that is not an insubstantial task. We have to keep our voices directionally pointed out toward the audience and rarely toward the wings or the back of the stage. We also have to be in sync with the orchestra and with one another at all times. Fortunately, the prompter is there to help, along with as many as ten television monitors placed around the stage and in the theater, so that the conductor's baton can be seen from any position. We must act our emotions and control them at the same time. No matter how devastated we may feel at any given moment, we cannot give way to tears as our lover leaves us while we're on our deathbed, because we still have to sing, and singing and tears can be a highly incompatible combination. The moment the audience suspects that I, Renée, am grieving is the moment it forgets about Violetta's grieving.

We count on our audiences to suspend their disbelief in many ways. First and foremost, we ask them to believe that it is a natural thing for us to be singing rather than speaking; second, we must do such a convincing job with our singing and our acting that they are willing to overlook the fact that we so rarely fit the physical requirements of our characters. People marvel at Meryl Streep's ability with accents and her adeptness at physically inhabiting her roles, but could she play the teenaged virgin in *Faust*? The first time I sang *Manon* in Paris and introduced myself as a girl of sixteen, several in the audience snickered, but then, most opera heroines are sixteen and no opera sopranos are. At the height of our careers, we are typically in our midthirties at the very least, and no one is surprised to see a singer taking on an ingenue role at fifty or even sixty. This is one aspect of the profession that I love dearly. All of the qualities demanded by a given role can be suggested by a believable performance and, more important, a suitable voice. After all, who ever doubted that Mirella Freni, singing late in her career, was the embodiment of the very young Tatyana in *Eugene Onegin*?

One of the hallmarks of sensitive, intelligent people is that they don't make sweeping generalizations about others based on physical appearances—unless, of course, the people being generalized about are opera singers. Put me on an elevator in any music school in the country, and I can tell you almost immediately who the singers are and who the instrumentalists are. You may say I am stereotyping, but when the passengers on that elevator declare their majors, you will also say that I was right. Instrumentalists have been practicing long hours since they were children, with the kind of discipline that demands a dedication and a seriousness that belong to a certain kind of personality. Singers often don't discover their voices until they're sixteen or seventeen, and their ability to project their voices isn't limited to the theater—an elevator will do just fine. When I was in school, Miss Texas seemed to be the soprano ideal: big hair, lots of makeup, high heels, and dressed to the hilt, with all components doubled, from hair height to heel height, for auditions. I tried to add an element of hipness to the image with my thrift-store vintage dresses, until Beverley drew the line at moth holes, after which my father only added insult to injury by tossing out my favorite dress when I wasn't looking.

We have other, more familiar stereotypes to deal with as well—first and foremost, of course, Brünnhilde, with her breastplate, long blond braids, horned helmet, and the spear. When most people think of a soprano, they think of a big woman with a comparably big voice, and historically, we are not for the most part small in stature. Marilyn Horne said it best: big rockets require big launchers. We're the weight lifters of the vocal arts. What we do, in fact, does feel very close to heavy lifting sometimes, making a sound that is substantial enough to carry to the farthest reaches of the balcony. On the other hand, I was amazed when I met Birgit Nilsson, Leontyne Price, and Renata Scotto, none of whom is particularly tall or large at all. (And as long as we're trafficking in stereotypes, tenors are traditionally not very tall, while the basses very often are, which might be related to the lengths of their vocal cords.)

Whether or not carrying a certain amount of weight is necessary for singing is a controversial topic. Beverley believed that it was, as she thought that it was the fatty tissue in the soft palate that could literally make or break someone's sound. Fat can also create a natural support, just like pregnancy. When I listen to the telecast of the *Otello* I performed weeks after I had Sage, when I was decidedly heavier than usual, my sound is richer and darker. Then again, it could have been raging hormones that momentarily caused the change in color and weight in my voice.

There was a point in my life when I became completely obsessed with Maria Callas and how she lost her voice. I asked everyone I knew what they thought had happened to her, and many of them suggested that her voice had gone into quick decline after she lost sixty pounds (as legend has it, with the use of tapeworms). I have to speculate that, because she dropped the weight so quickly, she had been unable to develop a new means of support. In the few existing videos of her performances from that time, she often has her forearms pressed against her solar plexus while she sings, as if she is trying to create support externally, rather than through the abdominal wall strength and technique that are really needed. Of course, she also looks gorgeous, and in her new willowy body she became the Audrey Hepburn of the opera world and the darling of Balenciaga.

To one extent or another all performers are packaged, and like it or not, image is part of that package. Obviously the voice has to be there as well, but there's also stage presence, charisma, or what the German language calls *Ausstrahlung,* or "shining out." Then there has to be a distinctive sound—not just a good voice, but a distinctive and unique one—and, most important, an ability to communicate meaning and emotion to the audience. When I sit through a series of auditions, it's quite clear who has those qualities and who doesn't. Very few people, no matter how talented, really stand out. For a long time I didn't have every element of my presentation and my own image together, which was one of the reasons things moved so slowly for me. Matthew Epstein and I began working together shortly after the birth of Sage, when I hadn't managed to control my weight nearly as well as I had in my first pregnancy. (My line was "I thought she would weigh thirty-five pounds. You can imagine my surprise.") He sat me down one day and spelled it out for me: "I know you want this very badly. If you want it enough, for Manon, for Violetta, for Arabella, you'll lose the weight."

Of course, I knew I was overweight, but it was jarring to hear it in plain speech from a professional I admired. When Susan Graham explained the low-carb theory to me, things finally started to turn around. I discovered over time that I am most comfortable with a consistent low-carbohydrate, low-fat diet, focused on green vegetables, berries, and soy-based substitutes for other main pyramid foods. Recently, I added to that regimen the wonders of Pilates, with a terrific coach in New York. Margaret Velez has given me the functional strength for which this program is famous, enabling me to feel not only stronger but more flexible onstage, as well as on the blue hills of my favorite ski slopes. The best part of it is the intense focus on core strength, which we need almost as much as dancers do. Now that I'm a convert, I only wish I had started years ago.

Matthew wasn't the only person to offer an opinion on the subject of my image. When I signed on with Mary Lou Falcone as my publicist in 1995, she had her own suggestions: "I would like you to streamline the way you dress. Prints and cut velvet are not becoming to you, and you might like to consider giving away the coat you have on."

Oh, to see yourself as others see you! She was right, of course, and I was reminded of some of my earlier experiences with the matter of my image, such as when my budding "diva" persona was humbled during my two summers at Glyndebourne. My sense of humor has always been self-deprecating, but this was really too much. In the festival atmosphere, a young singer has the added benefit of attending other performances, absorbing repertoire, and learning by observation. On one such afternoon, during the long intermission, I stepped out of the ladies' room and noticed that the rather grand woman in front of me was trailing a long strand of toilet paper from her delicate shoes. *Tsk tsk,* I smugly thought. As I wandered alone around the grounds, practicing my studied expression of serious artistry, a gentleman tapped me on the shoulder and said politely, "Miss, your skirt is tucked into your pantyhose in the back." He meant the *waist* of my pantyhose, of course. Some weeks later at another intermission, while I was trying to speak intelligently to patrons, a large bird deposited its contribution to the conversation on my forehead. I tried to think it was an anointment of sorts, hailing the arrival of the next great soprano. I finally gave up on ever having the sort of gracious image I craved when I arrived late for a performance of *The Rake's Progress*. The usher kindly allowed me to enter the box after the performance had begun. It was very dark, and I took great care to enter silently at all costs, not disturbing in the least the quiet recitative that was taking place. I quickly aligned myself with the heads in front of me and those to my left and began to take my seat. Unfortunately, there was no chair in my place. After the loud crash, Murphy's Law of humiliation dictated that several audience members in the rows ahead recognized me, all of whom asked with concern, "Miss Fleming, are you all right?"

It was then and there, once and for all, that I gave up the notion of developing a "persona." I stopped practicing the sort of English that would place me geographically somewhere on the moon, using that high, sing-song voice attributed to only the best sopranos, and I decided that humility and humor must surely be the only real strategies for surviving such a rarefied existence.

With Mary Lou and Matthew, my instinct for recognizing good advice served me once again, and I listened, for part of being a great student is never allowing one's ego to take precedence over the experience of other professionals. When my *Strauss Heroines* CD came out, one of the photos featured me glamorously dressed and lying across a bed. Soon after its release a journalist in the UK asked me during an interview, "Okay, how do you feel about using sex to sell your recording?" And the first thing out of my mouth was "Really? Do you think I did that? Thank you!" I was stunned, but I was also thrilled, never having been perceived as anything approaching sexy.

Andrew Eccles is the photographer with whom I have the greatest rapport. He has an eye for the most flattering angles and lighting and has photographed most of my CD portraits, requiring an entire day for a shoot that will supply the cover and publicity photos for between one and two years. I have also learned through experience how important it is to give to the camera, for an unfocused, tired, or dull expression does not an interesting photograph make. Hours of this takes a great deal of discipline and concentration, but if an alluring photograph encourages someone to pick up a CD of Strauss scenes and listen to it, then so be it. We live in an entirely visual society now, and the consumer is known to buy music with his eyes. If the expectations for women today, in particular, are often depressing and unrealistic, at the same time refusing to acknowledge that I am subject to those standards isn't going to make them go away, no matter how much I may resent them.

I have always been drawn to beauty, in whatever form it takes. Through my dear friend and Czech coach Yveta Synek Graff, I met one of Gianfranco Ferré's assistants at a postperformance party during a San Francisco production of *Rusalka,* and I told her of my interest in couture and how much I admired Ferré's work. I have always loved fashion, and never more than when I compiled my vintage collection at a Potsdam thrift shop for fifty cents per paper bag. I was especially taken with men's jackets and rhinestones and with fabulous cocktail dresses from the forties. My fashion sense was not unlike my singing back then: I had a lot of natural talent, but I just didn't have my style worked out.

Unbeknownst to me, this wonderful woman, Susan Mele, spent the next two years pleading my case, and in 1998, Ferré himself agreed to design a gown for me. It was burgundy, with a long train and a very simple silhouette, half velvet (though not cut velvet) and half wool crepe, and wearing it made me feel as if I were having a glass of superb Champagne after a lifetime of sweet pink wine. That marked the beginning of our relationship, and since then Mr. Ferré has generously designed one or two gowns a year for me. This is an aspect of my concert career that would otherwise have involved a great deal of effort in fittings, in decisions, and in cost. Instead, Mr. Ferré or an assistant and I meet before the upcoming season and decide on designs, and sometime after that a beautiful gown is delivered by post from Milan to my door without any fittings being necessary. Fashion's stork . . . Because my new concert-heavy schedule requires more gowns than any one designer could provide, I have more recently and fortuitously worn concert gowns designed by Issey Miyake and Oscar de la Renta, as well. When people tell me my life is glamorous, my first thought is usually of all the time spent in airports and rehearsals, but couture is one element of divadom that I gratefully embrace. In exchange, the designers receive valuable exposure, and exposure that speaks directly to their clientele, who are often concertgoers. My relationship with Rolex is based on the same premise. The company's aim is to align itself with excellence in the arts, sports, and science and exploration. In exchange, I receive invaluable amounts of print publicity.

A real diva also has a colorist who travels to Paris, London, Houston, and Chicago to keep up appearances. Michael Stinchcomb of Vartali Salon has been equally important in developing my image. It seems that, after all, hair requires more effort than clothing.

In all of these relationships, the greatest benefit is in feeling wonderful onstage, which enables me to focus completely on the performance at hand. It has always fascinated me to learn about the different needs that artists have when it comes to performing. Some singers require an incredible amount of time to focus their concentration before they go on, coming to the theater hours before the beginning of the overture, while others can sit backstage playing cards, set aside their hands, walk onstage, sing a bloodcurdling high C, murder the heroine, and then go back to their hands. Some brilliant singers have admitted that they're putting together their grocery lists during their most difficult scenes. Valery Gergiev asks his chauffeur to leave him off blocks away from the Maryinsky Theatre to clear his mind before the performance, much to the worry of his administration, since he also prefers to arrive seconds before the downbeat. Joan Sutherland worked at her needlepoint right until the moment she walked onstage, and I don't think it was because she imagined Lucia di Lammermoor enjoyed the craft. Everyone has her own way of preparing for the rigors of a performance. Ideally,

I will read through the entire role silently the day I appear in an opera, to review and find new insights. Whenever possible, I prefer a quiet dressing room, with as few distractions and interruptions as possible, and at least an hour and a half to prepare my voice and my appearance. I try to "force liquids," forgoing my favorite, coffee, and eat a moderate meal ninety minutes before the show. The time between leaving home and finishing the performance can often last as long as six hours.

While born with a vivid imagination that enables me to put myself in a particular character's situation, I had to work to learn how to realize that identification physically. When I sang Carlisle Floyd's *Susannah* at the Met, I was still struggling with the last vestiges of stage fright and the end of my divorce proceedings, and the tears were streaming down my face during the first act. Under the circumstances, my emotions were easier to access than they've ever been. Charles Nelson Reilly had been the first person I called when the heart of the crisis began a year earlier, and he reassured me, "The stage is where everyone lives out his sorrow, but it's safe. It's a refuge for those who suffer in their real lives." He loves to quote Emily Dickinson: "My business is to sing." "Make this your mantra," he said. That night I was making singing my business, giving it my heart and soul, yet a trusted friend said to me afterward, "You know, you really have to work on your acting." She didn't realize I was 100 percent involved with and connected to the heartbreak and isolation Susannah was feeling. That's when it clicked for me: It wasn't enough for me to feel a character's emotions; I had to be able to express them in such a way that the audience could feel them, too, especially in a big house, where no one can see my face past the tenth row without a pair of binoculars. Emotion has to be conveyed through every facet of body language, gestures, and movement. This was an important breakthrough for me, an aspect of performing that I am continuing to explore in every performance. Being innately inhibited, not to mention awkward, I have devoted a great deal of attention to this subject in recent years, once I began to get my voice under control.

I remember, years before, seeing a performance of the play *Wuthering Heights* as a student, and going backstage afterward to meet the actor playing the brooding, smoldering Heathcliff. I asked him how he could possibly give such a high-intensity performance night after night, and he said, "It's my job to make you feel that way, but if I actually became that person every night, I couldn't survive it." Jan De-Gaetani used to say that she did her crying in the practice room and the studio. She would get the emotion out of her system in the rehearsal so that the audience could then experience it during the performance: "They cannot experience the same emotion in the work which you experienced if you are indulging yourself and can no longer perform." Jan's other great piece of advice was to stop striving to be perfect. "Give yourself about a ten percent leeway," she used to say. "Having perfection as your goal will only set you up for failure. Once you realize an error, and then begin to contemplate the fact that because the performance is no longer perfect, it's been ruined, the next thing you know it really *is* ruined, because your concentration is gone. You are no longer actively performing." She believed it was much better to calculate in a margin for error because, after all, we're only human. I've never experienced what I would consider to be a perfect performance. There are far too many variables: vocal, interpretative, dramatic, physical. Opera is simply far too complex an art form.

A great theatrical experience onstage can be extremely cathartic. As I am by nature a person who prefers to avoid conflict, slipping into a character when I go out onstage enables me to open up. I can experience a host of different emotions that are not a part of my own life, and that can be liberating. The first time I ever met Plácido Domingo was in 1994 when I stepped into a rehearsal for the confrontation scene in *Otello*. Carol Vaness had injured her back, and I had been begging desperately for rehearsal time since the role was new to me, until management said, "Renée, you're on!" and suddenly there I was, onstage with Plácido in the confrontation duet. His acting was so terrifying in its intensity that I thought he really was going to strangle me an act in advance, which left my legs shaking so hard that I could barely stand up and needed help to leave the stage. When it was all over, he shook my hand and said brightly, as if greeting the new neighbor on the block, "Hello, I'm Plácido Domingo. It's a pleasure to meet you." I learned so much about artistry from his commitment to every level of the performance, and he brought me along with him to a much higher level of my own. Those few *Otello* performances served as another turning point in my development and career.

When singers find roles that are particularly well suited to them, they have the luxury of performing them for ten to twenty years and in countless different productions. In order to stay emotionally and intellectually connected to a particular role, I have to find ways to keep developing and enriching my interpretation. The layering process of bringing out the nuances of complex characters is endlessly fascinating, just as adding layers onto the characters that aren't as well written is an endless challenge. Every production and every cast is a new experience, and just because I've sung the Countess a dozen times before doesn't mean I can just phone in the performance. Recently, fashion dictates that productions are often set in the time period in which the composer wrote the piece, instead of the period he intended it to be set in. Although ancient Greece and the eighteenth century were originally favorite settings, togas and panniers do not appeal as much to the modern sensibilities of directors trying to make their controversial mark. Some operas are also set in present time, or at least in the twentieth century, with the fifties being especially popular, on the theory that these operas will then seem more relevant to the audience. Peter Sellars's contemporary Mozart cycle and Jonathan Miller's famous "Little Italy" *Rigoletto* both made a powerful connection to the libretto.

I don't really have a preference when it comes to period settings, but I'm always grateful when a new production has integrity. The director's concept needs to connect consistently to the opera at hand, supported by a detailed and thorough analysis. We have all seen productions that look as if last night's nightmare was arbitrarily executed on the stage today. For several decades, productions, especially in Europe, have been expected to make an impression through shock and outrage, and booing was the most favored response. These sensationalist practices are beginning to wane simply because very little is shocking now, and they are slowly being replaced with quality theatrical ensemble work from the performers. My wish is for musical values once again to hold equal importance with visual elements.

Once we've rehearsed a production for anywhere from two to four weeks, we're ready for stage rehearsals, which means it's time to dress the part. Fittings are arduous, both time-consuming and tiring. Standing still and serving as a dressmaker's model for two hours, perched on high heels, usually wearing a very tight corset adorned with heavy, warm fabrics, while every nuance of cut, shape, and trim is discussed in exhaustive detail, can be difficult. When I sang Amelia in *Simon Boccanegra* at the Royal Opera one year in July, before the recent renovation, temperatures reached 100 degrees backstage, and luck would have it that we were all costumed in wool, leather, and fur, with long coats. I was in my seventh month of pregnancy at the time and spent every free moment in front of the small fan in my dressing room, hoping I wouldn't faint before my next entrance. Sometimes a costume is made specifically for me, while other times a dress from a past production must be altered. For the new production of Strauss's *Capriccio* I recently sang in Paris, I suddenly realized, standing during a fitting, that two men, both the designer and the head cutter, had been poring over the points on the bra for my newly fashioned corset for at least ten minutes. Let's just say that Mae West would have had a field day. And while new costumes will be advantageously built on me, old ones are certainly equally thrilling. Every time a soprano wears a dress, her name and the date when she wore it are sewn inside on a small tag, and there will often be as many as eight names in a line. Will some young soprano be excited to pull a costume marked "Renée Fleming" over her head years from now? I will never forget the first time I was laced up in a gown that had been worn by Kiri Te Kanawa. Who wouldn't sing better in a costume with that history?

Over the years, I've tried to develop an eye for what is most flattering and what will make me feel the best, but it's certainly not a science, and I've often been frustrated when I later see a telecast and discover that my instincts were entirely wrong. Fabrics look completely different on camera, and under lights in the theater, than they do in a fitting room. I've often wished some magician would appear who could travel with me and discern immediately what works best in each theatrical situation. The closest I've found to that is director/ designer John Pascoe, with whom I've sung in six different excellent productions, beginning with Rameau's *Platée* at the Spoleto Festival. He also designed the collared green taffeta dress I wore when I made my television debut for the Richard Tucker Award—the equivalent of a debutante's coming out, and my introduction to most of the opera-loving public. When he designed new costumes for me for the Met's Franco Zeffirelli production of *La Traviata*, it was with an eye toward helping me stand out a little more onstage and yet be dressed in a less decorative way. I felt that his instincts were exactly right.

A costume fitting usually involves the supervisor of the costume shop, the cutter who is assigned to a particular costume, a specialist in jewelry, a specialist in shoes, a milliner, and the wig master, all of whom eventually peek in to check on the progress of the total creation. The designer is at the helm, guiding them all. When I was a beginner, I felt fortunate simply to be there and not have to throw my own costume together from bits and pieces in a trunk in the back of the theater. Now I stay very involved in costume decisions, because once I realized I had some influence over these choices, I was finally able to get over my fear of objecting to being asked to wear leather miniskirts, spikes, and chains onstage or, more likely today, to appear nude.

However carefully performers attempt to take charge of their images onstage, they are ultimately subject to the idiosyncrasies of any given production and the accidents that befall them. I've been dressed in fish scales and "authentic" period stockings that fell to my ankles once in every scene. (They didn't last long.) I've applied fake blood, glycerin to reproduce the sweat of fever, makeup to put me at death's door, and glitter and sequins (borrowed from my daughters, who have more than I do) to place me in a fairy-tale world. I once needed to extricate the hem of my dress from Susan Graham's buttons during a performance of *Der Rosenkavalier*. Once, during a rehearsal of *Rusalka*, I lost my skirt, which simply came unhooked and fell off, and I was too much in the moment—or the opera house was too warm—for me to notice the unaccustomed cool breeze on my legs. I've gotten stuck in doors, since walking with a French pannier that is six to eight feet wide can be a little bit like driving a car: it takes several attempts to execute a three-point turn correctly. My spike heels have been caught in everything from the hems of costumes and cracks and holes in the stage to the Styrofoam sand used for the Lyric Opera of Chicago's *Thaïs*. After making copious and permanent stabs in the popcorn-colored foam, I finally learned to walk on my toes. I've had to learn how to use a fan properly, as well as how to walk, sit, and lie down in a fully boned corset while singing a pianissimo B-flat. I've had to navigate stairs, raked stages, and lacquered floors. My own personal signature on any given night at the opera is to trip over my own gown, something I think I manage with unparalleled flair, and even after ten years of ballet lessons I can only be grateful that it's not worse. I've had to wear towering white wigs that have gotten caught in the scenery and in other characters' clothing.

One of my early experiences in Germany had me as Konstanze, singing "Martern aller Arten" from *Die Entführung aus dem Serail* while standing on top of a table with the stage curtains closed to its edges. Red-gloved hands came out from behind the curtains and undressed me as I sang that fiendishly virtuosic coloratura tour de force. Since I really couldn't sing the aria well, I was grateful for the knowledge that the audience would be completely distracted by the staging. In the same production I sang an extraordinarily difficult duet while bound to the middle of a chain-link fence. In one production of a baroque opera, I had to sing an equally difficult aria while climbing over a chain-link fence (it was a big year for chain link in opera, apparently). I've often sung in any number of positions: on the floor, with my head upside down. And while I would be willing to try it, I have yet to be flown, nor have I made an entrance or exit through a trapdoor, but then everyone needs something to look forward to.

In 2001 I sang *Arabella* at the Bavarian State Opera in Munich, which was comparable to performing Tatyana in St. Petersburg, Manon in Paris, or Eva in Bayreuth in terms of its geographical associations, and was one of the great thrills and risks of my career. Munich was the home of Strauss, whose music every year means more and more to me, so to be able to sing this role in this city made me feel as if I were singing for the master himself. Despite the wonderful cast, the rehearsal period was taxing, because the set consisted of an enormous pile of paper, which was supposed to represent the stacks of bills that Arabella's family couldn't pay. It made a steep hill that rose at an angle of about forty-five degrees on both sides, and we, the cast, were directed to climb all over it while we sang—mountain goats, one and all. One of the problems was that the paper, which had been glued onto the hill, would simply rip off when we stepped on it, so it was literally on a slippery slope that we rehearsed for the entire six-week period. I don't think that union laws would have permitted such a thing in the United States, but generally speaking, European singers are expected to meet more physical and theatrical demands. Eventually, and unsurprisingly, I had to spend two days in bed with back pain, and by the time a single four-minute-long scene that involved five singers took nine hours to stage, I was about ready to pull my hair out.

Still, I tried never to lose sight of where I was and what this engagement meant to me, as I scampered and slid over the bills in a performance that ultimately was very successful for us all. On opening night Carlos Kleiber called me on his cell phone. I was just about to go out onstage when his call came, and he said to me, "Do you know where I am?"

"No, where?" I asked.

"I'm in Garmisch," he said quietly. "I'm holding my cell phone up now. Can you hear the church bells?"

I listened very hard, and sure enough, from far away I could hear the sound of bells.

"I wanted to tell you we wish you well tonight," Kleiber said.

By "we" he meant himself and Richard Strauss, for he was standing at Strauss's grave site in the cemetery in Garmisch. I closed my eyes and listened to the bells, and in that wonderful moment I felt I had the support of both a legendary conductor and a legendary composer.

CHAPTER TEN

·PERFORMANCE·

*I*N THE COURSE of my career I have appeared in many different venues. I've sung for a small roomful of people and I've sung in giant outdoor arenas, but whether I'm performing for a group of twelve or a group of twelve thousand, my goal is the same: communicating with the audience. When the evening is going well, I feel larger than myself. It's as if the boundaries of my body have dissolved and I can reach out through my voice and touch the audience in an almost physical way. For me, the singer's art is the art of expression—expressing the music, expressing the text, projecting my voice into a large space, and then using it to make that space between me and the audience grow smaller and smaller. My voice becomes a wide net, which I spread out across all of us to draw us closer together.

If everything is going right, there are moments in a performance when the audience is absolutely silent, and you know you have it in your hand. Those are the moments performers live for. They typically occur only in certain places, in certain operas, and sometimes they never happen at all. When the members of the audience are single-mindedly focused on what they are hearing, I feel a tremendous surge of gratitude. I know I have reached them, and with that knowledge comes freedom, the absolute freedom to go where my imagination leads me. That is the goal, the purpose of all those years spent working to develop a strong technique. Freedom means that I'm able to be spontaneous with a phrase. I can hold a note longer, sing it softer or louder, try a *messa di voce* or a decrescendo on a whim. I can turn a phrase or place an accent on a certain word. In those moments imagination comes to the fore, and the hours of hard work and discipline in which I've learned every note and shaped every nuance exactly actually free me instead of confining me to the page. The more skill I have, the more I can trust my voice; and the more I trust my voice, the more risks I'm willing to take. Sometimes I'll look back on a certain performance and think, *How did I manage that?* What made me think I could hold that note for so long or sing that phrase so softly or not take a breath where I should have taken one? Because these are moments of inspiration, they are ephemeral, and the next performance will never be exactly the same.

When I'm touring, giving recitals, the performing context changes every night: the city, the hall, the audience, the piano. How I feel, how I slept, how much time there was to rehearse, the orchestra, the conductor, everything figures into how the evening will go. In recitals my singing is affected by whether the lid on the piano is up or down. Sometimes I'm working with a piano that sounds too percussive, which will in turn make me push my voice ever so slightly. If I'm lucky, I'll be able to diagnose the problem quickly, and we'll find a different tone quality for that particular instrument in that particular theater. The acoustics in an empty hall vary greatly from those in a packed hall. Even after all these years I can be fooled into thinking I'm having a bad night when in fact it's that the acoustic of the theater has deadened with the presence of an audience. On sometimes the acoustic is too live, which can cause me to sing in a strangely high-resonance position, and that's even worse than an acoustic that's too dead. A very bright, live acoustic sounds harsh after a while, and I find myself getting tense. The second that something doesn't feel or sound right, I start down my mental checklist: Am I feeling okay? Is the air-conditioning too high? Is it blowing on my face and drying out my throat? Am I pushing, and if so, why? Is a muscle tightening somewhere?

Along with all the external conditions, I have to account for whatever subtle changes in my voice require tweaking and readjusting. I have to factor in fatigue, tension, and any bad habits that can creep into my voice in one night, on one note. If I'm very lucky, I have the time to warm up slowly and go over whatever moments I thought were weak the night before. Most often I'll come up with strategies for dealing with the problem. It's as if my voice were a bubble of air inside a level, and I have to constantly tap on one end (the bubble shoots too far to the right) and then the other (I've overcompensated and sent the bubble too far to the left), trying to find the balance, the target spot at dead center.

As an example of the type of maintenance I now need, during a recent concert in Germany, I ran into trouble with two high B-naturals while singing an aria from *Manon*. Out of the blue they had left their normal track and somehow slipped into pure head voice. The next night I had to pull them back down in order to balance them between mouth and head resonance. Since high notes have always been a bit unsure for me, I have to be extremely vigilant to keep the fear factor from creeping into my singing, even now. Once I become overly aware of a note and the ways in which it might fail me, chances are it *will* fail. If a pitch has gone off one night, I'll tense up when I have to sing it the next, no matter what my strategy is, so unfortunately I have to deal with that as well. In this particular case, I managed to figure out what I had done the night before to get them in the wrong place, which was a tiny adjustment in my head position. In my dressing room, I caught myself still doing it unconsciously, by singing the phrase into the mirror, just the way Ubaldo Gardini had suggested all those years ago when I first sang Musetta. When I turned away from the mirror and sang the same phrase again, I felt my chin go up slightly and thought, *There it is*. I had probably been too aware of the lighting the night before and had lifted my chin half an inch too high. It's this constant reworking of technique every day that fosters longevity.

Once I identified the solution to the problem, I created a strategy to use it. When I got to the first B-natural, I tried to keep the back of my neck open and released the note without lifting my chin. I also had to release my breath and not tense up at the same time. The task I gave myself for that performance was to sing an umlaut on the lower preceding pitch with very little breath pressure just before connecting to the troubled B, and then open it up horizontally as I went up, while still not adding any breath pressure. I practiced that a few times, because muscle memory is a key aspect of singing. When I stepped out onto the stage, part of me really didn't believe I was going to be able to reproduce what I had managed in the dressing room, because I still worried about becoming tense, and the slightest bit of tension would send the note shooting straight back up into my head voice. But in the end the strategy worked beautifully, and I was gratified that my solid training had enabled me to figure out a way to fix a problem that I hadn't been able to solve before. The rest of the performance was a complete joy, because I could then concentrate on the business of expression. I was the only one who was aware that I had had something to worry about, and with any luck, that will continue to be the case for a few years to come.

Of course singing isn't the only thing that concerns me when I'm onstage. I'm also thinking about acting, my physical presentation, the meaning of the text, my pronunciation and diction, and the audience. Because I'm not an extrovert by nature, it helps me tremendously to receive from the audience as well as give to them. Sometimes their love is abundantly evident, while during other performances I feel as if they are the judge and I'm the defendant. I can practically see them out there with their scorecards, noting every tiny flaw.

I constantly have to remind myself that the audience is, on the whole, a benevolent group, especially when I'm singing a demanding program. Likewise, I don't ever go to Carnegie Hall to hear a recital in hopes that I'll have the opportunity to be critical. Most of us attend concerts or operas hoping that the experience will be a positive one, even a transformative one. When I perform I always try to seek out at least one person in the audience who looks engaged, who is smiling—in much the same way that Edith Wiens connected to me at her *War*

Requiem rehearsal. On the nights I scan the hall and can't find anyone to sing to, my heart sinks into my shoes. When that happens, it's always in a recital or a concert, because the lights are less blinding, there is no orchestra pit to see over, and the house is smaller and more intimate—all of which bring me much closer to the audience. I tend to avoid very small halls now, because early in my career, I sometimes became intimidated by a cultivated audience whose members seemed to sit back, fold their arms, and say, "Show us." As the person up on the stage, I need a vote of confidence—at least a little smile or look of engagement. During one winter concert, I bemusedly watched as nearly one-quarter of the house began falling asleep. I didn't think the performance was quite *that* dull.

There are also times when I completely misjudge an audience. They can seem brutally serious while I am singing, only to applaud rapturously at the end. Occasionally the audience members are so intent that I mistake their focus for criticism, but then I'm pleasantly surprised to find out they've enjoyed themselves. Experience has taught me to be more open-minded, because it's often happened that what I have feared to be the most excruciating performances have reaped the most gratifying results.

The truth is, I think most of us who perform do it for the applause, for what we get back. We have a great need to be loved, and preferably by a huge group of people simultaneously. There are, of course, a few performers for whom the audience is completely superfluous, and making music—and, as an aside, earning a living—is their only concern. I'm not as pure as that. I want and need the love and validation. I wasn't a natural performer, but I was a natural student, and I think I took my student need for straight A's and transferred that over to the audience.

Singers have a long and complicated relationship with applause. Taking a bow is certainly part of any performance, and one that I'm not always comfortable with. In a way it is a seduction. It's very interesting to observe different singers' styles. I've read long, elaborate descriptions of how famous singers took their bows, of how some great sopranos used only the simplest gesture to bring an end to the evening, while others went for a bow that was grander and more artful than the entire performance that came before it. Sometimes a bow has more of an effect on the audience than the music itself. Picture the singer who grasps the curtain with both hands and drags herself to peer around its edge, as if this required a supreme effort after enduring the emotional upheaval the performance cost her. It seems too much to even attempt to step onstage again, and she looks as if she is just about to faint from exhaustion . . . until she suddenly becomes aware of the audience. She hears them cheering for her. Her eyes grow wide with astonishment, and with a single, questioning gesture, she lightly touches her heart. "Me?" she seems to say. "All this love is for me?" And at that point, of course, the audience members are driven mad by their desire to scream, "Yes, you!" They thunder their approval, their shouts of "Brava!" echoing through the night. They will leave the theater convinced that they have never been so moved in their entire lives—not completely realizing that it was as much the bowing as the singing that had enticed them into surrendering their hearts.

There are other ways to connect to an audience. I'll often sign CDs after a performance, which gives me a chance to make face-to-face contact with the people for whom I've just been performing. Audience members have the opportunity to tell me their stories, that they found comfort in my music when suffering the loss of a family member or throughout a difficult illness—or sometimes it enhanced a joyful event, such as a wedding or the bonding of a relationship. It is an extraordinary privilege to know that people who love music turn to me in the most important moments of their lives. When I'm close to an audience, I feel as if I am completely open to them, and in turn, they can see me for who I really am. With my heart and soul expressed through my voice and the music, all else fades away.

There are two primary ways that the audience tends to perceive a soprano onstage. There's the group that wants to put her up on a pedestal, that regards her as a sort of gift from God on high, come to earth to bless the masses with her golden tones. The other group, which I think of as the larger public, views a soprano, if not as the girl next door, then certainly as a real person. This is the image most people have of me—off the pedestal and down to earth. I often think about who it is I'm trying to be for the public. Do I want to be imperious, difficult, temperamental? Do I want to take physical stances that are grand? Do I want to be warm and gracious? Do I want to be loving, sexy, giving? I'm sometimes aware of my own role in how I am perceived, and while my presentation depends on the piece I'm singing, a choice must always be made.

I believe that the ultimate goal of an opera singer is to create a legacy. In the case of Maria Callas, her legend has remained strong and vibrant after the success she achieved in her lifetime, and that was already tremendous. Her singing could often be uneven, and her voice was not universally considered beautiful. Some have said that it wasn't even particularly large, but as a consummate musician she used it effectively to place her own personal stamp on everything she sang. Once, when I was in Paris, I asked Michel Glotz about Callas's acting. He had been her manager, and they were close friends. What made her so unforgettable onstage? So little videotape of her exists. Did she chew the scenery? Was she given to pounding the floor? What was it about her that captured the imagination of so many opera lovers? What he told me was quite to the contrary of what I had assumed. He said that she did almost nothing. Onstage, she was still, and therefore any movement or vocal gesture had enormous impact. For that reason, people couldn't take their eyes off her. She seized the focus from the blur of the activity around her. For me, in purely vocal terms, it was the sound of sadness in her voice that was most moving—something in its chiaroscuro sound is like a knife in my heart. It's impossible to know if that was the sound her voice was naturally imbued with, or if it was the heartbreak in her life that colored it so. She set the current standard for what a great singing actress could be. Callas also didn't perform very often, which generated its own kind of frenzy, with fans running after her car, forcing her to escape through tunnels beneath opera houses after performances. The myth of Callas has so overshadowed the life of the real woman that it's difficult to be objective about her. While she often engenders opinions that are either too worshipful or too critical, in the end she had what any singer longs for: her own distinctive, irreplaceable spot in history.

When I first started singing, it was sometimes said that our particular era was completely bereft of great singers. Everyone talked wistfully about the 1950s, or those who were extremely knowledgeable about historical recordings mooned over singers in the first half of the twentieth century. Real aficionados looked to an even earlier Golden Age and tried to imagine through letters and descriptions just how the originators of our favorite repertoire sounded before recording began.

In truth, it's the importance of the music itself, and of the work of the composer, that is the creative gift, while the role of the singer is relegated to that of *l'umile ancella*, the humble handmaid. From that perspective, singers are not artists themselves but merely interpreters of art. A few, however, can transcend craft and the efficient employment of a natural skill by honing that skill to the highest level. The reason that some singers go on to become great artists has very little to do with their voices, but rather with the fact that they have used their instruments as tools for detailed communication. They further take advantage of every aspect of their talents, including their talent for living, to capture the audience's imagination. Perfection often creates such a flawless surface that there's no place for the audience to enter into a piece, while the idiosyncrasies of individual style are like windows into the singer's heart. Part of why we watch these performers with such passionate intensity is the same reason we can't tear our eyes away from the girl on the high wire or the man with his head in the lion's mouth: the thrill that comes from witnessing someone taking chances.

There are nights when I perform a recital and everything has gone perfectly. I feel that I've sung my best and have been able to make the leap from interpretation to artistry. I've made a real connection to the audience. I look back on the entire evening and wouldn't change a thing. And yet those can be the very nights when I go back to my hotel and feel disoriented, for the juxtaposition is just too great. For the most part, I enjoy the time I spend on the road, as it gives me an opportunity to be on my own. The phone doesn't ring nearly as much as when I'm at home, and I'm not in the middle of the chaos of my regular life. Even though I thrive on chaos, everyone needs a respite from time to time. Still, after communicating so intensely with twelve hundred people, it feels strange to be alone in an unfamiliar room. I'm wide awake, wound up after the performance, and what I feel is an incredible void. Many concert performers have spoken about the loneliness of their lifestyle, and this is generally a very true observation. There's an enormous thrill that comes from a night onstage, when the hard work that goes into making a great performance comes into contact with the excitement and energy of the audience. But when I get back to the hotel there's no way to hold on to that elation. It's as if the whole evening has been erased with the single turn of the key in the lock on the hotel room door, and suddenly I can be negative and judgmental about the smallest error I might have made. By the next morning I'm usually fine, because I understand that this is part and parcel of the nomadic life that singers lead.

Opera's built-in social life makes for a less lonely existence. We are reunited with an ensemble of singer friends and familiar faces backstage at least every few years, creating a family of sorts for the month or two that we're working together. There's an inherent excitement in the adventure of it all, but underlying it is the constant desire for a connection to home and family. This is the supreme sacrifice we make in exchange for practicing this glorious art form. As a wise colleague once said to me, "What we do is so joyous, so satisfying, we would do it for free. We are actually paid for the grief of leaving our families and friends."

CHAPTER ELEVEN

·ROLES·

ONE OF THE OBSTACLES I face in learning any new role is finding a way to carve two hours each day out of the middle of a packed schedule to find time to practice. Rehearsing at the piano in my living room makes me grateful that I have developed such good concentration skills over the years, as the phone rings every two minutes and the doorbell only a little less often. My assistant Mary Camilleri tries her best not to interrupt, but every now and then something comes up that requires my immediate attention. While she juggles three phone lines she is also digging up copies of musical scores I need to look at and packing for my next trip to Germany. My other assistant, Alison Heather, is my liaison to the world, creating travel itineraries and putting together my schedule, trying to finesse the details of where I'll be singing and when, and arranging interviews, fittings, lunches with friends, practices, school plays, meetings at the Met, and the occasional date. My assistants have referred to me as anything from "the velvet whip" to simply "the hurricane," though if I didn't become so harried, I'd say that the overwhelming necessity for multitasking puts me more in the category of "Stepford diva." When my daughters come home from school, they swoop past the piano for a quick kiss and report on their day, covering everything from grades on pop quizzes to playdate and party invitations, to general gossip about who sat next to whom at lunch and what was said. It's the highlight of my day. After we catch up, they have a snack and head to their rooms to start their homework. Right now,

I'm rehearsing *Daphne* while also living through a complete renovation of my apartment, so not only is there a great deal of dust to contend with—not the best environment for singing—but constant banging, guys in baseball caps trudging in and out, and a lot of yelling in Russian, which makes me wish I'd been putting in a new kitchen while I was learning Tatyana. Meanwhile, the girls' nanny is doing the laundry, and Rosie, my Cavalier King Charles spaniel, is barking manically at the two designers who have just shown up to take measurements for the built-in shelves I'm having installed. This chaos is not the exception but the rule. After the kitchen is done, there will be something else to take its place. If I were a delicate person who needed quiet and concentration in order to work, I would be doomed to spend the rest of my life singing the Countess in *Figaro,* because there would never be an opportunity to learn a new role. My world is thrilling, rewarding, demanding, and almost never peaceful. When the work needs to be done, I simply need to find a way to do it, regardless of what is going on around me, and I probably wouldn't have it any other way.

Although I've always taken great pleasure in working with the different elements that go into making an operatic character, from the music to the costumes, the most gratifying aspect of developing a character is the moment of discovery. Just when I think I really know the woman I am singing, something will happen that reveals another facet of her personality. Call it divine inspiration or the exercising of a creative muscle, but whenever I suddenly see a novel way to react to dialogue or a different movement or an unsuspected motivation, I feel newly alive in the role. It can happen during a rehearsal or a performance, or it can be a layered experience that extends and grows across several productions, but the building process never ends. What makes it so exciting is that the combined effort of reading the original book or play on which a libretto is based, studying the period and historical context, and, most important, immersion in the text and music itself creates a completely whole and complicated person on the stage. The more you put into it, the more you and the audience will get out of it.

Fantastical characters, such as the water nymph Rusalka or the sorceress Alcina, are generally difficult to flesh out, since the essence of what they need or want must be uncovered and imbued with nuance. Performing Alcina for the first time seemed like a series of variations on "Fifty Ways to Leave Your Lover" (Ruggiero) and fifty ways—or, more specifically, five fiendishly difficult arias—to express the loss of love (Alcina). By today's standards, the sketchy, convoluted, or downright absurd stories on which some baroque and nineteenth-century Italian operas are based require the most imagination in staging and benefit from a director who can work conceptually. Some heroines are also virtuous to a fault, perched on an imaginary pedestal for all time. Contrarily, complex characters with real human lives, such as the Marschallin or Manon or Violetta, are the easiest and, for me, usually the most satisfying to bring to life.

I remember that the first time I saw a production of *Otello*, I couldn't help thinking that Desdemona had been the victim of a childhood lobotomy. What other explanation could there be for her utter obliviousness to her husband's jealous rages and to the real motivation for his line of questioning about the nature of her virtue? But while preparing the role, I came to see her as a true innocent: she believes so completely in the love she shares with Otello that she can't conceive of anything coming between them. That realization enabled me to play her with enormous love and confidence. Our director in Chicago, Sir Peter Hall, took her confidence in her marriage a step further, having Otello implicitly assign her to the role of the one and only calming influence on him. She then interprets his rage against her as a sign of anxiety, needing only to be soothed with loving words. She realizes too late the seriousness of his accusations. Every time I sing the role now, I look to find even more goodness and trust in her, and in doing so I hope that my portrayal helps to explain to the audience the depth of her nature.

Singing Dvořák's *Rusalka* is the equivalent of a sensuous moon-light swim, but bringing the character and the story to life is a challenge. The ending of this opera, particularly, took me a great deal of time and discussion to understand. What happens to her? Or to the prince, for that matter? Add to that a second act in which the protagonist is mostly mute, necessitating that Rusalka express everything she is experiencing with her face and body alone, and I can honestly say that I needed all seven productions in which I have performed in to get to the heart of this role. Robert Carsen, the director of the Paris Opera production, seized on the implicit sexuality of the story and on Rusalka's attempt to "become a woman" and made a finely wrought psychological drama of the opera, in which the Water Gnome and the Witch became Rusalka's parents. I asked the choreographers of several productions to help me find a physical language to express her despair and what she terms her "neither woman nor nymph" state, once she is partially transformed into a human, for performing an act without singing seemed at first to be comparable to a violinist's performing a concert without a violin.

The final scene in Günther Schneider-Siemssen's design for the Otto Schenk production, the version I have appeared in most often, is my favorite of all the realizations. In it Rusalka appears to be walking on water, though in fact it's a sheet of Plexiglas that's artfully lit and is embedded with metallic ribbons and threads. Rotating machines under the set gently move similarly decorated Mylar sheets to simulate the rippling of water under moonlight. The complete effect is really quite convincing, and what soprano wouldn't like to walk on water just once? In the end, she can neither die nor go back to being a water nymph, and so she's doomed to spend the rest of her days seducing men and leading them to their death from a dark place, deep in the water. At the heart of *Rusalka* are the themes of love and redemption, as is true of all of my favorite theatrical works, but one has to "dive" in to find the opera's meaning. Rusalka swears she will not kill her lover, and yet she does so with a kiss, because he begs her to.

He wants release from the shame and pain he has caused her, in the form of death. She asks God to take his beautiful human soul and returns to her own infinite, dark existence, to the tune of one of the most beautiful postludes in the entire operatic repertoire. Dvořák's nymph is a far cry from the perky Little Mermaid in the Disney film, which is based on the same fairy tale of Undine, who winds up getting both her legs and her man.

Sometimes the challenge of taking on a difficult role can lead to such a high level of success with a particular production that it becomes a favorite, as was the case when I sang *Alcina* with the Paris Opera at the old Palais Garnier in 1999. Susan Graham sang Ruggiero, the object of my affection, or rather obsession, and for each of us, it was a first attempt at a Handel opera. We were fortunate to have Robert Carsen as director and William Christie at the helm with Les Arts Florissants, his baroque orchestra, in the pit. When I first met Christie, I fully expected that he would ask me to sing the role very purely with no vibrato and a very white sound, which I was more than willing to try, but he was adamant: "This music made people swoon when it was premiered. People fainted. That's what we're going for." He told me to bring everything I had to the score, every bit of expressive wallop I had, all the sex, all the jazz, everything. I kept nervously protesting, "No, no, no. Wait, you can't be telling me this. You can't mean that. This is not stylistically correct." But he insisted, and so finally I tried to sing as I would jazz, bending a phrase here, flattening out a note there. I would begin a tone without vibrato and then add it later on. Performing in this manner was such a shock because it was Handel, after all, who I thought would be stylistically in line with Mozart, but Christie assured me otherwise. The end effect was successful, because we were willing to risk failure by opening up.

Christie's harpsichordist, Emmanuelle Haïm, and Gerald Moore and I worked out the embellishments and cadenzas for each of the da capo repeats of Alcina's arias. This was a matter of tailor-making decorations that were expressive, interesting, and a perfect fit for my capabilities. By far the most time-consuming aspect of preparing a bel canto or Handel opera is memorizing, practicing, and reworking these embellishments, which usually go on until opening night. If I could, I would improvise them myself during every performance. The brilliant soprano Natalie Dessay, who sang Morgana, could, and did throughout rehearsals. When I mentioned to her that I was simply astounded by her singing and musical imagination, she laughed and demurred: "Oh, I sing them differently every day because I can't remember what I did yesterday."

Rehearsals are always fun for me, because there's no yardstick against which we have to measure ourselves. It's all about exploration. Performing before an audience is wonderful, because you can draw upon their energy, but you expose yourself to their perceived judgment as well; as you are working out your concept of a role, it's better to be free of that. The basis of Robert Carsen's talent is his vast cultural education and impeccable taste. He's fluent in several languages, is wonderfully imaginative, and never hesitates to push me to give my best, even if it means creating tension in rehearsals. That tension never lasts, because I know that his motivation is to force me to take risks, and in doing so he gets results. Handel offers a tremendous challenge to a director in that his operas contain few ensembles or even duets, and their confusing and complex stories move forward slowly and usually only in the short recitatives between multiple long arias. This can be impossible for a director who needs to work realistically, but it is a wonderful opportunity for an abstract and imaginative thinker. Not only was this production musically perfect, it was also visually beautiful, thanks to the designer Tobias Hoheisel. The *Alcina* set was a white box, with doors that would open onto images of green forests and meadows, pictures of gorgeous and glimmering nature projected onto the back wall to give the illusion of depth to infinity. Thirty or forty men were arrayed onstage to portray Alcina's victims as "rocks" (which also served as the real furniture), as Alcina is a sorceress who feels it is her calling to seduce and destroy men, until she falls in love with Ruggiero. Many of the men were naked, which, although slightly distracting at times for Susan and me, was certainly never dull. *Alcina* was one of those magical events in which the ideas were genuinely fresh, and both the critics and the audience loved it—a rare combination.

There is a fine line between pushing myself creatively as an artist, by taking on new roles and by trying to find greater expressiveness in singing, and pushing my voice too hard, which means agreeing to a role that will ultimately be damaging. It is essential for any singer to know her own voice and abide by what she knows. It can be very flattering when impresarios tell me that I would make a perfect Salome or Isolde, and yes, I could most certainly sing all of the notes in those roles without any difficulty right now—but only without the orchestra, without emotion, without the stentorian colleagues I would share the piece with, and without the little voice in my head telling me I'd better live up to great past performances, so I'd better "sing out, Louise."

The greatest challenge I have faced vocally is without a doubt the bel canto repertoire, the roles composed for virtuosic singers in the nineteenth century by Bellini, Donizetti, and Rossini. When choosing arias for my *Bel Canto* recording, I was surprised to realize that I had already performed so many of these roles, most of them early in my career, and each of them was an education in vocalism and dramatization: all of the requisite perfection of tone and style of Mozart with a greater range, real coloratura fireworks, trills, and expressive bravura. Add to that the spare plots and my least favorite conceit—the heroine as victim—and only true dramatic commitment will sell these works. However, what attracts me most about this repertoire is the freedom of the cantabile line, which really does hearken back to jazz in my taste, and back to William Christie's maxim that nothing but the entire expressive gamut will do. One can veer away from the often minimal contribution of the orchestra and stretch and pull the melody to one's heart's content, as long as it doesn't stray too long and the underlying pulse remains. The composers themselves indicated few expressive markings, so what is left? Imagination! How would Amina sound if she was asleep, or awake, in my favorite scene from *La Sonnambula*? What does heartbreak sound like in a voice? Despair? How can tears be expressed vocally? Can the voice speak directly from the heart, without the slightest intermediary? This is the freedom of bel canto, and this is why the recitative of "Ah! non credea" on my *Bel Canto* recording is the work I'm proudest of to date. The late, great producer Erik Smith and I spent hours in the studio finding the most expressive takes, so that we could most artfully flesh out those scenes.

For a soprano bel canto also requires a mastery of singing in the passaggio, the stamina to sing long, dramatic scenes without interludes—six of them in the case of *Il Pirata*. The last page is, of course, always the most demanding, and just when one's larynx feels as if it's risen to eye level. It is uncomfortable, to say the least. I always tell young singers to have a sense of leading their tone and not pushing it, using those small points beside the nose, and to keep their sound slim, with as much head voice as possible. (Just as with a piece of luggage, it works better when you pull rather than push.) When the voice is pushed, chances are too much breath pressure is being applied through too small a space. In early lessons, a yawn is usually used to indicate the needed space, but it's important not to "yawn" too aggressively and push down on the larynx, either. Finally, this must all be executed with enough support to keep the sound buoyed, but not pressed. I stay constantly involved in regulating the airflow as I sing a difficult passage. The process is practically unconscious at this point, but the effort persists: "No, the sound has just turned a bit grainy. Ease off on the breath now," "Stop pushing," "Maintain support," "Lift your chest and relax the back of your neck and trapezius," "OK, feed a little bit more breath," "Keep the resonance high." This is the type of technical attentiveness that will also get me through passages like the final scene of *Capriccio*. The goal is always to have singing be as effortless and as efficient as possible. This requires attention to both how the voice feels and how it sounds. The difficult thing to understand is that harm from faulty technique doesn't show up immediately, and it might even be the case that it doesn't feel wrong at the time.

Protecting my voice doesn't mean seeking out undemanding roles, but rather singing roles that are a perfect fit for me. Often what is right for me would be nearly impossible for someone else, and vice versa. I only discovered halfway through a rehearsal period in Paris that I could indeed sing the rangy and very long Manon of Massenet. Until then, I had visions of myself apologizing to the audience on opening night before the Cours-la-Reine scene, delivering a humble speech about not knowing my limitations, and assuring them that they'd never have to see me again, as I beat a hasty retreat. Fortunately, I discovered instead that I had grown into the role, and it would soon become an absolute favorite. What a feast! Manon and I met during a long period of exploration of French repertoire: Marguerite, Thaïs, Louise, Anna in *La Dame Blanche*, Salomé in *Hérodiade*, as well as roles in *Platée* and *Médée*. After English, French is the language I most enjoy performing in, for its nasal vowels help me to maintain the high placement that is safest for my voice, and the fluidity of the vocal line lends itself especially well to singing. I also find myself continually intrigued by the complexity of Manon's character. Her ability to acknowledge her shallowness and then to go on blithely being shallow is a somewhat refreshing change after all of the archetypally virtuous heroines I usually play. I'm also challenged by the enormous journey she takes, from innocent coquette to runaway adventurer, from fame-seeking gold digger to repentant lover, who finally boldly decides she should have it all, and is punished with imprisonment and ultimately death.

Once I could manage Manon's vocal hurdles, stamina became an issue, which meant carefully gauging the use of my energy and voice in the early scenes. The first season in Paris, I almost didn't make it through the final scene in the first few performances and had to drop a few pitches just to survive. I eventually found my stride, as I did during one of my first performances of this role at the Met, when I discovered that I was in an unexpected duet. I made my entrance for the grand Cours-la-Reine scene in the Jean-Pierre Ponnelle production's enormous red corseted dress with wide pannier. As I began singing I heard what I thought was someone joining me from backstage, but in a mocking way. It was a man's voice, and I thought that it must have been some new stagehand who hadn't yet been indoctrinated in the distinctive sounds of opera. As it continued, I became more and more annoyed by the distraction—until suddenly I realized that audience members were tittering, for the sound had actually carried out to the house. In that scene the chorus shares the stage with me in tableau, meaning without moving, and in my peripheral vision I saw one of its members sheepishly leading a very large borzoi off the stage. It was then that I realized that my partner was a dog, which had begun to sing with me, or howl. (The audience howled, too, though not in the same way.) For my part, I was more than slightly concerned about the fact that the dog's high notes were rather good. When the curtain came down, and I said firmly to members of the artistic management who came running backstage, "It's the dog or me," I was sure I detected some hesitation.

Richard Strauss has become my core composer, in a sense, replacing Mozart. I've never completely understood the label "Mozart/Strauss soprano," because the music is so different, but historically it is true that many Countesses and Fiordiligis have also become Arabellas, Marschallins, and *Capriccio* Countesses, as the roles do require similar vocal weights and, more important, temperaments. For me a stretching of comfortable limits is also important from time to time. A good example is the title role in *Daphne*, which presents a great challenge because it is so fiendishly composed. Four of the five principal roles in this opera are what I would call "extreme Strauss," with writing that tests the absolute limit of each voice type in range, tessitura, and volume.

Daphne's tessitura lies uncomfortably high. I sing other repertoire containing higher individual pitches—Daphne's highest pitch is only a high C—but the average may be considerably lower. This is one of the absolute keys to knowing whether a role is suitable: an appropriate tessitura, not whether the actual pitches are too high or too low, which is a secondary consideration. One of the most important strategies I've found to deal with a tessitura that is too high is to use an equally higher resonance. In other words, I'll sing more in head voice with less mouth and chest resonance in order to remain relaxed and vocally unstressed.

Ten years ago I could not have survived this opera. As my technique has improved, roles such as Manon, Violetta, Daphne, and the bel canto heroines have more comfortably entered my repertoire. Usually singers take on these roles when they're very young, as the voice tends to get lower and darker with age. I've had the opposite experience. Recall the image of the vocal tapestry, in which the higher colors are woven into the fabric of the tone and the lower colors are woven out for the period in which the high tessitura is sustained. Physical relaxation becomes more important than ever in a role like this, which often means being vigilant about stress in and around performances.

Musically, Daphne is slightly more chromatic than other Strauss roles, so it took longer to learn the pitches, and though the text itself is simple, the harmonies move so quickly that it takes the precision and speed of an acrobat just to keep up with the score. When I'm first learning a role, I work simultaneously with the text and the music. In a perfect world there would be enough time to divide these tasks in a more painstaking fashion, but I usually put myself under more pressure than that. A huge role to learn in a month and a high tessitura to navigate were not my only obstacles in preparing this part. The score for *Daphne* is so complex that my first priority was simply finding an accompanist who could sight-read or who knew the music. I can remember a time (and it doesn't seem like that long ago) when my problem wasn't so much finding an accompanist as being able to afford one. I always encourage all young singers to study piano, because they'll save themselves a bundle of money, and the ability to teach yourself your own music is an incredibly useful skill. I have many colleagues who are truly fine pianists, and as a result they have the musicianship that enables them to learn a wide variety of difficult repertoire (although some of the greatest singers in history couldn't even read music).

A month before we began our rehearsals, in order to get a head start on interpretation, I had a reading session of the score with Semyon Bychkov, who would conduct *Daphne* in Cologne. A great conductor like Semyon will work with a singer to find colors in the voice, along with dynamic variety, rubato, and every other element that distinguishes one performance from another. Semyon suggested, for example, that I emphasize the *schein* ("shine") in *Sonnenschein* ("sunshine") with a "smile in the voice," and perhaps a lingering on the *sch* sound. (A "smile in the voice" is one of my favorite tonal ideas; the effect is produced with more lift in the cheekbones, or an inner smile. Victoria de los Angeles was the best representative of this technique, which is a beautiful way to illuminate a phrase, so to speak.) Likewise, I'll sing the word *tanzen* ("dance"), which has a dotted rhythm, in a light, springy way. If the word is *Trauer*, which means "sad" or "sadness," and it's on a minor chord, then I'm going to lean on that pitch and invest my sound with a much darker quality to bring that word to life.

The most interesting aspect of Daphne's character is that she begins the opera as a true innocent—unconnected with the human world, and desiring only to be a part of nature, which makes her uncomfortable with her own coming-of-age. Unfortunately, she realizes too late that her childhood friend Leukippos would have been the appropriate suitor for her—too late, because Apollo kills him with a bolt of lightning in their fight for her affection. In the monologue she sings after Leukippos's death, she matures before our very eyes and ears, her music taking on a dramatic heft that intensifies her grief. This shift in the character of the music shows the brilliance of Strauss as a dramatist. Daphne is finally granted her wish, as she is transformed from human to tree. In the eerily repeated phrases that end the opera I always imagine her voice combining with the rustling of the leaves depicted by the violins.

Arabella, another of Strauss's great female creations, is entirely human and strong. She knows what she wants and buoys her entire family through a trying financial period, finding solutions to every heartbreak as well. I found her difficult to like when I first began learning the role, as my modern sensibilities couldn't accept what seemed to be a callous rejection of her other suitors once she decides that Mandryka is *"der Richtige,"* the right one. But once I studied the period in which she lived, I came to appreciate her unusual degree of emancipation. It is *she* who is deciding who will be her mate, at a time when few matches were based on love or desire. Being sensible and highly responsible, she feels that it is her duty to end cleanly her other potential liaisons. In the last act, it is Arabella who takes charge of the situation—not Mandryka and not either of her parents. She forgives his distrust and encourages her family to accept Matteo as an appropriate mate for Zdenka. Arabella's soaring soprano resolves the humiliation of the evening and of her family, and allows Mandryka to rise to the occasion as well, so that they can forever-more prove the adage that opposites attract. Vocally, this role lies similarly to the *Vier Letzte Lieder*, with some of the same sustained high singing in the stunning first-act duet, in Arabella's monologue, and in the final scene. I imagine Arabella as a young Marschallin: a woman of great integrity, the very soul of graciousness.

Capriccio's Countess falls, perhaps, somewhere between the two—still young but intelligent, witty, and searching for love and the essence of art at the same time. I have come to adore this score, having been indoctrinated in its subtleties. Underneath the rapid fire of this conversational text is as much desirous rapture as one finds in any of Strauss's operas. Phrases in both Flamand's and Olivier's declarations of love haunted me every hour of the day throughout the Paris Opera rehearsal period when I first sang this role. The trick is to know *Capriccio* well, since these moments are too fleeting to catch easily on first hearing. I also imagined Strauss to be burying himself in the "longing for beauty of our thirsting hearts," as the Countess sings in the penultimate scene, when he composed this piece in 1942.

The role that breaks my heart is the one that expresses loneliness. It's very easy to become the Marschallin while I'm singing her. Forget about the inevitability of the end of her affair with Octavian: it's her isolation, her crisis of time and beauty, aging and losing her sense of self-worth, that are so crushing, and that are fairly universal concerns for women. When she looks at the clock and asks it to stop, I can identify with her predicament, for I'm no less affected by that clock than she. The chances are slim that I'll die of tuberculosis or be strangled to death by my husband, so while those sorts of dramatic roles can be exhilarating to play, they don't lead me to look into the mirror of my own life. But playing out the Marschallin's grief, her fears, and finally, her heartbreaking dignity—those are the moments when I feel the most exposed. There are nights when it can be hard to admit those fears to myself, much less to a crowd of strangers, and on those nights it can be equally hard to leave her sadness behind at the end of the performance.

When I canceled my scheduled debut in *La Traviata* at the Met in 1998, I regretted having backed out of the production since, like all diligent students, I had been conscientious about turning my papers in on time. Violetta is an extraordinarily demanding and complicated role, with a long history of brilliant interpreters, and I knew that when I got to it I wanted to give it the full force of my attention, and not let it fall at the end of the most difficult year of my life. When the Met kindly rescheduled the performances for the fall of 2003, the Houston Grand Opera equally graciously agreed to allow me to premiere the role there some six months earlier.

I have seen *La Traviata* performed many times, and I've always felt strongly that the vocal demands the role makes on the soprano are so enormous that it's difficult to get far enough past them to concentrate on Violetta herself. The role is generally acknowledged to require almost three separate voices: the lyric coloratura of act 1; the *lirico spinto* of act 2, scene 1; and the lyric soprano of act 2, scene 2, and act 3. If sopranos like myself find "Sempre libera" uncomfortable, then the rest of the role will come as a gift; conversely, sopranos who love act 1 will find the remainder of the opera to be a difficult dramatic stretch. As an audience member, I have also always wanted to love Violetta more. I wanted to see her vulnerability and to root for her and feel crushed by the heartbreak of her situation; I wanted to believe that Alfredo's love could make her well. As a singer, I wanted to get to a place where I felt so in control of the music that I could think beyond it and find the dramatic essence of Violetta, leaving open every possibility for the interplay of my imagination with the role. For example, I had always thought that Alfredo would present her with a flower at the beginning of act 2, which she would tenderly put in her hair. Otherwise there are few opportunities in the opera for the couple to show their happiness and the basis for their intense love. Whenever I thought about interpreting this role I thought about the flower, how it represented the freshness of Violetta's life with Alfredo in the country, and how deeply she felt the joy of being alive. I very often imagine dramatic moments in the staging while learning a role, even if it's difficult to achieve all the goals I set out for myself in an actual performance.

One of the primary reasons I longed to perform Violetta was for the opportunity to sing "Dite alla giovine," which occurs at the moment in act 2 when Violetta succumbs to Germont's demand that she leave Alfredo. For me it is the most heartbreaking music in the opera, and rather than making this the stormy confrontation we might expect, Verdi turns his heroine's sacrifice into something that feels entirely intimate. Through the music, we can see her baring her soul; we can feel her vulnerability. I have always pictured Violetta taking the flower from her hair and crushing it unconsciously in her hand, just as her happiness is being crushed, in full awareness that she is dying. Violetta is a woman of tremendous integrity, unlike Manon, who is cheerfully decadent and has only glimpses here and there of the moral road not taken. Violetta makes the right choices at her own expense, so we feel she is victimized by class and circumstance and the men who love her. She is one of the most sympathetic characters I have ever played, while at the same time fully three-dimensional and therefore endlessly interesting to inhabit night after night.

Much of the information I need to create a role comes from the music itself. Verdi's writing constantly gives the impression of breathlessness, which correlates perfectly with both the symptoms of Violetta's disease and the excitement of new love. It took many performances before I began to explore fully these tiny pauses in the vocal line. While each scene, each phrase of Violetta's music offers a range of choices, both musically and dramatically, the second and third acts are most comfortable for me—although most of the opening act is a joy to sing and, in a sense, a wonderful warm-up for the rest of the opera. But in an unusual choice, Verdi closes act 1 with Violetta alone onstage, in a scene that requires both stamina and strength, not to mention a high tessitura and no interludes for rest. Ultimately, I decided the only way to survive this and be vocally consistent was to lighten the color and weight of the high Cs in the cabaletta, and then proceed cautiously in the final pages of the act. The end requires enormous concentration on these technical challenges, which are made all the more difficult by the fact that they must be sung with a wanton air. The reward for pulling this off is, of course, the rest of the role, which is an absolute treasure.

I was helped enormously in my preparation for Violetta by my discovery of several books on the subject of courtesans in nineteenth-century France. I was surprised to learn that these figures were not prostitutes as we imagine them today, but women who lived alongside the crème de la crème of society in lavish lifestyles. In their fine homes they hosted some of the greatest minds of the day—poets, composers, men of power. They were turned out to the highest standards of fashion, they had the best carriages and jewelry, and they wielded power and influence over the men who admired them. If they were fortunate, they managed to save enough money to live on through retirement, or they had generous patrons who continued to support them through their later years. The less lucky courtesans died in their early twenties of tuberculosis, or consumption, as it was then known, a disease that left them thin and pale with blooming cheeks—in short, looking quite stunning. This research subsequently led me to Marie Duplessis, the real-life courtesan who is often regarded as the model for Violetta. Marie was a French farm girl whose father abandoned her by the age of fifteen after her mother died. She went on to become the toast of Paris, even conducting a love affair with Franz Liszt, who cherished her memory for the rest of his long life. She died at the ripe old age of twenty-three.

To help shape my performance I also took up my usual practice of polling, and I asked everyone what they thought about Violetta. Charles Nelson Reilly was helpful in discussing the spittoons she would have placed around her apartment. He also came up with a number of small tasks for her to perform, such as pouring tea for Germont and hiding pills in her bloodstained handkerchief. Even the movie *Camille* offered valuable insights. I loved Greta Garbo's performance, her frail beauty, and her sadness, which are so touching against the Baron's stern coldness. It's useful to seek inspiration from all available sources and absorb their influence, for the more I have tucked away in me, the more likely I am to come up with my own ideas on the spur of the moment.

Of course, when a soprano goes looking for inspiration, one of the best places to start is with other sopranos. Historic recordings are essential resources, and when I start preparing a new role I want to listen to every interpretation I can get my hands on. The beauty of listening to historic recordings is that one can hear authentic Italian and hear just how clearly style has changed from sopranos such as Tetrazzini, Muzio, Melba, Olivero, Farrar, Caniglia, Carteri, and Ponselle. Performances were far more original and by today's standards sometimes even eccentric, but what a joy to hear so much personality shining through in a work we already know so well. I don't love Callas's studio recording of *La Traviata,* which strikes me as oddly careful, almost pristine, and lacking in all the qualities for which she's famous. Her live recording from La Scala with Carlo Maria Giulini, however, is wonderful and compelling. My favorite *La Traviata* recording is that conducted by Carlos Kleiber, with Plácido Domingo and the Violetta of Ileana Cotrubas, who has a shimmer in her voice that projects vulnerability in spades. I listen to these recordings and analyze the performances to see what secrets I can cull. I don't mind stealing an especially moving turn of a phrase or dramatic idea, and other times I learn equally well what *not* to do.

I may study too much, as I still engage in a constant battle with myself as to whether as an actress I should be simple or layered, histrionic or direct. I go back and forth between these two alternatives on almost a line-by-line basis. One famous Violetta offered help directly. For me Renata Scotto always displayed remarkable musical intelligence and artistry. Her acting, imagination, and use of the text made her a fascinating artist to watch and hear. She generously agreed to coach me on the role of Violetta before I went to Houston and was especially helpful with language, the way to use words most effectively. Singing in Italian isn't as easy for me as singing in French or German, because I speak those languages, and therefore I was grateful for the guidance from a native speaker.

One of the wonderful things about Violetta is that she is so mercurial a character that she can be played in many different ways. When I first sang the role in Houston it was fortunately under the direction of Frank Corsaro, who had very original things to say about her. In this production, for example, Violetta was angry and bitter in act 1, drinking too much and staggering across the stage with a Champagne bottle in one hand and a glass in the other, which made her not entirely attractive. There is much validity to this interpretation, because the truth is, Violetta has a great deal to be angry about. Just being able to think of her in a new way gave me the freedom to keep exploring, and I went infinitely further with her than I would have on my own. Violetta is a different woman altogether in the Met's production, and I knew I was prepared and flexible enough to accommodate this version thanks to my experience in Houston.

If I had one wish as a performer, it would be to divide myself in two for a night so that I could be both onstage and in the audience, watching myself perform. If I could judge myself from the theater objectively and determine which turn of phrase was most successful, which look, which gesture, I could improve my interpretation. While it's helpful to sing in front of a mirror, and having a teacher in the audience provides a useful critical voice, there is nothing that reveals the strengths and weaknesses of a performance quite so clearly as videotape. I remember the first time I sang the Countess at the Spoleto Festival in Italy (back to Italy again!) with a girlfriend. The local newspaper dubbed us the "two ladies from Baltimore," which implied all too clearly that we lacked certain essential aspects of nobility. When I had a chance to see a tape of the performance, I was shocked to see how ungainly I looked onstage. A large part of the problem was how I used my hands, which unbeknownst to me were full of tension, with my fingers spread wide apart and thumbs sticking straight up. Seeing that tape taught me to observe how other singers used their hands and conveyed a sense of delicacy. I had to learn to release the tension, especially in my thumbs, and gesture gracefully.

Athletes have the advantage of instant replay and game tapes that can be studied later. I really believe that if I could watch more performances, I could be a much better performer than I am now. Unfortunately, the rules are such in theaters that no recording or videotaping is allowed for fear that illegal copies would be sold. Every time there's a telecast from the Met, however, three scratch versions are made before the final taping, and I've learned so much about acting and performing just from studying them. Brian Large, who directed the Met telecast of *Otello,* helped me immensely when I nearly vaulted out the window after viewing the first scratch tape. The improvement between this initial effort and the actual taping was immense, because he helped me to find the best angles and use of lighting. Further, I took copious acting and performance notes after each viewing. These tapes are as painful for me to watch as it is for most people to hear their voices on an answering machine. But I force myself to do it, because without such direct feedback, I cannot continue to improve other than by guessing and second-guessing.

CHAPTER TWELVE

·BACKSTAGE·

*A*s MUCH AS I long to know what a production looks like from the house, most audience members wonder how the whole business of preparing a performance looks from backstage. The relationship between the world behind the curtains and the operagoers in their velvet seats is a little like that between the flaming hot, frantically busy, and completely well-organized kitchen of a five-star restaurant and the elegant customers who are enjoying their meals. The two tableaux seem so disparate that you could hardly imagine them sharing the same building on the same night, except for the fact that everyone is there for the same reason—in one case, the food; in the other, the opera.

The stage door to the Met is in the parking garage, where we all eventually file through. I'm lucky to have a driver, Richard Burns, to whom I can entrust even my children. (I once realized halfway home to Stamford from the Met that I'd forgotten to pick up my daughter back in the city. Richard turned around so fast, we had whiplash.) I usually try to arrive anywhere from an hour and a half to two hours before curtain to get ready, for there are many aspects of the preparation of a role, including the physical transformation, getting my voice ready after a quiet day, and, most important, entering into the role mentally.

I greet the guards and make my way down a long cement hallway lined with lockers, as I head for the dressing-room area. For all the gorgeous chandeliers and gilt boxes in the front of the house, this part of the house is low-ceilinged, lit with fluorescent bulbs, and decidedly unglamorous, though in a comforting and familiar way. The dark red carpet is worn, and the waiting area outside the dressing rooms is furnished with chairs and tables that must have come from a dentist's waiting room in the midfifties. From down the hall I can hear that other singers have arrived before me, for they are already vocalizing on scales and lines from the opera.

Warming up is something I need to do every time I sing, unless I'm singing for long hours every day. If I'm rehearsing for an opera, then I find that the act of rehearsing itself provides the same kind of warm-up as a twenty- or thirty-minute session. There is never a single prescribed way to go about this, because the body itself is different every day. So many factors contribute to the ease and well-being of the voice: how well one has slept, what one has eaten, the moisture in the air, fatigue, altitude, change in climate, the difficulty of the music at hand, stress, and even small reactions to food, pet hair, or the weather. Flying can wreak havoc on a voice, as it's all too easy to get off a plane with some sort of respiratory illness. Even if one doesn't get sick, there's the very dry air to contend with, not to mention jet lag. Whenever I'm on a plane, I make it a point to tell myself I'll be fine. I drink plenty of water and try to stay away from caffeine and alcohol, and when I arrive, I listen to my body if it needs sleep.

With all the traveling I do, I have found there is a real art to finding an optimum singing place on a daily basis. It requires tremendous sensitivity to the body and the coordination of sensation with sound. I listen carefully while I vocalize and keep carefully attuned to my physical condition. Where is the muscular tension? Is my breath right? Warming up the muscles that enhance the breath is a big part of the process, particularly if I don't have a lot of time, as is loosening up the jaw and facial muscles, which enables a free sound to resonate in the mask. Then I loosen up the back of the neck, trapezius, shoulders, and chest, making sure there is no tension in the back. It's a process that requires the most minute adjustments, because the smallest problems can have enormous effects.

Sometimes I'll use a mirror. I stretch my palate, loosen up the tongue, engage in a couple of good yawns. I rely on the Alexander technique to make sure that my alignment, particularly in my back and neck, is released and free, and on my recent Pilates training, which has been extremely helpful for building core strength and stamina and even my breath control. I know a lot of singers who prefer yoga, which is to say we've come a long way from the image of the pampered diva living on chocolate and the chaise, not that both aren't wonderful; you have to be at least moderately healthy to withstand this lifestyle. I focus intently on releasing the abdominal wall and the intercostal muscles to allow an optimal intake of air. I make sure that my chin is at the correct angle for the back of my mouth to be open properly. These are tiny adjustments, and only experience and years and years of singing have enabled me to make them quickly and efficiently. I'm still amazed at how often I'll find that I'm heading in the wrong direction and conclude that the solution to a flat pitch is one thing, when in fact it's a completely different strategy. Sometimes I'm simply having a bad day, and an extra three minutes of concentration on releasing the breath or on resonance can produce the exact results I've been searching for. This constant fine-tuning of the voice continues to be fascinating, rewarding, and satisfying for me. It's a skill, a craft, and an art all rolled into one.

Next, I have to clear my mind so that I can focus exclusively on the text and the concentration of meaning in a foreign language. If I'm worried about a trip I have to take the next day or about one of the girls who is struggling with her homework, I'll fail to find the calm I need. Any distraction can hamper the flow required for a satisfying performance.

These days I am constantly involved in questions of interpretation, and of emotion in music and how it is transferred. I am always trying to determine the greatest level of expression for a given phrase. James

Levine and I have talked about the difference between a performance upon which interpretive elements and emotions are placed and a performance in which those elements are relayed to the audience in a way that feels natural and organic. He said the goal was for the personality to be completely present but not self-conscious. I am so often haunted by the difference between Beniamino Gigli singing "Ombra mai fu," which is the simple, thrilling deployment of a great voice, and the interpretation of singers like Dietrich Fischer-Dieskau and Elisabeth Schwarzkopf, who performed with highly detailed, intelligent, and imaginative artistry. Who can say which approach is best? It's a matter of subjective opinion, of taste.

Part of the process of warming up takes place calmly and privately in my dressing room—maybe a full five minutes. The rest of it takes place while people are running in and out, the phone on the wall with the extraordinarily long cord is ringing, and the cell phone in my purse is adding its own noise to the clatter. The little room with its huge makeup mirror, ancient space heater, two humidifiers, and shabby sofa turns into Grand Central Station. Someone pops in to see if I need anything. Victor Callegari, who has been head makeup artist at the Met for thirty-five years, walks in with his huge tackle box to give me a face that can be seen at least one hundred yards away.

"They're taking pictures tonight," I tell him. "Give me a little more color."

"You looked very nice the way you were the last time."

"I was too pale."

He simply shakes his head and starts with a ghostly white foundation. With his long experience of seeing what people look like under the lights, there really is no arguing with him. As he's gluing on the false eyelashes, Amelia calls. She's sick and doesn't want to go hear James Galway play at Carnegie Hall tonight, but since she sounds worse than Violetta in her final moments, I suspect a possible fake. I tell her she has to go, and she sighs and says okay, fine. It was worth a try.

Juliet Veltri comes in to apply my wig. She's held this position for

ten years, and her mother held it before her. Anyone who is employed
there will tell you that overall the Met is a great place to work. When
you're on, the days and nights are long, but the season ends and then
there's plenty of time to regain your energy. Juliet whips my hair into
pin curls and then slips on the first-act wig. A few of the bobby pins
seem to go directly into my scalp, but at least I am assured this wig
isn't going anywhere tonight. Needing to warm up more, I head over
to the little Yamaha upright piano in the corner while Juliet trails
along behind me, trying to slip the jeweled picks into the back of my
chignon. I play a few notes from the first-act aria and begin to sing.
James Levine calls to say how much he enjoyed the Schubert program we performed together a week earlier; we laugh about a couple
of things, but he doesn't keep me on the phone, for he knows what
time it is. I am not ready to go on. I am not ready at all. The girls and
I went skiing the day before, and now I'm worrying that all that cold,
fresh air and physical exertion have stripped the tone from my voice.

Dmitri Hvorostovsky taps on the door and sticks his head inside.
"Decent?"

"Decent," I say.

He is Germont from the waist down, in formal gray trousers and
gleaming shoes, but he is wearing a white T-shirt and his suspenders
are hanging down around his waist. He doesn't have his mustache on.
"How are you, darling?"

I give a happy sigh and tell him I'm fine. I picture all the swoony
girls who wait outside the stage door for his autograph every night,
and I think about how they would die to hear the word "darling"
from his lips, even in a professional capacity. Dmitri is the closest the
opera world comes to Richard Gere. When he goes back to his dressing room, I can hear him warming up through the thin walls. It is an
inspiring sound.

The next arrival is Vicki Tanner, my dresser and all-around right-
hand woman. Like Victor, she's been on the job for thirty-five years.
She asks me if I've eaten, and I remember that my dinner is in a plas-

tic box at the bottom of my bag. If I don't eat it right away, it will be too late. I really can't have a meal five minutes before walking onstage, especially when the first act is such a challenge, but if I don't eat I'll run out of steam long before the opera is over at eleven. Someone comes in and asks me to sign some programs for patrons and a few CDs, and I do that while Vicki gets me a tall Styrofoam cup of hot water and tells me she can't find any tea bags, which is fine because I have a few in my purse.

If an opera singer wants to be a so-called diva in the negative sense, and demands that the air-conditioning be turned off in an entire shopping mall in July so she won't get a sore throat, I think, *Fine*. But where I have no tolerance for diva behavior is backstage, which is, unfortunately, the place a person is most likely to see it. It is the responsibility of the singers to repay the respect and courtesy of the Met's professional staff in kind. I admire people like Victor and Vicki greatly because I know how much time and dedication they've put into their work. I'm grateful for that, and truthfully, they inspire *me*. An opera production is an enormous machine, and even if my name is on the front of the program, I am not putting the show on by myself.

In the middle of all of this, I suddenly remember I have to tape a segment for a tribute to Fred Rogers (Mister Rogers of television fame) in the morning and I haven't looked at the piece I'm singing yet. Vicki has microwaved the food I brought over, and I take a few bites, sit down at the piano, and try to play and sing the piece. It's a song Fred wrote himself, and it's really lovely. I think of how in a perfect world I'd rehearse it for a few days, preferably with someone who can play the piano better than I, but the moment is now and there's nothing to do but take what I can get and be grateful. I feel lucky to have found a minute to go over it at all. Ramón Vargas, who is singing Alfredo, comes in wearing spats, a blue silk vest, and a red striped tie, holding a top hat in both hands like a respectful suitor. He looks absolutely polished and ready to go, and it makes me realize how far behind I am. He gives me a kiss.

"Do you feel good?" he asks. "You look good."

I tell him I feel better than I look, because at this point I am Violetta from the neck up and Renée Fleming from the neck down. Ramón leaves, and Vicki is back, telling me it's time to get into costume.

Gone are the days when I couldn't sing Musetta without a silk gown on. I could now sing Violetta in sweat pants, but I do love the costume. First Vicki puts a giant petticoat over my head, and then she laces me into my corset. I am no Scarlett O'Hara; there is no bedpost to hold on to, and I will never be squeezed down to seventeen inches, but this thing is *tight,* although nothing compared with the corsets I wore in *Platée.* Some singers want their corsets loose, and some like to have the breath pinched out of them. I prefer mine snug, giving me something to push against when I sing and offering one more level of support for the breath. Vicki now drops John Pascoe's enormous white-on-cream silk confection of a dress over my head and laces that up as well. Then there are the gloves, rhinestones big enough to be seen in the back row of the Family Circle, three rings the size of quail's eggs, two bracelets, a necklace, a brooch. It is any eight-year-old's fantasy of costume jewelry. Vicki gives me my fan and handkerchief, and I stand back to judge the total effect. I am a wedding cake, covered in layers of frosting and piped-on roses. For all of the excess—wretched or glorious, depending on your perspective—I think it's beautiful.

I apply a little more blush from my own personal stash, because I still think I'm too pale, no matter what Victor insists, and I go back to the piano to run through a few tricky lines in the first act. I'm standing now, for sitting is just too much work once the costume is on. There is very little time left, and I run through what sounds like a fast-forward version of *La Traviata's Greatest Hits.* It is at this point that I start to talk seriously to myself, since there's nobody else around to give me a pep talk. I focus on my first bad note.

"Look—*this* is what you did wrong the last time! You ran out of breath on that line. Don't humiliate yourself. Remember, you're still going to have a lot of those little black notes to sing when this line is over." I tap the piano again. "What key are we in, Renée? Okay, let's get that high C." I let one out, and it doesn't sound too terrible. "There you go! That was interesting. Now, attach that high C to your gut!"

Maybe there are people standing in the hallway listening, but I doubt there is anything going on in this room they haven't heard before. I sing two more lines.

"Correct that. Again. Big breath. There you go."

Over the loudspeaker I hear the call. "Violetta onstage with a hankie." Vicki knocks on my door again. It's time.

Vicki walks behind me like a maid of honor, holding up my skirt. In the waiting area outside the dressing room, courtesans and ladies' maids and gentlemen of the high life are sitting around, telling stories about their dogs and what they did last weekend. Gorgeous young women in bright silk gowns wear tatty cotton bathrobes over their costumes to keep them neat. Everyone is dressed to the nines. I hear bits of Italian, Spanish, Russian. "Good luck!" they say, and I wish them luck. I walk past the wig shop, the wardrobe room with its rows of irons, the carpentry shop, down narrow cement walkways lined with ladders and dollies, walls covered with coils of black electric cords as thick as rattlesnakes. It's hard to imagine that this is the path taken to reach the most glamorous spot that I know, and that every great singer of the past forty years has walked these hallways too. As I near the stage area I encounter so much activity and so many people—people with headsets and clipboards, people talking on cell phones, people in costumes and others in black T-shirts and jeans, guys with hammers and scaffolding, women at the light board and men carrying around extra canister lights, ballet dancers in tights, and girls with tambourines.

It is amazing to think almost every night a production involving so many intricate details comes together in a perfect performance. The curtain goes up; the lights come on. Although it is rare, things can also go hugely wrong. When I made my debut at the Royal Opera in *Médée*, one of the front pieces of a steeply raked set hadn't been properly fixed to the stage. I had the first aria in the opera, so I sat down to sing it directly on the loose scenery, and it tipped forward with me on it. There was a loud gasp from the audience, because if I had been an inch farther front I would have been tipped into the orchestra pit. In *The Ghosts of Versailles* at the Met in 1991, a heavy piece of flown scenery fell. Had we been rehearsing a loud section of the opera we never would have known, but fortunately it was a quiet moment, and we heard the initial crack before it fell, and we ran. Two other young singers and I had been rehearsing directly beneath the spot where it fell and could have been crusted. Teresa Stratas was so upset at the thought of what might have happened to us that she burst into tears and couldn't go on. Two years ago, in a Paris production of *Rusalka*, an enormous wall of scenery that was six feet deep and two stories tall came crashing down onto the stage. I didn't realize I could run quite that fast. The members of the backstage crew generally do a remarkable job of keeping us safe. They manage a set change in five minutes, attaching a set of rickety stairs to a piece of scenery with a couple of clamps that have to support the entire chorus, and somehow it works.

When we get to the edge of the stage, Vicki drops my skirt and I am on, stepping out onto the bridge between the front of the world and the back.

The world onstage is oversized. Like our voices and our jewelry, it must be easily accessible to every row. A giant chandelier looms overhead. The furniture is overstuffed with big, floppy pillows everywhere. This Zeffirelli production, with its red walls and gilt trim, paints a scene you can sink into, lush, soft, and beckoning. I begin singing, taking my energy from the audience and the other performers onstage and giving them mine in return.

Even though this is the penultimate performance of my second appearance in the role of Violetta, I still discover five or six new interpretive refinements in the first act. In the first duet with Alfredo, I realize I haven't fully explored the coloratura. Ideally anything we sing must have some purpose behind it. It isn't enough to sing the notes well; there must be meaning in every phrase. For example, take the cadenza that falls at the end of the first duet. It can be interpreted as laughter, as ardor, or as hysteria; it can represent Alfredo's pulling Violetta close and her pushing him away—any of those choices are valid. Nowhere in the score does Verdi specify: "This is the way I meant for this to be." That's exactly what makes the music so exciting: it's intangible, it's enigmatic, and it gives me the space to stretch out and experiment, to play it different ways on different nights and see what feels organic to the character, or even what feels organic on that particular night. At this performance I decide to let Violetta's consumptive breathlessness also come to represent her yielding to romance, so I make her breathless in an almost aroused way. I see how I can associate these two ideas: she's ill, but she's also under the spell of a very charismatic young man. Creativity is like a muscle—the more often you use it, the stronger it gets, and the more you come to rely on it, even unconsciously. I believe that everyone is creative, but we have to train ourselves to be so in a comfortable and confident way. If I exercise my creativity frequently, keeping it as limber as I do my voice, I'm much more likely to make discoveries and improve my performance. That's the real joy of performing: you do something for so long and with such discipline that it actually begins to look, and at times even feel, effortless.

Another chance for expression comes at the cadenza at the end of the cavatina in the big aria, which offers me one of the most powerful opportunities in opera: to make the audience wait. If a performance is successful, the audience feels that it is experiencing something real, something that is happening in front of it for the first time. On the stage, we experience a similar sense of reality. One of the ways to maximize this potential for identification is with time and surprise. It was Frank Corsaro again who gave me my favorite surprise, the long pause before "È strano! È strano!" The guests from the party have left, the evening dies down, and everything is quiet again. Normally, the door shuts, Violetta turns around, and before she can forget the pitch, she sings, "È strano! È strano!" immediately. But Frank had a different notion of the scene. I want you to take off your shoes, he said, and go look at the fire. All of this sets up an element of tension with the audience, and tension is essential to the drama of music.

In the musical line, I learned about tension from Hartmut Höll, who referred to it as *tragen*, German for "to carry." Think of music as a piece of taffy that can be pulled and stretched. Rather than sing the line in a four-square, pedantic way, the heartstrings of the audience can be pulled with dynamics and legato, anticipating the next pitch just slightly or delaying it just a touch, to create tension in the line, giving voice to yearning and desire. This will actually draw the audience forward and bind them to you emotionally. Alternatively, an absolutely straight, pure, pristinely sung line will sometimes carry equal emotion for its sheer angelic quality. When Hartmut talked about *tragen*, he could demonstrate with his phrasing on the piano, which was infinitely more difficult to do than with the voice, because the instrument doesn't sustain. This is another means of expressing what's in our hearts and guts, and very few singers master it. When they do, I am more moved by this as an audience member than by all of the scenery chewing in the world.

Even in the moments when I'm alone onstage, as at the end of *Traviata*'s first act, I'm never really alone, for I have the enormous comfort of Joan Dornemann in the prompter's box. She averts train wrecks, gets people back on track when they're ahead or behind, cues us when we forget what we're supposed to say, and in a desperate case shouts out a word. As young singers we never had the luxury of prompters, but in the major theaters we become completely reliant on the extra security they provide, which makes their absence more than a little nerve-racking. I sang my first *Manon* in Paris without a prompter, which was especially stressful, given the dialogue in the piece. When James Conlon came in as the new music director of the Paris Opera, the first thing he did was install a prompt box. The prompter, after all, is an opera tradition, dating back to when performers sang different roles every night.

Once act 1 is finished, I breathe a huge sigh of relief. This is not to say that the rest of the opera is easy; however, the opening act is not only where my anxiety lies but also the most exhausting of the acts, and if I don't pace myself properly I start to wilt later in the evening. I also worry about injury in a demanding role. It's amazing how even now I'll sing a phrase slightly wrong and think, *That's it! It's over. My voice is ruined.* That may sound neurotic, but it's certainly possible: you never know exactly when you're going to oversing and shut down your vocal cords for good. Think of how a figure skater executes perfect double-axel–triple-toe-loop combinations all night long, only to slide her foot out the wrong way while skating straight ahead and pull a tendon.

The curtain comes down, and after a bow to encouraging applause, I'm back to the dressing room. Off comes the cream-and-white wedding cake gown of act 1. Vicki slips over my head the blue-and-green-striped dress for act 2, scene 1: the courtesan in the country. The rhinestones are traded in for a large cross, the upswept wig is now long loose curls, and the jeweled hair picks are replaced by a modest straw hat. Plácido Domingo knocks on my door. I had no idea he was in the audience tonight; I had just seen him the night before in *The Queen of Spades* because Sage was singing in the children's chorus. He gives me a kiss, takes both of my hands, looks at me seriously, and says, "You know I adore your voice." When he leaves, the conductor, Valery Gergiev, calls on the dressing-room phone to tell me I'm doing wonderfully. Even at this stage of my career I need and appreciate all the positive reinforcement.

I walk back through the winding hallways with Vicki carrying my skirt, past giant wooden storage crates labeled GÖTTERDÄMMERUNG and LUISA MILLER. The glamorous props of the first act have been pulled away, the chandelier now folded up and hanging two stories above our heads, safely out of the audience's sight. The high life is now bucolic, a sunny room with endless windows.

If you're lucky, there are dozens of times in your career when you think, *This is the best director I've ever worked with. This conductor is a genius. This tenor, this mezzo, this bass—I have never seen such talent.* In a way, being an opera singer is like being a very romantic sixteen-year-old who falls in love with great passion and conviction every month. I especially love to sing with Dmitri, who is famous for his breath control and ability to spin out long phrases. He's a perfect example of someone who understands *tragen* and can use it to pull and bend the very strings of your heart. If you lined him up against all the historic Germonts, you could discern his special gift immediately: he has perfect support and technique. Add to that the fact that he has a beautiful voice and he knows what to do with a phrase, and the scene passes like a dream. It also features some of my favorite acting in the opera, because it's so subtle and tragic. This is the moment when we see who Violetta really is, when her goodness shines out and the audience makes a deep commitment to her.

When the first scene of the second act is finished, I head backstage to change again, and on the way a woman stops me and hands me an envelope. The principal performers at the Met are paid at some point in the middle of every performance, and while getting a paycheck is always gratifying, I'm always distracted, to say the least, and I often forget where I've stuck the check in the rush of getting out of one costume and into another. Several days after a performance, my assistant Mary usually has to say to me, "Um . . . did they ever pay you?"—at which point we start hunting for the check.

Act 2, scene 2, starts with a party featuring the chorus and dancers. I'm not onstage at the beginning, and I have just enough time to get into the black gown that says "I have returned to the high life and now I am a miserable courtesan again." It's the biggest scene for the extras, and the costume people set up shop right at the side of the stage, ironing out jackets, fluffing up skirts. When the act is finished, I race back to get into my nightgown and prepare to die.

I've always struggled with how best to look emaciated and waiflike in the final act, and this year I took a great tip from Susan Graham—a bust flattener. She wears one when she sings trouser roles in Handel and Strauss, and it occurred to me that its use might aid me in appearing less healthy, so I put one on underneath my lavender nightgown. Victor comes in to take off the extra blush I put on before the first act and gives me dark circles, and then I get a long, disheveled wig that sends a clear message that I've been sweating through a high fever for days. I trade in my cross for a large, sentimental locket that no doubt holds a picture of Alfredo, along with the portrait I will give him as a keepsake of our love. The handkerchief I carry now is large and blotched with blood. I look like an Edward Gorey drawing. Vicki takes me back to the stage and helps me into bed. The carpenters have stuck an enormous wooden pole in the middle of the set and are noisily drilling something above my head, but it's the third act, I'm in bed, and everything is right with the world. The carpenters remove the pole, straighten up, and are gone. From the other side of the curtains I hear the music and try to rouse myself.

I am so grateful for the times I've been able to work with Valery Gergiev. Our artistic sensibilities are complementary, and we play off each other well. Valery has a way of bringing virility to the orchestra that I find gutsy and exciting, and in response I'll sing more passionately, which in turn inspires him. He gives the music a much more strongly rhythmic reading than what I usually encounter. We performed *Otello* together in 1994, and because I was in the second cast I was able to watch many of the rehearsals. The storm scene was so fiery and alive that I actually felt terrified. I don't have to watch him constantly, for he'll stretch a phrase, and then I'll hear it and innately feel that my next two phrases need to push forward to balance out that stretch. It's that constant give-and-take, the risk and trust, that can make a production of *La Traviata* feel like an opera you've never seen before.

My favorite performance analogy has to do with love. Leonard Bernstein said that conducting was like making love to a hundred people at the same time. I've also heard it said that to see Kleiber conducting Ileana Cotrubas as Violetta—the way he never took his eyes off of her, and the way they responded to each other musically—was to imagine that he was in love with her. And a jazz musician once told me that Miles Davis had said that his job wasn't done unless the women in the audience fell in love with him. No wonder we try to replicate the most powerful emotion in the human existence.

One of the moments requiring the greatest interpretive skill in the opera comes in the third act, when Violetta reads the letter she has received from Germont. The letter scene can make or break a Violetta, because it is so nakedly revealing. In Houston, Frank had her seriously angry that Alfredo hadn't come yet even though he knew she was dying, a powerful concept that led compellingly to her scream of "It's too late!" But at the Met, my reading was more pensive, in keeping with the production's overall gentler vision of Violetta. The letter reading is about the meaning and beauty of the language, as one is infinitely more exposed when speaking a language than when singing it. In singing, every vowel is stretched, and you can get away with a lot more and still sound authentic; but in speaking, there's no place to hide. It involves the kind of detail that I can get very obsessive about, even more so than with a difficult vocal passage.

Finally, Alfredo and Germont do return. Alfredo and Violetta reaffirm their love and all is forgiven. She has one brief instant of joy, thinking she's fully recovered and that they can have a beautiful life together, and then she drops dead on a high B-flat—difficult, to say the least, to make believable. When we walk out together from behind the curtain, the audience roars. It sounds like the ocean, like a single enormous wave of love and approval crashing down on us. People tear up their programs and throw them into the air, and though this is expressly forbidden at the Met, I am not about to be the one who tells them to stop. The pages rain down on us, and the applause seems to go on as long as the opera. Suddenly I feel that I could happily stay up all night.

And that should be where this story ends, with my resurrection in front of a loving audience, in the company of my colleagues and friends, but the evening is not quite over. Back in the dressing room, the wig is tacked onto its Styrofoam head and the nightgown goes back on its hanger. I take out the pin curls, wipe off the dark circles as best I can, and get back into my own clothes. When I am composed I open the dressing-room door and greet everyone whose name is on the backstage list, a group that ranges from Met patrons to someone I went to third grade with, other singers, fans from other states or other countries, close friends, friendly acquaintances, and almost everyone in between. There is an art to meeting, greeting, and keeping the line moving along, for while I appreciate these visits, I want to make sure the people at the end of the line don't have to stand there until two a.m. There are photographs and hugs and little presents. After I've spoken a few words with everyone, I go back to the stage door, where the long line of fans who didn't manage to get their names on the backstage list wait. These are the troupers. It is very late by now and very cold, but they want me to sign their programs. Many of them are young singers, and I remember the days when I used to wait at the door to tell someone how much I appreciated her performance. I try to talk to everyone for a minute. It is after midnight by the time I get to the end of the second line. These are the moments when I love New York the most. The city waited up for me. It doesn't feel lonely or in the least bit shut down. A friend has invited me to join her for a late salad and a glass of wine if I have the energy, and suddenly I have all the energy in the world, at least for a little while longer. I walk down Broadway, away from Lincoln Center, and chalk this one up as a good night.

CHAPTER THIRTEEN

· CODA ·

I CANNOT IMAGINE a more satisfying calling than my own: beauty, humanity, and history every day, combined with the cathartic joy of singing. And as a classical musician, I have the luxury of a long career, if I can maintain my voice. The complexity of the art form and the ability to grow artistically can hold the attention of a loyal following for between twenty and forty years, which is not usually the case for performers of more popular music. The greatest advantage it has given me is choice: what role or concert to accept, when, and, to some degree, with whom.

I will continue searching for new and challenging repertoire and developing other operatic and concert world premieres. How can any art continue to grow if the flow of enriching new material dries up? Imagine if every year we had two or three new operas to record, with major stars and an eager and hungry public as interested in these releases as they are in a new book by Ann Patchett or a new film by Pedro Almodóvar. As I grow as a recitalist, I will explore the endless reams of song literature while continuing to savor the opportunity for creating a recorded legacy. The same qualities that have made me so eager a student are also enabling me to expand my horizons and explore theater, art, and an interest in education and the importance of music and the arts in our culture.

Only recently have I felt secure enough to appreciate how truly fortunate I am. I think back to Jan DeGaetani bringing every class to tears when telling us what a privilege and an honor it was to be a musician, to be an artist. At the time, we could scarcely relate to that sentiment, since at that point in our careers we were lucky to reach the end of a single aria without coming to grief, but I understand it very well now. Often in the middle of a performance I find myself completely overcome with a deep feeling of gratitude for the fulfillment inherent in this work. Music enabled me as a fragile young person to give voice to emotions I could barely name, and now it enables me to give my voice the unique and mysterious power to speak to others.

I am also fortunate to be grounded by extraordinary friends who provide an interpersonal exchange that rejuvenates me and allows me to gather strength for the pressures I face every day—a veritable oasis. There are treasured friends from my youth, colleagues, new friends who face similar challenges of high-profile careers, and admirers and friends from all strata of society who are highly educated appreciators of the arts. I'm an Olympic ruminator, and without the sounding board of this loving, sensitive inner circle, my sister, and my family, I'm not sure I could withstand the rigors of my life.

The central challenge I face in all of this is making sure I have enough time with my children. I openly discuss everything about my work and my traveling with Amelia and Sage. They know exactly when I'm leaving and when I'm coming home and when they get to go with me. We make calendars; we e-mail and call each other every day. We never lose our sense of connectedness. I stay completely informed about everything that's going on with them. I work very hard to make it clear to my daughters that they come first with me, and they seem to know that they do. They're also at an age now when they're aware of my Herculean work ethic and the necessity for multitasking to the extreme, but they also know deep down that if push came to shove, there would be no choice: it would always be them. I never close the door on them when I'm rehearsing. They can come and sit in my lap. They can interrupt me if they need to. I've never wanted them to feel they were competing with music for my attention, and so far, so good. They love music. I don't push it, but it's always there, and they're welcome to it.

My general philosophy as a parent is to expose them to as much as is humanly possible—as many kinds of interests, as many kinds of people, places, and situations.

Untold amounts of love go into making sure their needs are met on a daily basis, and happily, I'm now finding it possible to better balance my personal life with my professional life overall. I feel grateful that my mother worked and instilled in me an understanding that while she was different from my friends' parents, I could be proud of her. We don't teach our daughters to be dependent anymore, but that wasn't the case in my mother's generation. Recently, Sage performed in the children's chorus of a Russian opera, and when I went backstage to pick her up after the accolades, I said, "Sweetie, you're skipping rope onstage and you're supposed to be having fun. May I please have one of your most stellar smiles next time? And sing out!" I had to laugh when I realized that history was repeating itself. I'm not only caretaker of the girls; I'm also their role model. I tell them that I hope they'll find a life's ambition that makes them as happy as mine has made me: something they feel passionately about.

One beautiful day in Connecticut, I was driving the girls on errands when my older daughter, who was ten at the time, started singing one of the Queen of the Night's virtuosic arias from *Die Zauberflöte*, complete with high Fs absolutely perfectly in place. I keep a pitch pipe in the car, because I often warm up while driving (make a note to stay clear of sopranos on the road), and with it I verified that she was even singing in the right key. I looked at her and said, "Amelia, that's amazing! Where did you hear that?" I had taken them to see the opera, but that was a year earlier.

She smiled and answered, "Oh, I saw it on television the other night. It was in a movie."

"Oh, so you saw it a few times throughout the week?" I asked, thinking it must have been on the Disney Channel.

She shrugged, seeming totally unimpressed with herself. "No, just once."

Musical memory is such an interesting gift. Of course, for a week after that both girls sang the Queen of the Night's aria every time we got into the car, driving it into higher and higher ranges. It was hilarious to me, but deeply puzzling to any little girlfriends of theirs who were riding along with us.

Every time she sang, I told Amelia she was doing a wonderful job, until finally she said to me, "Well, you know, Mom, I *am* considering becoming an opera singer."

Of course, being an opera singer was the furthest thing from her mind three days later, but for a second at least she had seen it, this thing I have known all along: there must be at least one note in my range that belonged to my grandmother, and certainly my mother's soprano and my father's deep love for new music have given much of the color and depth to my sound. Their voices are our inheritance, part of the amalgamation of who we are and what we have learned. We are unique, each human voice, not because we are completely self-generated, but because of how we choose to assemble the countless factors that made us. My voice carries in it the generations before me, generations of my family, of brilliant singers I have admired, of dear friends. It goes on in this book, not the sound of my singing but certainly the work and thought and passion of the discipline. Tiny slivers of my voice will be incorporated into a student I teach in a master class or into the young singer who listens carefully, just as little glimmers of Leontyne Price's shining high C and Dietrich Fischer-Dieskau's expansive breath came into me. If this is the past of my voice, then I must believe it is the future as well. My voice will go forward in the same way, not only through recordings but through my daughters and through their daughters and sons as far as the line will take us. It doesn't mean that everyone will be a singer, but that every one of us will find a passion in life to drive us ahead, and just maybe part of that passion will rest in the voice. People will hear it even in a word that is spoken: the wealth and wonder of all the music that came before.